LIVING WITH HIV AND DYING WITH AIDS

Offering compelling evidence of the inadequacy of biomedical models for the AIDS response, this book provides a clear and lucid look at the inequalities that drive growing rates of HIV infection and the inadequacy of existing systems to address them. Bringing to life the old adage the 'personal is political', it provides valuable evidence of the social and economic realities faced by HIV-infected people everywhere.

Sofia Gruskin, University of Southern California, USA

A powerful combination of qualitative empirical data, sensitive sociological insights into diverse contexts of living and dying with HIV/AIDS, and a clear explication of the relevance of human rights both within nations and globally. Collaborative work between medical and social science researchers is the suggested path to deeper understanding of the profound burden of social suffering that extends beyond biomedical considerations.

Solomon Benatar, University of Cape Town, South Africa, and University of Toronto, Canada

A wide-ranging analysis of what makes HIV such a potent agent of human suffering, and why the remarkable biomedical progress of the past 30 years must be matched by advances in human rights, equity and access for there to be real progress. Here is a contextual backcloth against which clinicians can re-evaluate treatment and care for HIV.

Jane Anderson, Homerton University Hospital NHS Foundation Trust, UK

No other source provides such an insightful, integrated, broadly-focused analysis that uses an explicit conceptual framework to take context and differences into account, systematically connecting human needs, human rights and inequality. This brilliant, accessible book is essential reading for policy-makers, practitioners and academics, whether or not they are interested in the specific case of HIV and AIDs.

Pat Armstrong, York University, Toronto, Canada

Global Health

Series Editor: Professor Nana K. Poku,
University of California, Berkeley, USA

The benefits of globalisation are potentially enormous, as a result of the increased sharing of ideas, cultures, life-saving technologies and efficient production processes. Yet globalisation is under trial, partly because these benefits are not yet reaching hundreds of millions of the world's poor and partly because globalisation has introduced new kinds of international problems and conflicts. Turmoil in one part of the world now spreads rapidly to others, through terrorism, armed conflict, environmental degradation or disease.

This timely series provides a robust and multi-disciplinary assessment of the asymmetrical nature of globalisation. Books in the series encompass a variety of areas, including global health and the politics of governance, poverty and insecurity, gender and health and the implications of global pandemics.

Also in the series

Informal Norms in Global Governance
Human Rights, Intellectual Property Rules and Access to Medicines
Wolfgang Hein and Suerie Moon
ISBN 978 1 4094 2633 2

Ethics and Security Aspects of Infectious Disease Control
Interdisciplinary Perspectives
Edited by Christian Enemark and Michael J. Selgelid
ISBN 978 1 4094 2253 2

Migrants and Health
Political and Institutional Responses to
Cultural Diversity in Health Systems
Christiane Falge, Carlo Ruzza and Oliver Schmidtke
ISBN 978 0 7546 7915 8

The Political Economy of Pharmaceutical Patents
US Sectional Interests and the African Group at the WTO
Sherry S. Marcellin
ISBN 978 1 4094 1214 4

Living with HIV and Dying with AIDS

Diversity, Inequality and Human Rights in the Global Pandemic

LESLEY DOYAL
University of Bristol, UK

with
LEN DOYAL
Queen Mary, University of London, UK

ASHGATE

Published by
Ashgate Publishing Limited
Wey Court East
Union Road
Farnham
Surrey, GU9 7PT
England

Ashgate Publishing Company
110 Cherry Street
Suite 3-1
Burlington, VT 05401-3818
USA

www.ashgate.com

British Library Cataloguing in Publication Data
Doyal, Lesley.
   Living with HIV and dying with AIDS : diversity, inequality
   and human rights in the global pandemic. -- (Global health)
   1. HIV-positive persons--Cross-cultural studies.
   2. HIV-positive persons--Psychology. 3. HIV-positive
   persons--Social conditions. 4. HIV-positive persons--
   Economic conditions. 5. HIV-positive persons--Medical
   care. 6. Discrimination in medical care. 7. Right to
   health. 8. HIV-positive persons--Civil rights.
   I. Title II. Series III. Doyal, Len.
   362.1'969792-dc23

The Library of Congress has cataloged the printed edition as follows:
Doyal, Lesley.
   Living with HIV and dying with AIDS : diversity, inequality and human rights in the global pandemic /
by Lesley Doyal with Len Doyal.
      pages cm -- (Global health)
   Includes bibliographical references and index.
   ISBN 978-1-4094-3110-7 (hardback) – ISBN 978-1-4094-3111-4 (pbk.) – ISBN 978-1-4094-3112-1 (ebook)
   1. AIDS (Disease)--Political aspects--Comparative studies. 2. AIDS (Disease)--Government policy--
Comparative studies. 3. HIV infections--Political aspects--Comparative studies. 4. HIV infections--Government
policy--Comparative studies. I. Doyal, Len. II. Title.
   RA643.8.D69 2013
   362.19697'92--dc23

              2012043455

ISBN 9781409431107 (hbk)
ISBN 9781409431114 (pbk.)
ISBN 9781409431121 (ebk – PDF)
ISBN 9781472400147 (ebk – ePUB)

Printed and bound in Great Britain
by MPG PRINTGROUP

Contents

Introduction and Acknowledgements

This book had its origins in an invitation from Professor Jane Anderson to give a lecture on gender to health workers involved in HIV care. Having coffee afterwards she talked about how she wanted to carry out a wider sociological study involving the many African women she was helping to care for. However she was afraid she did not have the relevant skills. But I did – leading us to begin what was to be a lengthy collaboration resulting not only in several studies of African migrants living with HIV in London but also in Jane adding anthropological skills to her very considerable clinical ones. The difficulty we had in obtaining funding for this work offered an early warning of the fact that priority is usually given to biomedical research. However it also highlighted one of the central themes of this book: the value of bringing social science into the study of HIV and AIDS, especially when this is based on interdisciplinary collaboration.

Our first study of women was followed by one of men who defined themselves as heterosexual (who had hardly been studied at all in any setting) and one on men who had sex with men. This latter group had been almost totally ignored in African contexts, though they had of course been extensively studied in the USA. As our studies proceeded, my exploration of the background material raised many questions about the bias in existing studies. The most obvious was the lack of available information on the experience of living with HIV and dying of AIDS in the global south. At this early stage (2005) the global spread of the pandemic was already clear, especially in the African region. However the literature on the experiences of those infected was sparse and focussed almost entirely on what were seen as practical policy-oriented issues such as 'safe sex' and the 'proper' use of antiretroviral therapy (ART).

As I continued to review the literature, other problems began to emerge. Most importantly it seemed to be extremely fragmented, with very little connection between the different dimensions of people's lives. Moreover some very important topics were almost entirely ignored, including both paid and unpaid work and experiences of reproduction and parenting. It appeared that these were not deemed relevant to HIV-positive people despite the fact that the beneficial effects of ART were beginning to extend their lives. The key themes still appeared to be 'stigma' (used in what was often an overly simplistic way), sex and death – especially in the poorer settings where the majority of those affected by the pandemic were now to be found. They were still being treated as an undifferentiated mass whose illness was largely their own fault and whose individual experiences were of little interest or value.

From 1994 onwards I was lucky enough to spend several weeks a year in South Africa at the Women's Health Unit at the University of Cape Town. This highlighted for me the importance of understanding the different epidemics in their social, economic and cultural contexts. In the early years in particular the lack of available treatment threw the circumstances of what were now millions of HIV positive people into sharp relief. I vividly remember visiting the clinic funded by Médecins Sans Frontières (MSF) in the township of Khayelitsha, where ART was just beginning to be rolled out. This was taking place against the background of extreme reluctance on the part of the government to provide the necessary drugs, as well as dire warnings from richer parts of the world that this was an impossible challenge. On a visit to a maternity hospital the same year I sat with a 16-year-old girl who was HIV positive as she gave birth, and watched her walk away a few hours later. The baby had been treated to prevent mother to child transmission but there was no therapy for the mother: their future seemed intolerably bleak and entirely unfair.

By the time I had finally decided to write the book, circumstances were beginning to change for the fortunate ones, but for many more they remained hopeless. Researchers were gradually beginning to explore the situation in different parts of the world but their results were narrowly focussed, with little integration of different aspects of living with HIV and almost no comparison between settings. My aim was to combine these diverse and usually small-scale studies into a more holistic picture. This could then contribute to an evidence base for the implementation of broader policies as well as bearing witness to the tragedies that were continuing to engulf so many people's lives.

As the book progressed it felt like new research findings were exploding around me (as witnessed by the eventual size of the bibliography). My main concern became one of synthesising these into a form that would be accessible to activists, clinicians, other health workers and policy makers as well as social scientists and, of course, students. A key theme was the relationship between diversity and difference on the one hand and universality on the other. How did the experiences of HIV positive individuals differ across social groups and nation states? And what needs did they have in common which would have to be met if they were to realise their potential in what were often desperate circumstances?

The authorship of the book has been somewhat unusual, as evidenced by the names on the front cover. It began life as a solo project but ended up as a much more collaborative venture. As I advanced further into the text I became aware that it would be much better if some of the more conceptual/philosophical debates underlying it were made more explicit. Expanded discussions of the universality of basic human needs, inequality, disadvantage, human rights and global injustice were clearly central to any understanding of life and death in the context of the pandemic. But there had so far been relatively few attempts to make these connections in any systematic way.

Fortunately issues such as these are one of my husband Len Doyal's areas of expertise as a philosopher and medical ethicist. Hence we agreed that he would help me extend the scope of the book to include a number of topics that had been referred to only briefly in early drafts. I cannot thank him enough for his huge contribution in this and in so many other ways. His love, moral support, technical skills and continued enthusiasm for helping me tease out the many intellectual puzzles that inevitably arise in a project of this kind were invaluable. Indeed they made it all possible. We hope that this work together will further highlight the importance of moral and political philosophy in current debates concerning HIV/AIDS policy in this time of crisis.

Throughout the writing of the book Sara Paparini has played a major role as a researcher, confidante, supplier of references I might have missed and all-round supporter and friend. Despite the fact that her first language is not English she was especially good at 'vetting' the political correctness (or not) of my own language in a field that is notoriously full of pitfalls. My visits to South Africa were made more fun as well as more enlightening by the advice, help and hospitality of many friends, including Margaret Hoffman, David Coetzee, Solly and Evie Benatar, Toni and Ivan Strasburg, Helen Schneider, Lucy Gilson, Paul and Belinda Roux and Naeema Abrahams.

During the writing of the book I needed more than my fair share of complex medical and dental care and most of this was delivered not just with expertise and professionalism but also with real humanity. For that I want to thank Dougie Clark, Habib Ellamushi, Fazeela Khan-Osborne, David Osborne, Leigh Stephens, Adella Shapiro, Mike Swash, David Vasserman and Lloyd Williams. My son Daniel Wilsher was a huge source of support throughout this period, pushing my wheelchair, sitting in doctors' waiting rooms, sharing snatched lunches and providing essential advice on international law.

When the going got tough, eating, drinking, laughing and loving with others was always a special treat, and for that I especially want to thank in London Evi Campetella, Reno and Soraya Cerio, Joel Gladstone, Peter and Sue Kopelman, Ania Korszun and Ian ('Chef') McKenzie, Lucy Parham, Sara Paparini and Chris Passeroti, Jane Smith and Sybil Williams. The same applies in Perugia to Elisa Ascione, Pierluigi Buratta and Sonia Bittoni, Laura Formeniti, Luigi ('Gigio') Montelione and Barbara Belfiori Montelione, Margherita Taticchi, Marcella Giogliali and at Faula, Paul Mackay and Luca Colautti.

Over the last three years so many other people have given me helpful and critical advice and support that there is not enough space to name them all. You know who you are and I thank you for your help. I want to thank Jane Anderson and Vin-Khim Nguyen for their valuable comments on the manuscript. Peter Aggleton was especially helpful in sending important and detailed suggestions, while Sofia Gruskin went out of her way to help at what was a difficult time for her. Thanks also to an anonymous reviewer for encouragement to turn a 'good' book into an 'excellent' one. Special mention also to Gary Morgan for support and technical assistance above and beyond the call of duty.

I owe everyone a huge debt of gratitude.

As series editor, Nana Poku's enthusiasm for the book has never wavered, despite huge pressures on his own time. I am also immensely grateful for the speed, professionalism, patience and personal support of all those at Ashgate Publishing. Thanks especially to Margaret Younger, Kirstin Howgate, Elaine Couper, Maria Anson, and Michael Drapper. What a team!

Finally, I am very grateful to Andy Clark for allowing me to use his amazing photograph which is on the cover of the book. It perfectly captures the reasons for writing it and points toward the urgency of resolving the problems of all of the adults and children who live with HIV or die of AIDS. Whenever I wavered in my work, the young man in the photograph appeared to be telling me to get on with it. I hope that he has the same effect on all who see him and read this book.

Dedicated to Hannah Doyal and Daniel Wilsher

For your love, support and understanding

Chapter 1
Posing the Problems

As we pass into the fourth decade of the global pandemic of HIV and AIDS, much progress has been made in understanding it. The retrovirus responsible for HIV has been identified, enabling biomedical therapies to ameliorate the symptoms and extend the lives of many of those who have been infected. However, millions more remain uncared for and uncared about. At the same time the resources available to meet their needs are shrinking as financial storms break over much of the world. If this challenge is to be met we will need to know much more about the economic, social and cultural contexts within which HIV epidemics continue to spread.[1] A broader global policy agenda can then be developed to tackle the preventable inequalities and disadvantages that still constrain the lives of so many HIV positive individuals whether or not they go on to develop AIDS.

Where Are We Now in the Pandemic?

The early history of HIV and AIDS has been well documented (Shilts 1987). It was first identified among gay men in the US and it was quickly linked to what were seen as 'lifestyle factors.[2] The disease became emblematic of a stigmatised sexual identity, with many of those infected being blamed for their own misfortune. No treatment was available and many died extremely painful deaths as the illness ravaged relatively small and close-knit groups. However these experiences did engender high levels of political advocacy by and on behalf of those affected. And, as we shall see, this has continued in various forms as the infection has spread.

The late 1980s brought major changes, with positive developments in the therapeutic arena – but also huge increases in the numbers of those affected around the world. The introduction of antiretroviral therapy (ART) in the form of Zidovudine (AZT) in 1987, followed 10 years later by highly active antiretroviral therapy (HAART), allowed those already infected to 'cheat death'.[3] Though life

---

1   The use of the term 'HIV epidemic' is recommended by UNAIDS as the most inclusive formulation to include both HIV and AIDS (UNAIDS 2011).

2   Of course it is likely that others were already affected in different parts of the world but they remained almost entirely invisible.

3   Unless there is a need to be more specific, the general term antiretroviral therapy (ART) will be used throughout the book to refer to the various drugs used for treating HIV.

expectancy remained uncertain, HIV and AIDS could now be treated as potentially separable entities rather than the inevitable continuum implied by the use of the term HIV/AIDS. Thus those who were able to access these new drugs began to rebuild their lives on a reasonably firm basis.

But over the same period the shape and size of the original epidemic had changed dramatically. By the beginning of the new millennium it had been transformed from what was frequently referred to as a 'gay plague' into what more closely resembled a 'disease of the poor'. The vast majority of the 27 million who were now HIV positive were living in middle or low income countries, with sub-Saharan Africa at the heart of what could now be defined as a 'pandemic'. And most were unable to access the drugs that were creating new hope among those infected in the 'global north'.[4]

The significance of this inequity was reflected in the Millennium Development Strategy, which called for universal access to ART by 2010 and a halt to the spread of HIV and AIDS by 2015. Over the following decade this aspirational approach encouraged the creation of many new prevention and treatment developments. This included, among others the WHO's '3 by 5' initiative which focussed on treating 3 million with HIV by 2005 (WHO 2003). However these targets can now be seen as unrealistic. Access to treatment did increase dramatically, with the numbers on ART rising to around 6.2 million in middle and low income countries by 2010. The annual number of new infections declined from a peak of 3.4 million in 1997 to 2.7 million in 2009, while deaths from AIDS-related illnesses also dropped from 2.2 million in 2005 to an estimated 1.8 million in 2010 (WHO, UNICEF and UNAIDS 2011).

However serious challenges remain. Despite the 'roll out' of ART more than half of those in need are still not able to access it. By 2010 around 34 million people were estimated to be HIV positive and 1.8 million died from AIDS during that year (WHO, UNICEF and UNAIDS 2011). But, most importantly, the total number of people living with HIV is continuing to rise as a result of new infections as well as the greater longevity associated with ART (UNAIDS 2012c). For every two individuals currently starting HIV treatment five more are newly infected. This situation poses two major challenges: how to prevent the further spread of HIV and how to support those who are (knowingly or unknowingly) already infected.

The need to slow down the numbers infected has received increasing attention as the gap between available resources and projected needs has widened. However there appears to be no simple solution, and the different types of biomedical, behavioural

---

4   There are now many challenges to be faced in distinguishing between the geopolitical statuses of different countries. The terms 'developed' and 'developing', for example, no longer stand up to critical scrutiny, while 'rich' and 'poor' are often too simplistic. Where collective terms are needed we will therefore use 'global north' and 'global south' where appropriate or high, middle and low income countries as the alternative found in most official documents.

and structural/social approaches to prevention continue to be extensively debated (Bekker et al. 2012; Coates et al. 2008; Padian et al. 2008; Hankins and Zalduondo 2010; Collins et al. 2008b; Gupta et al. 2008).[5]

An even more urgent challenge is posed by the circumstances of the millions already infected with HIV. Though the availability of ART has increased, there is still a long way to go in meeting current needs. This will include the initiation of care for all those who have yet to benefit from these new technologies. Most importantly it will also mean ensuring sustainability of a range of therapies for the increasing numbers of survivors who will need therapy over a lifetime. This has led one commentator to talk of 'a ballooning entitlement burden' which will be extremely difficult to achieve within existing financial constraints (Over 2008).

To make matters even more complex, it is clear that drugs alone will be limited in their effectiveness, especially in the deprived settings where the vast majority of positive people now live. Individuals may not feel able to be tested; they may not take up therapies (even if they are available); or their circumstances may prevent them from using them properly. Some will be able to 'normalise' their lives with continuing treatment after diagnosis, while others will not. These variations reflect the vast differences between positive individuals in their capacity to meet their own needs and those of their dependants in the face of a distressing and disabling disease. It is these differences and their origins which will provide the major focus of this book.

The account that follows will draw on a wide range of literature from across the biomedical, behavioural and social sciences to explore the experiences of positive women and men in the global north and the global south. Comparing those from different social classes and ethnic groups who express their sexuality in diverse ways, it will identify the complex links between these individuals and their wider biological and social environments.

How do HIV positive women and men in different settings develop their survival strategies? What resources are they able to access, and how? What health care services are available to them, and how do they use them? How do those living with HIV (re)shape their identities and their sense of themselves in the context of bodily changes, psychological and physical illness and fears about the future? And how do they (re)align their emotional attachments and their relationships with others? What are the factors influencing their major life decisions, especially those involving sex and reproduction? And how do they die?[6]

---

5 For a very useful overview of the many different prevention strategies now available see Bekker et al. 2012.

6 This final question will be the most difficult to answer since there has been so little research investigating the diversity of experiences surrounding death among HIV positive people.

Understanding the Biological Foundations

Knowledge of the biological characteristics of the HIV virus is clearly an important starting point for answering these questions. Mediated through the bodies of individuals living in very different circumstances, the (changing) nature of the virus has been the necessary but by no means sufficient condition for the spread of the global pandemic.

The human immunodeficiency virus (HIV) is located within the broader group of retroviruses. It can only be transmitted through infected body fluids and the process is not easy since the virus must enter the body in sufficient volume through the skin or mucous membranes and then gain entry to the bloodstream. The main modes of transmission are unprotected vaginal or anal intercourse; transmission from an infected mother to her child; the use of infected blood or blood products; and injecting drug use with contaminated equipment. As we shall see, the proportion of infections transmitted through these different routes will vary markedly between settings. In well-resourced circumstances the risk of transmission from a single heterosexual sexual act is estimated to be around 0.04 per cent for females to males and around 0.8 per cent from males to females. The risk of transmission through anal sex is considerably greater (Baggaley et al. 2010). There is also evidence that all of these rates can be as much as four to 10 times higher in very deprived communities (Boily et al. 2009).

Once the virus enters a cell it makes DNA copies of its own RNA. These new viruses then attack other cells, focussing in particular on the destruction of CD-4 receptors that cluster on the T cell lymphocytes necessary for normal immune response. Hence the importance of a CD4 count for measuring the degree to which such compromise has occurred. The virus is able to both reproduce and mutate rapidly, making it especially difficult to develop pharmaceutical strategies for prevention or cure.

The first stage of acute or primary HIV infection involves what has been called an 'unseen and unfelt war' between the virus and the immune system (Whiteside 2008). This can last from several weeks to several months and during this period the individual concerned is highly infectious. Yet their seropositivity is not obvious to them or to their partners and can rarely be medically diagnosed. Some people experience a flu-like illness at the end of this phase, but this is rarely identified as a marker of HIV.

Positive individuals then move on to a long period of clinical latency which is marked by rapid destruction and reproduction of the retroviruses themselves as well as the cells they attack. During this period the infection can be diagnosed through the discovery of antibodies to HIV, but only a minority of those infected will be tested. When the CD4 immune cells are destroyed more quickly than they can be replaced, the individual is susceptible to a wide range of opportunistic infections. They are said to have acquired immune deficiency syndrome (AIDS) when the CD4 count falls below 200 and/or they have one or several of what are called AIDS defining illnesses.[7] Without treatment, infections and malignancies increase in frequency, severity and duration until death intervenes.[8]

There is continuing debate about the length of time between initial HIV infection, illness and death if the infection remains untreated. During the early phase of the pandemic US findings indicated that illness usually occurred about 10 years after infection, with death following 12–24 months later. The period of survival without treatment has always been assumed to be shorter for those in the poorest and least healthy settings, but data on this remain unclear (Isingo et al. 2007; Morgan et al. 2002). A recent review found the average survival after the onset of untreated AIDS in resource-poor settings to be about one year (Zwahlen and Egger 2006).

Thus the biological characteristics of HIV and AIDS create a range of constraints within which individual men and women will have to manage their lives. These limitations will of course be felt especially strongly in communities where the prevalence of infection is high and available resources are scarce.

Taking a Historical View: Comparisons with the Black Death

We can place the particularity of the HIV pandemic in a historical context by comparing it with the 'Black Death' that first swept through Asia and Europe between 1349–50 (Lane 2004). Both have killed vast numbers of people: the Black Death is said to have claimed some 40 million over this period (amounting to between 30 and 60 per cent of the population of Europe). AIDS had killed around 30 million people by 2010 and the annual death toll is currently around 1.9 million, or 7,000 per day.

However the timescapes of the two are very different. The Black Death 'burned out' over a very short period (though similar epidemics recurred several times between the fourteenth and the seventeenth centuries). HIV on the other hand is usually described as a 'long-wave event' whose ultimate death toll cannot yet be estimated (Barnett 2006; Barnett and Whiteside 2006). Hence it will have harmful effects that may only emerge over decades. In this sense HIV has been described as partially 'self-replicating' in that its social effects engender the very

---

7   These include PCP pneumonia and the virus-induced cancer Kaposi's sarcoma. In women, cervical cancer is also regarded as an AIDS-defining condition when it occurs along with HIV infection.

8   Relatively little is known about the differences between women and men in the biological development of HIV and AIDS. However the evidence indicates that for men the first opportunistic illnesses are more likely to be cytomegalovirus, Kaposi's sarcoma or oral hairy leukoplakia, while for women they are more likely to be oesophageal candidiasis or toxoplasmosis. See Fact Sheet: Sex Differences in HIV/AIDS from the Society for Women's Health Research at www.womenshealthresearch.org/site/PageServer?pagename=hs_healthfacts_hiv.

conditions of poverty and deprivation that play a part in promoting its biological continuation.

These differences in timescape between the two diseases also apply at the level of individual experience. Those infected with the Black Death took only a very short time to die. But, as we have seen, HIV positive individuals are infected for a lengthy period before they are even aware of their illness: indeed many suffer and die of AIDS without ever being diagnosed. This has a major impact on their own quality of life as well as potentially increasing both the risk that they will infect others and the burden of caring to be borne by the rest of society.

The two pandemics can also be distinguished by their mode of transmission. Most experts agree that the Black Death was spread to humans by fleas which themselves were carried by rats. But, as we have seen, the major route of HIV transmission is sexual intercourse. Hence it is spread not by chance encounters with insects but through the most intimate and compulsive of human activities. This has obvious demographic consequences. While the Black Death hit all age groups, HIV infection is confined mainly to the sexually active – the young and middle-aged. It therefore leaves a 'black hole' within the age structure of those populations that are severely affected, limiting their collective capacity for waged and unwaged work and damaging household survival strategies.

At the same time, the connection with sex (and especially with sex between men) has been influential in creating a particular stigma around the disease itself. In the religious context of the Middle Ages the Black Death would certainly have been regarded by many as a punishment from God. However this would have had little effect on those infected, since death came so rapidly. The impact of hostility and discrimination directed towards individuals living with HIV, on the other hand, has been extreme. Despite this being a 'scientific era', responses have frequently been both primitive and punitive. As a result, social exclusion and hostility have been identified as serious challenges facing those with HIV and have led many to delay seeking tests or revealing a positive diagnosis.

Finally we need to note the difference between the Black Death and HIV and AIDS in terms of the relationship between infection, survival and existing social inequalities. It would appear that the impact of the plague was relatively indiscriminate and many of the rich died quickly, despite their attempts to escape to safer places. Similarly, infection with HIV is not confined to the poor. However the vast majority of those who are positive do live in the most deprived parts of the world.

The development of effective biomedical treatment has further widened the gap between rich and poor: between those who can acquire the means to mitigate their symptoms and extend their survival and those who cannot. Such inequalities did not exist in the Middle Ages, when all those infected faced the same fate. Thus there are arguments for identifying the HIV pandemic as the most diverse and also the most inequitable yet experienced in human history. The evidence for this claim will be provided as the book progresses.

Bringing in the Social Sciences: Adding Value

Not surprisingly, most of the early research on HIV and AIDS was undertaken within a biomedical paradigm as doctors scrambled to find a cure. Psychologists or 'behavioural scientists' also became involved but remained in the back seat.[9] Many worked on preventive strategies for changing individual sexual practices, while others examined the 'coping mechanisms' adopted by those infected at a young age with a stigmatised, highly distressing and terminal illness.

Reflecting the distribution of the disease itself, most of this research was done in the USA on (mainly white) gay/bisexual men. As ART gradually became available in the 1990s many of these same researchers moved on to explore the realities of daily life under the new medical regimens. But they were still operating in the shadow of doctors, mainly measuring individual risk behaviour and adherence to therapeutic drug protocols. And again the studies were concentrated in the USA and other rich countries.[10]

However as the global nature of the pandemic became apparent the research focus gradually shifted towards low and middle income countries in the global south. Within this context the importance of social processes quickly became apparent, drawing attention away from more individualistic approaches. Not surprisingly, the African region has been the location of the majority of recent studies, with an impressive body of social science research building up in South Africa in particular.[11] HIV epidemics in other parts of the world are also coming under increasing scrutiny, with the numbers of studies increasing in Central and Eastern Europe – where the epidemic is expanding most rapidly – and in the South and South East Asian regions. Some of this new research is focussed on the structural determinants of HIV and AIDS in the broader context of globalisation. But there is also a growing body of ethnographic work producing qualitative analyses of life with HIV in small-scale settings.

These detailed accounts have generated important new insights into the diversity of experiences of HIV and AIDS between individuals and communities. However, the emerging literature is inevitably partial and fragmented due to both

---

9   The term 'behavioural science' should not be confused with 'social science'. Though they sometimes overlap, the term behavioural science will be used here to refer to psychological research focussed directly on individuals, while social science will refer to those studies that place individuals in a broader context, exploring the wider structures and processes that shape their lives.

10   While therapeutic progress was made mostly in what would be called the 'developed' countries of the global north, some of the richer 'developing' countries in Latin America were also beginning to widen access to treatment during this period.

11   While some of this was initially led by researchers from the north, the need to tackle HIV and AIDS has played a crucial role in building a critical mass of excellent social science researchers in Southern Africa in particular. Studies in West and East African settings are also increasing rapidly (Samuelsen et al. 2012).

geographical and disciplinary variations. This can make it difficult to distinguish between those experiences that are context specific and those that are more generalisable. In order to make better sense of these differences, methods and insights will be needed from a range of socially oriented disciplines (Coates et al. 2008; Imrie et al. 2007; Kippax and Holt 2009; Mykhalovskiy and Rosengarten 2009a, 2009b).

Some studies will be quantitative in approach, identifying and measuring the structural variables that shape the everyday reality of HIV positive individuals. These will include access to income and wealth as well as entitlement to a range of commodities and services. However, quantitative methods can tell us only part of what we need to know. We also need to understand the complex cultural and symbolic processes that shape the ways in which individuals experience the disease and how they respond to it. Hence more qualitative social research will also be required (Lockhart 2008; Scheper Hughes and Bourgois 2004; Moatti and Souteyrand 2000).

The use of both quantitative and qualitative social science will create more nuanced understandings of the external realities of the different epidemics as well as the internal worlds of the individuals who are affected. This will be essential if biomedical and social interventions are to be both efficient (that is to say that they work in principle) and also effective (that they work in practice in the environments in which they are to be used). Most importantly, it will have the added advantage of making visible the lives of millions of men, women and children whose individuality continues to be lost in what is often the vast abstraction of the pandemic.

Inequality and Disadvantage: A Conceptual Framework

The most obvious connection between inequality and HIV might be assumed to be the poorer health of those who are seropositive compared with those who are negative. But those receiving treatment for HIV in a well-resourced and supportive environment may be in better health than those with other serious illnesses (especially if they are untreatable). Indeed their quality of life may be superior to that of people who are not suffering from a specific illness but who live in such deprived conditions that they will never reach the state of health that more privileged people take for granted. Hence differences in well-being between HIV positive and negative people will not be our major concern here. Instead we will focus on structured patterns of inequality within HIV positive populations themselves.

Even a quick glance shows that it is those who are not only positive but also poor and unsupported who are the most disadvantaged, with those who have untreated AIDS being in the worst situation of all. As we shall see in what follows, this is of moral as well as personal significance. Those with the lowest levels of well-being and the least access to resources will have the lowest life expectancy as well as the most constrained capacity to 'flourish' as human beings. Hence they can be seen to symbolise the inequality and injustice that continue to characterise so many lives under global capitalism.

These patterns of disadvantage can be found both within and between communities and can originate in both local and global arenas. Their impact is evident in the narratives of individuals as they struggle to devise personal or collective strategies to meet their own needs and to help those to whom they have a duty of care. Of course such inequalities are not 'natural' in any sense but are based on existing economic, social and cultural divisions both within and between societies. Understanding their origins as well as their impact will be the central theme of this book.

Inequalities in Action: Case Studies of Diversity

In order to provide a conceptual framework for making sense of the more personal accounts that will follow we need to undertake a brief excursion into what is meant by 'inequality' and how it is linked to issues of human need and human flourishing.[12] This will be done through an analysis of four (invented) case studies. The people imagined here all share the common experience of living with HIV but they are doing so in very different circumstances. Ultimately they all have the same basic needs that will have to be met if they are to optimise their well-being despite their infection. But their access to the necessary resources for achieving this varies dramatically.

Stephen is a white gay man living in Manhattan. He is 35 years old and works as a policy analyst in a US foreign aid organisation. He has been in a long-term relationship with his partner Philippe, who is a chef in an upmarket French restaurant and is HIV negative. Stephen was first diagnosed HIV positive in 2007 after a routine test and has been on ART therapy since 2009. He has not yet experienced any serious symptoms.

He is part of a wider community of gay men, several of whom are also HIV positive. They talk frequently about new developments in treatment and try to make sure they are receiving the most effective therapies. His (very large) medical bills are paid through his occupational medical insurance. He eats well and exercises regularly, as well as visiting a number of complementary therapists.

Of course Stephen wishes that he had not been infected with HIV and frequently worries about the future progression of his illness. He is also concerned about the side effects of the drugs – especially those that are visible to others, such as changes in body shape. But the limitations on his life are not currently severe and most relate to the quality of his relationship with Philippe. Although they have worked out sexual strategies to avoid putting Philippe at risk, both are sometimes frustrated by the reduction in intimacy this involves. And Stephen worries about whether Philippe might seek more excitement elsewhere.

---

12 Some of the more detailed arguments in this section are placed in footnotes, with references to further reading for those who wish to follow them up.

Sumalee is a Thai women living in Bangkok. She is 28 years old, has a basic level of education and works long hours in an electronics factory. She has two children, aged seven and four, but separated from her partner when he began to beat her. She recently heard that he had died from an unexplained illness and hesitated a long time before having an HIV test. Her own diagnosis was made only a year ago and she has recently been given ART. She has found her situation very difficult to come to terms with as she has never had sex with anyone except her husband.

Sumalee spent a great deal of time trying to decide whom to talk to about her situation. She was afraid to tell anyone at work in case she lost her job and could not support the children. Her sister, with whom she now lives in a small two-room apartment, has become her closest confidante, along with another HIV positive woman who lives in the same street. She is reluctant to tell anyone else since she is terrified that they will think she has been promiscuous.

Sumalee is able to access free health care at a neighbourhood clinic. While she trusts her carers to protect her privacy, she often feels inferior when they talk to her about future treatment options. They do not always make themselves clear and this make her feels ignorant. While she can read, she does not have access to written material for further clarification. She would like to join an HIV support group, both to share her experiences and to learn more, but has little time free from work and the children. Her main symptom is fatigue and she is also beginning to have headaches but is not sure whether these are a direct result of her HIV. Her biggest worry is whether she can survive long enough in reasonable health to see the children grow up.

Lena is 22 and lives in Kiev, the capital of Ukraine. She was abused as a child, has some secondary education and has been an injecting drug user since she was 18. She lives in one room in a crowded and rundown squat with her boyfriend Boris, who is also a user. She is prone to respiratory and skin infections and does not have a regular job. She undertakes intermittent transactional sex either in exchange for drugs or to get money for food. She is currently five months pregnant.

Her HIV was diagnosed at the beginning of her pregnancy and the shock was very great, even though she knew she was at considerable risk. She is extremely worried about her own health and that of her baby. She has tried to eat well and look after herself but because of her social circumstances she is finding this very difficult.

The health workers at the maternity hospital have not been supportive. Lena is uncertain about whether or not they will provide drugs to prevent transmission of HIV to the baby, while also worrying about the damage her own drug habit might cause the child. She has tried several times to get help in becoming clean but has been turned away because so few services cater for women.

The doctors have told her she does not yet need ART, but she is concerned that when she does supplies will be irregular and she may not be able to get them at all. She recently made contact with one of the few women's projects in Ukraine and is hoping they will help her when the baby is born. Drug users frequently have their babies taken away and she will need legal as well as practical help if she is to keep her child.

Simon is a former miner. He is 38 but looks much older. He was brought up in the rural Eastern Cape in South Africa and married a woman from his home village when he was 20. With the end of apartheid he hoped to be able to get a decent job but things changed very little in his part of the country. Soon his wife became pregnant and he was forced to leave home and try to earn money elsewhere. Joining up with a number of his friends, he moved across the country to work in a gold mine in Carletonville. The work was hard and he lived in a cramped hostel with 80 other men. When things got too hard for him he would occasionally turn to cheap alcohol and local sex workers, but never really felt good about this. He missed his wife very much and felt he was letting her down.

After five years of going back and forth between home and the mine, Simon began to feel weak and found it difficult to keep up with the others on his shift. After some delay, and with considerable fear, he visited the doctor at the mine and was diagnosed not only with HIV but also with tuberculosis. He was treated for TB in the mine hospital but was then sent home.

Simon's wife now cares for him and their three children but they live far from a health centre and life is very difficult. His children and other relatives are frightened of his illness and try to minimise their contact with him. His wife grows food and sells some in the local market but Simon is too ill to make any contribution to their survival. He is in a great deal of pain but no palliative care is available and few people visit him. He knows he will die soon and cannot really see the point of living much longer.

Inequalities and Well-Being in the Context of HIV and AIDS

These people are living with HIV (and in Simon's case dying of AIDS) in very different circumstances. They vary in their sex and gender as well as their sexual preferences. They speak different languages, have been raised in different cultures and have access to different levels of resources to mention just a few of the variations between them. But from a moral perspective one of the most significant factors is the very marked inequality in their capability to make choices about what they define as the most important activities in their lives and to put them into practice.

The most important of these activities will relate to what Ronald Dworkin has called their 'critical interests': 'interests that it does make their life genuinely better to satisfy, interests that they would be mistaken, and genuinely worse off if they did not recognise' (Dworkin 1993 pp.199–208). Examples of such 'constitutive activities' (Doyal and Harris 1983) are universal and include different types of production and consumption, caring for and about others, loving and learning. They also involve avoiding harm and helping others to do the same, being and feeling creative and doing all of these things in ways that promote both self-respect and respect from others (Nussbaum 2011 Chapter 2; Powers and Faden 2006 pp.16–29; Wolff and de Shalit 2007 Chapter 2).

We will use these ideas throughout the book to develop a more systematic understanding of the inequalities and the consequent advantages and disadvantages that characterise the daily lives of too many HIV positive people. But in order to clarify them a little further we should first return to the example of Stephen, who appears to have the highest levels of well-being while living with his illness. Three key aspects of Stephen's circumstances are the most salient in explaining how well he is doing.

First, and most important, Stephen successfully participates in many different aspects of social life (including labour in the form of paid work) and this enables him to develop his understanding of himself and his potential. All human activity is ultimately social in character either because it is initially learned from others or because it is done in collaboration with them (Doyal and Gough 1991 pp.50–56, 76–80). The capacity for sustained and secure social interaction is therefore the vital critical interest that all human beings share. For Stephen (and for anyone else) the inability to maintain this will lead to very serious harm.

Second, Stephen's survival is not currently threatened by his HIV status. Despite his infection he is asymptomatic and has no other debilitating or painful illness. In this sense then, his physical health is good enough to allow him take part in the activities he values most in relation to his critical interests. His positive status is not a barrier to successful participation, so that he can reasonably be said to be physically 'fit'.

Third, Stephen is 'autonomous' in the sense that he has the knowledge and understanding required to formulate goals and develop methods for achieving them, along with the emotional confidence, cognitive capacity and other aspects of mental health necessary to translate his strategies into action. He also has the social opportunities to act accordingly. Hence he is able to make realistic choices (at least in principle) both about his own critical interests and other aspects of his life that he deems important. (Doyal and Gough 1991 pp.59–69; Sen 2010 pp.231–2; Sen 1992 p.40).[13]

---

13   This account of the importance of survival/physical health and autonomy as basic needs for sustained and potentially successful social participation is derived mainly from Doyal and Gough (1991). While not underplaying the differences, there is significant overlap between this work and the 'capabilities' approach developed by Sen and Nussbaum (Nussbaum 2011), the 'well-being' approach of Powers and Faden (2006) and the 'genuine opportunity for secure functionings' approach of (Wolff and De-Shalit 2007). For reasons of space this analysis will minimise the differences between these approaches and use some related terminology interchangeably. While their analyses have varied emphases, their common vision remains the same: the universal moral importance and good of human flourishing in the development of each individual and the role that survival/physical health and autonomy (or freedom) play in its achievement. For a comparison of some of these approaches, see Alkire (2002); Brock (2009) pp.63–71; Dean (2010) pp.24–6, 82–9; Gasper (2007) and Gough (2003).

Autonomous individuals such as Stephen will be able to avoid many of the harms that others will fall prey to. This does not mean that he would never do anything that could potentially harm himself or Philippe: they might decide for example to have unprotected sex on Stephen's birthday. But the key factor here would not be the substantive choice that Stephen might make but rather the fact that he has the capability to make it at all.

When we look more closely, Stephen's potential freedom of action reaches even further. For instance, he could choose to leave his job because he fundamentally disagrees with his manager's decision to cut back the provision of condoms to Malawi. Thus his options are not confined to those contained within his current social or cultural boundaries. He has what can be called 'critical autonomy' (Doyal and Gough 1991 pp.67–9, 187–90). This is very important for all individuals if they are to avoid what for many may amount to an intellectual and emotional prison.[14] It also goes to the heart of the idea that critical autonomy in particular can never properly be explored except in the context of a democratic and participatory society (Held 1995 pp.141–218).

Overall then, Stephen's case illustrates the fact that survival/physical health or 'fitness' (in the sense referred to above) and autonomy (including critical autonomy) are basic human needs that must be met in order for any individual (whatever their HIV status) to optimise their freedom and well-being. Unless these needs are met they will be unable to engage in the social participation necessary for them to flourish as human beings: to lead what has traditionally been called a 'good life'. But in order to satisfy these basic needs a range of what have been termed 'intermediate needs' will first have to be met (Doyal and Gough 1991 pp.155–9, Chapter 10).

The core list of these has now been laid out in many international documents concerning well-being and is little disputed. It includes: nutritional food and clean water; accessible sanitation; environmentally appropriate and safe housing; non-hazardous work and a safe physical environment; effective health care (including safe birth control and childbearing); significant primary relationships (especially in childhood); and appropriate levels of knowledge and understanding alongside emotional, physical and economic security and privacy (Doyal 1997).

These intermediate needs can be met by access to an *adequate* supply of material, social or personal resources with 'universal satisfier characteristics' that are the same for everyone, everywhere. They are 'those properties of goods, services, activities and relationships which enhance physical health and human autonomy in all cultures' (Doyal and Gough 1991 p.157).[15] These characteristics

---

14   This concept may be especially important in making sense of the lives of many poor women whose lack of critical (or even basic) autonomy may threaten their physical and mental well-being in the most extreme ways. Later chapters will illustrate this point in a number of ways in the context of HIV.

15   What 'adequate' supply means in this context is complex and disputable. In the wide spectrum of literature either sympathetic to or compatible with our approach,

will be determined by what are deemed to be the most accurate natural or social scientific findings. In the context of nutrition, for example, they will reflect the levels of macronutrients (carbohydrate, protein and fat) and micronutrients (vitamins and minerals) estimated to be necessary for the maintenance of the levels of physical health required for sustained survival and well-being. The appropriate levels of satisfiers related to non-material factors such as the education required for particular tasks *within* a given culture will be relatively straightforward. However, when we include the critical autonomy required to make choices *between* different forms of social life the equation educational requirements will rise considerably. Satisfiers such as emotional security will be even more difficult to measure, but indicators based on more qualitative studies can provide useful guidelines for comparison across different settings.

In this sense then, these intermediate needs will be the same for all according to the nature of their critical interests in the circumstances in which they find themselves. However, they can, of course, be satisfied in many different ways. The same nutritional requirement can be met through consuming different types of food for example, while houses with very different designs will provide appropriate shelter according to varying climates and local terrains. Thus an emphasis on the universality of basic and intermediate need satisfaction for the preservation

---

definitions include terms such as 'sustenance', 'a dignified and minimally flourishing life', 'a decent life', 'a good life' and so on. We believe that the standard of adequacy of basic need satisfaction should be set high, and hence the same applies to levels of intermediate need satisfaction. *In principle*, such satisfaction is adequate when using a minimal amount of appropriate resources, it optimises the potential of *each* individual to sustain their participation in those constitutive activities important for furthering their critical interests. What this means *in practice* is that levels of intermediate need satisfiers should be linked to what has been shown to be possible in countries with the best physical, cognitive, emotional, environmental and political indicators. The Scandinavian countries remain good examples.

Of course there will be a range of socio-economic constraints in middle and poor income countries which make such a high standard unrealistic. As always in these matters 'ought implies can'. Yet in trying to establish 'thresholds' at any given time, we must be careful not to aim too low. Aspirations concerning intermediate and therefore basic need satisfaction can of course be adjusted with reference to what is achievable by the best performing nations within any particular socioeconomic range (e.g. high, medium or low income). But within poor countries there can be no justification for complacency and every reason for political struggle to reduce or eliminate arbitrary constraints on the well-being of individual citizens. For example, there is no reason to believe that the optimum level of need satisfaction deemed suitable for the potential to flourish within a particular social form of life should be constrained to the level of 'participation' rather than the more 'critical' level demanded for capability to criticise, reject and remove oneself from such forms of life (Doyal and Gough 1991 pp.159–70).

For other approaches to 'thresholds' or levels of 'sufficiency' of basic need satisfaction (or 'capabilities' or 'well-being' or 'decency') below which no one should be allowed to fall, see (Nussbaum 2011 pp.32–42; Powers and Faden 2006 pp.57–64; Ruger 2010 pp.45–50, 88–95; Wolff and De-Shalit 2007 Chapter 5).

of critical interests is perfectly compatible with cultural relativity in how such satisfaction is achieved.

We can now see why Stephen is apparently living so well and is relatively advantaged despite his positive status. He is physically healthy and autonomous because he is well nourished, well educated, securely and safely employed; has access to excellent health care; is in a supportive primary relationship; and has a strong sense of himself and his abilities. He is capable of making and acting on choices about the things he values, and his critical autonomy reflects his capacity to challenge views that are different from his own. Sadly, the same cannot be said for many millions of other HIV positive (and negative) people around the world.

In order to take this analysis a stage further we can examine the unequal and more disadvantaged circumstances of Sumalee compared to Stephen. For the moment she is well enough to work, though this may not continue as she is already beginning to feel the strain. The family have sufficient food and clean water for their immediate purposes and, so long as she does not become too unwell, she has some degree of security in her job. Her accommodation is adequate despite its limited size. Hence some of her most important physical needs are being met.

However the level of satisfaction of her intermediate need for appropriate health care is not adequate. For example those health professionals with whom she engages are not supportive enough to allay her insecurities or to enable her to make optimal sense of the information required to make appropriate choices. Further, she has no extra time to attend local organisations that could help improve her understanding. This has a negative impact on her overall autonomy, and her critical autonomy is especially limited.

Her close relationship with her sister and her friend are important in providing support, but she is afraid of further extending her network in case her HIV status becomes common knowledge. She has close relationships with her children and sees them as central to her existence. However they also represent dependants whose own intermediate needs she has a 'special obligation' to meet along with her own (Jeske 2008). Her intermediate need for primary relationships is therefore partially met, but is limited by her maternal responsibilities as well as the particular stigma attached to women with HIV in her community.

When we move on to compare Sumalee and Lena the reality of the 'corrosive disadvantage' that blights the lives of so many positive people becomes clearer (Wolff and De-Shalit 2007 Chapter 8). Because of her poverty and addiction, Lena is undernourished and already suffers from a number of infections that weaken her immune system. Hence her physical health was already problematic before the HIV began to take hold. Her standard of housing is very poor, generating high levels of anxiety. She has trouble feeding herself adequately and in order to do so she has to risk her health and physical safety still further. All of these disadvantages corrosively reinforce each other.

And so they continue. Since she was an abused child and was poorly educated, Lena has little self-esteem. Despite her access to health care she has a very poor understanding of her illness. This is reinforced by the inadequate communication she has with her doctors and nurses, who appear to be unresponsive to her needs because of their prejudice against drug users.

Lena has had very little access to positive primary relationships either in childhood or in the present. Indeed this is one of the reasons she finds it so difficult to quit drugs since addiction is her key bond with her partner, who offers her some degree of emotional support and physical protection – albeit to a minimal level. She desperately wants to keep her baby but knows that without help and support from elsewhere this will be impossible.

When compared with Sumalee, Lena's physical health is not nearly as good and she is significantly less autonomous because so many of her intermediate needs are very poorly satisfied. Her capability to make choices concerning herself, her baby and her future is extremely limited due to the hostile nature of her social environment. She is not helpless but understandably feels close to it. She needs institutional support that is not available. Lena is more disadvantaged than Sumalee and has fewer opportunities to improve her situation.

Simon's situation is of course even worse. His physical condition is terminal as a result of both the TB and the HIV that has now progressed to AIDS. In theory he might be treatable, but in practice such a choice and its realisation are way beyond his capability. He has no means of getting to the closest health centre, which itself is without a consistent supply of ART.

His health is so poor that he has lost any sense of physical or emotional security. He knows that he is dying, as does everyone else with whom he interacts. Because he can contribute nothing to the family, their feelings toward him are often ambivalent. Since she knows how he contracted his illness, his wife's care is often affected by her anger and desperation. Because of their fear and the desire of his wife and her relatives to protect them, we have seen that his children have little contact with him. Hence he lacks positive primary relationships just when they are most needed.

As his sickness moves inexorably on, Simon becomes even more undernourished, dehydrated and weak. With such extremely low levels of physical health, and lacking even basic levels of autonomy, he no longer feels human; a useless outcast with no respect, no dignity and minimal choices. It is not surprising that for Simon, death cannot come too soon. Life itself has lost its value.

These cases have highlighted both the commonality and the diversity of living with HIV. There are many differences between these four individuals. Yet they are bound together by their common humanity – by the fact that they all have the same basic and intermediate needs.[16] Again, in this sense Stephen, Sumalee, Lena and Simon are all 'equal' but there are major inequalities in their ability to satisfy these needs which in turn create massive differences in the quality of their lives and their deaths. These differences reflect the patterns of diversity and disadvantage that

---

16   Throughout the rest of the book we will ordinarily speak of 'basic need satisfaction' since this empirically requires the adequate satisfaction of 'intermediate needs'. At times, however, context will dictate that we refer to the latter alone.

characterise the wider pandemic. But of course there are many more Simons than there are Stephens and it is here that much of the problem lies.

Poverty and 'Structural Violence' in the Pandemic

It is a central feature of the pandemic that the vast majority of those living with HIV and dying from AIDS do so in situations of relative or absolute deprivation. Even among those who live in rich countries, many belong to marginalised groups and are worse off than their compatriots.[17] But, most importantly, the vast majority of those infected live in the poorest countries with very few resources at their disposal. Hence HIV (and the conditions associated with AIDS) are not diseases of poverty so much as diseases of the poor.

This social and economic reality reflects the historical processes of colonialism, neo-colonialism and slavery that have impoverished so many parts of the world. It is also linked to more recent global restructuring which has exacerbated old problems while simultaneously creating new ones. The mechanisms by which these changes occur are complex and multifaceted, but the overall impact has been to put severe constraints on those aspects of development needed for improvements in population health.

Global inequalities in income and investment have intensified over the period of the pandemic with the gap between the richest and the poorest widening. These trends are difficult to measure but a study from the United Nations University estimated that the richest 1 per cent of people in the world now controlled around 40 per cent of assets while the richest 10 per cent controlled around 85 per cent (Davies et al, 2008). Conversely the poorest 50 per cent owned only 1 per cent. Looked at from the perspective of individuals, the World Bank has recently estimated that around 1.4 billion people are now living on less than $1.25 per day. In South Asia this represents 36 per cent of the population, while in sub-Saharan Africa it is nearing 50 per cent.[18]

Millions of people are moving within and between countries in pursuit of sustainable livelihoods. By 2010, 214 million were living outside their country of birth, and almost all nations were affected in some way or other by internal and/or external migration (United Nations Department of Economic and Social Affairs 2011). While this has meant better lives for some, it has contributed to the breakdown of traditional support networks and enhanced vulnerability for others.[19] Paul Farmer has described this as 'structural violence', with individuals

---

17　The main exception here will be the relatively affluent 'gay men' in the global north of the type represented by Stephen.

18　http://data.worldbank.org/topic/poverty.

19　For case studies of how these complex factors play out in South Africa see Marks (2002). For a very powerful example of how they shaped the life of one street boy in Mwanza, Tanzania, see Lockhart (2008).

being harmed because the social arrangements under which they live deny them the opportunity to meet their own basic needs: 'historically given (and often economically driven) processes and forces conspire to constrain individual agency. Structural violence is visited upon all those whose social status denies them access to the fruits of scientific and social progress' (Farmer 2001 p.78).

Under these circumstances, millions of poor and disadvantaged individuals will be at heightened risk of sickness and premature death, with HIV and AIDS high on the list of potential hazards: 'poor people are vulnerable biologically, socially, and economically to a disease occasioned by their most intimate acts. They make love on the edge of a cliff in a deadly game of Russian roulette' (Baker 2008 p.12). For those who lose out on this gamble, structural violence will also limit their access to therapies and to palliative care.

Outline of the Book

This first chapter has provided an introduction to the study of living with HIV and dying with AIDS. It has highlighted the need for an interdisciplinary approach to understanding and tackling the pandemic while highlighting its complex relationship with wider patterns of inequality and disadvantage. A conceptual framework has been outlined for making sense of the links between HIV and AIDS, inequality and human needs across a range of social and economic settings

The second chapter will map the 'global pandemic'. It will identify each of the smaller constituent epidemics with their different patterns of transmission and the resulting variations in the social groups that make them up. It will then move on to explore the characteristics of these different HIV positive populations through the lens of socio-economic status, sex/gender, race/ethnicity and sexual identity as well as injecting drug use and age. Each of these characteristics will be linked to particular patterns of advantage and disadvantage in relation both to the acquisition of HIV and to the capacity of individuals and groups to mitigate its effects.

The third chapter will focus on individual narratives, offering an overview of what we know (and do not know) about the physical, psychological and social journeys of those who have been infected. How has illness altered their view of themselves, their past and their future? What are the challenges faced by individuals as an HIV diagnosis damages their social identity? Some will be shown to successfully achieve 'normalisation', with some of these reconstructing themselves as positive activists. However significant numbers will face extreme difficulties in managing what may be last phase of their lives. The chapter will include a critical evaluation of the concept of stigma and its implications for narratives of HIV across different cultures.

Chapter 4 takes up the issue of access to health care and its implications not just for ultimate survival but also for the quality of life of those dependent on it. It will place considerable emphasis on the economic social and cultural obstacles to care. This will be interwoven with a discussion of the appropriateness and effectiveness of medical therapies through the lens of individual experiences. The chapter will conclude with a discussion of the complex effects of ART on autonomy through the notion of 'therapeutic citizenship'.

Chapter 5 will then explore the implications of HIV and AIDS for the livelihoods of those infected as well as those who care for them and those who are dependent on them. It will highlight the implications of illness and death for the intensification of poverty in settings where work is scarce and often involves hard physical labour. The chapter will also explore the effects of HIV and AIDS on wider household groups with resulting changes in the gender division of labour and the transfer of work between generations. There will be a particular focus on the implications of caring both for the carers themselves and for those who are dependent on them.

Chapters 6 and 7 will be concerned with some of the most invisible aspects of the lives of HIV positive people: sex and reproduction. Chapter 6 will explore the implications of an HIV diagnosis for sexual life. It will examine the varying constraints placed on sexual activities and the implications this has for the maintenance and development of intimate relationships. The analysis will bring together accounts of the impact of HIV on individuals with very different sexual identities and practices. Chapter 7 will then examine issues associated with the reproductive needs and desires of people living with HIV. It will examine the challenges of conception, fertility control, pregnancy and childbirth in the broader context of global inequalities in reproductive rights. There will also be a detailed examination of the experiences of positive women as they take responsibility for new (and possibly damaged) lives in the context of their own (often untreated) illness.

Finally, Chapters 8 and 9 will revisit some of the key themes of the book from a number of different philosophical, methodological and political perspectives. Chapter 8 will focus on the origins of the concept of human rights and its implications for HIV and AIDS advocacy. It will explore both the value of human rights discourse and also the current limitations of human rights practice. The chapter will finish with a discussion of the potential contradiction between the universalism inherent in the human rights approach and claims for 'AIDS exceptionalism'.

The concluding chapter will highlight the current dilemma of growing needs and declining resources within the global HIV and AIDS arena. Potential solutions will be explored in the form of more accountability and transparency in resource allocation, and more effective collaboration between biomedical and social researchers. It will then summarise the strategies needed to ensure that the existing human rights machinery is used more effectively in both local and global contexts.

Chapter 2
Mapping the Pandemic

This first 'pandemic of globalisation' is made up of a series of separate (though sometimes overlapping) epidemics.[1] The main routes of transmission of the virus vary between epidemics, as do the numbers and types of people affected. This chapter will draw a preliminary map of variations in rates of HIV and AIDS in different parts of the world. It will explore some of the main social and economic factors involved in shaping both the epidemics themselves and their impact on the lives of those affected. This will involve the presentation of many statistics which may at times seem indigestible. However they are an essential prelude to a deeper understanding of patterns of diversity and disadvantage within HIV positive populations.

Differences *between* Epidemics and their Populations

Most commonly, epidemics are defined geographically by region and by country and then by intensity: 'low level' (below 1 per cent of the population); 'concentrated' (high prevalence in a few identifiable groups); 'generalised' (between 1 per cent and 15 per cent prevalence and self-sustaining in the wider population); or 'hyper-endemic '(above 15 per cent prevalence). Here we will explore the state of the various epidemics using mainly WHO and UNAIDS regional data.[2] Though these are based on geographical criteria, it will be important to remember that the epidemics themselves are not just spatial but also geo-political.[3]

The Epidemic in the Global North

The number of new infections in North America and Central and Western Europe is now relatively stable, largely as a result of the increase in preventive services and wider public awareness of related risks. However the total number of people

---

1   Biologically they are characterised by a variety of retroviral types or subtypes. The main types in the pandemic are HIV-1 (most common and most easily transmissible) and HIV-2 (found mostly in West Africa).

2   Because of the relative invisibility of HIV and AIDS in North Africa and the Middle East, systematic regional data are scarce. However, for a useful discussion of the particularities of the epidemic in the Middle East see Obermeyer (2006).

3   The data sources used here are WHO, UNICEF and UNAIDS (2011) and UNAIDS (2012c) *World AIDS Day Report* unless otherwise indicated.

living with HIV in the global north continues to rise, reaching an estimated 2.2 million in 2010 – about one-third more than in 2001. This reflects the widescale availability of antiretroviral therapy (ART), which has significantly reduced the number of AIDS-related deaths. About 90 per cent of those estimated to be in clinical need in the United States now have access to these drugs.

The USA still has one of the largest epidemics in a single country and is home to more than half (about 1.2 million) of the positive people in the region. In 2010 sex between men was still the major mode of transmission, at around 60 per cent, and the incidence has been increasing among younger men in this group in both the USA and the UK (Crepaz et al. 2004; Dodds et al. 2004, 2007).[4] Infection through unprotected heterosexual contact has been increasing over time and now accounts for about 27 per cent of all new cases. As a result the number of positive women has risen and they now make up about a quarter of those newly infected. The proportion of those (mainly males) infected through injecting drug use (IDU) has declined markedly and now stands at around 9 per cent (Kaiser Family Foundation 2012).

Viewing the US epidemic from a different perspective, African American and Hispanic women and men have been disproportionately affected. Relative to their numbers in the population, they are over-represented among the newly infected and among those living with HIV as well as those dying from AIDS (Kaiser Family Foundation 2012; Peterson and Jones 2009). Indeed the rates of HIV among African American men who have sex with men (MSM) now rival those among the general population in many high prevalence countries (Centers for Disease Control and Prevention 2006).

In Western Europe around 730,000 people are now estimated to be living with HIV, with unprotected sex between men (around 40 per cent) unprotected heterosex (around 39 per cent) and injecting drug use (about 4 per cent) currently the most common modes of transmission (van de Laar et al. 2008).[5] As in the USA, the number of new HIV diagnoses attributed to unprotected sex between young men has recently risen sharply in several countries (Dubois-Arber and Moreau-Gruet 2007; Gebhardt 2005).[6] While the overall number of new infections is relatively stable, national trends vary across Western and Central Europe. Rates of diagnosed HIV cases doubled between 2000 and 2009 in Bulgaria, the Czech Republic, Hungary, Lithuania, Slovakia and Slovenia and increased by more than 50 per

---

4   The term 'men who have sex with men' (MSM) will be used here in a narrow technical sense to describe the epidemiology of the various epidemics. The problems with the use of the term will be discussed later in the chapter and other formulations will be used in line with particular data sources.

5   Care should be taken in comparing data from the European Union and the World Health Organization (WHO) European region, which includes Central and Eastern Europe. See European Centre for Disease Control (2010).

6   For further discussion of the implications of this see Chapter 6 on sexuality.

cent in the United Kingdom. On the other hand, new HIV diagnoses decreased by more than 20 per cent in Latvia, Portugal and Romania (UNAIDS 2012c).

A major feature of the epidemic in the Western European context is the growing number of those diagnosed positive who are migrants from sub-Saharan Africa (European Centre for Disease Control and Prevention 2010). These women and men now make up the majority of those infected through heterosexual contact in many European countries. In the UK, for example, migrants from the African region now constitute nearly one-third of new diagnoses (UK Health Protection Agency 2011). Hence those from poorer regions bear one of the heaviest burdens of HIV and AIDS even when they are living in the richest countries.

Injecting Drug Use as a Key Driver in Transitional States

In Eastern Europe and Central Asia HIV infection is concentrated among IDUs, sex workers and their sexual partners and represents the fastest growing epidemic in the world. This reflects in large part the economic and social disintegration as well as the personal alienation experienced by so many in the post-Soviet era. In 2010 injecting drug users made up more than 62 per cent of people living with HIV and the number of positive women is growing in many parts of the region: by 2009 they made up 45 per cent of the HIV positive population in Ukraine (UNAIDS 2012c).

An estimated quarter of all the 3.7 million people (mostly men) who inject drugs in the region are living with HIV. Less than 1 per cent of infections are attributed to sex between men, though this is probably an underestimate (AIDSTAR-Two 2010; Caceres et al. 2006; Baral et al. 2007). Availability of ART in the low and middle income countries in the region has been estimated to be the second lowest in the world, with only about 23 per cent of those in need being able to obtain it.[7] The number of people living with HIV has tripled since 2000 and reached around 1.5 million by 2010, reflecting the growing numbers infected. Deaths have also increased over the same period in the absence of treatment (WHO, UNICEF and UNAIDS 2011).

Significant Progress with ART in the Central and South American Region

Around 1.5 million people are estimated to be living with HIV in the region, with five countries having an adult prevalence higher than 2 per cent. The majority of new infections are said to be occurring in and around urban networks of MSM (Bastos et al. 2008). In Mexico these men are estimated to account for 57 per cent of all diagnoses to date (UNAIDS 2012c). However rates of infection have also been growing among IDUs and among those living in rural areas.

---

7   For regional estimates of ART availability in all middle and low income countries see WHO, UNICEF and UNAIDS (2011). The region with the lowest coverage is the Middle East and North Africa, at only 10 per cent in 2011.

The countries of Central America are the most heavily affected, with research uncovering hidden epidemics among MSM (Caceres 2002). An increase in the number of positive women has been observed in the same countries as well as a rise in incidence among marginalised groups, including indigenous populations.

Brazil contains one-third of all HIV positive people in the region and has made considerable progress both in stabilising the epidemic and in providing treatment for those infected. Beginning in 2002, it was the first country in the world to guarantee free, universal access to antiretroviral drugs.[8] In the region overall about 68 per cent of those in need are now able to access ART, with the figure as high as 83 per cent in Brazil (WHO, UNICEF and UNAIDS 2011). This has been the major factor in the increase in the number of people living with HIV from 1.1 million in 2001 to 1.5 million in 2010 (UNAIDS 2012c).

Asia: Married Women at Risk in Densely Populated Settings

Around 4.8 million people were living with HIV or AIDS in Asia in 2010, of whom about 50 per cent were from India. Epidemics in the Asian region are particularly diverse both within and between countries (Steinbrook 2007). The number of people infected has stabilised over the past five years but remains very high, reflecting the very large size of the populations in India and China. At present, epidemics in the region are mostly contained within three overlapping groups: MSM, IDUs and female sex workers and their clients (UNAIDS 2012c).

It is estimated that around 75 million men in the region regularly buy sex from women (UNAIDS 2009). China has approximately 130 million internal migrants, and young men moving from rural to urban areas in search of work have been identified as one of the keys to the spread of the epidemic to the general population. This is of course exacerbated by the 'one child policy' which left a huge excess of men unable to find available women, and hence more likely to buy sex.

Those women who sell sex may do it to fund a drug habit, or they may have become involved in sex work as a survival strategy before turning to drug use (Sharma et al. 2009). Those who have been trafficked face especially high risks of contracting HIV, with a recent study in Mumbai showing that around half of all women and girls in this category had been infected (Gupta et al. 2009). The prevalence of HIV among IDUs is also very high, with the average being about 16 per cent but reaching 30–50 per cent in some settings (UNAIDS 2012c; Sharma et al. 2009).

In 1990 women made up some 17 per cent of the total HIV positive population in Asia but by 2007 this had doubled to 35 per cent. Most had only ever had one sexual partner (UNAIDS 2009).[9] Many men are infected through their interaction with female (or male) sex workers and then pass on the virus to their partners

---

8   For further discussion see Chapter 9.

9   Of course this is not only a problem in Asia but more detailed research has been carried out there. For similar evidence from South Africa see Abrahams et al. (2004).

(Saggurti et al. 2009; Schensul et al. 2006). These risks are exacerbated by the fact that many married men also have sex with other men but keep this secret.[10] Similar patterns can be seen among IDUs. A recent report estimated that some 50 million women in Asia are at risk by one or other of these routes, making sex with their husbands a major threat to their health (UNAIDS 2009).

Finally, China is the only country in the world where large numbers of people have been infected through contaminated blood. Following a ban on imported blood in the 1980s, many poor people in rural areas sold their blood as a survival strategy. However the techniques used were not safe and many of those involved as donors or recipients became infected. By 2005 they accounted for some 10 per cent of the HIV positive population in the country (Asia Catalyst 2012).

Availability of ART increased threefold in the region between 2003 and 2006. However by 2010 only a third of those in East, South and South East Asia in need of ART were receiving it (WHO, UNICEF and UNAIDS 2011). The number of people living with HIV or AIDS in the region has remained stable at around 4.9 million over the past five years.

The Heart of the Pandemic: Sub-Saharan Africa (and the Caribbean)

The sub-Saharan African region as a whole contains about 11 per cent of the global population but about 68 per cent of those infected with HIV. In 2009 it was the location for 72 per cent of all deaths from AIDS. There were an estimated 1.9 million new infections in the region in 2010, representing more than two-thirds (70 per cent) of all new infections globally. Average life expectancy at birth in parts of southern Africa is estimated to have declined to levels last seen in the 1950s. It is now below 50 years for the sub-region as a whole and most of this fall has been attributed to deaths from AIDS (UNAIDS 2012c).

The African region is the only one to contain low-prevalence, concentrated, generalised and hyperendemic epidemics at the same time. Significant progress has been made between 2001 and 2009 with the number of people newly infected falling by more than 25 per cent in 22 countries (UNAIDS 2012c). However the problems remain severe. South Africa has now stabilised the number of new infections but still has a generalised epidemic with the largest number of HIV positive people (around 5.6 million) in any single country, while Swaziland has the highest prevalence rate in the world at 26 per cent of all adults. There are now estimated be nearly 23 million people living with HIV in the region. Access to ART has increased markedly from a low of 2 per cent just eight years ago, and by 2009 services covered about 49 per cent of those in need (UNAIDS 2012c).

The main routes of transmission in the African region are sex between women and men and (to a lesser degree) mother to child transmission. Sex work and migration are important factors in shaping this pattern of infection. Women make up about 60 per cent of those who are positive and the prevalence among those aged

---

10   For further discussion of the point see Chapter 6.

15–24 is especially high. In South Africa 21 per cent of girls and young women in this age group are HIV positive, compared to 7 per cent of men of the same age (UNAIDS 2012c). This has led to high rates of mother to child transmission, with about 90 per cent of all HIV positive children in the world living in Africa. It has also contributed to a dramatic increase in the number of 'AIDS orphans' (Hosegood et al. 2007a).

Despite the predominantly heterosexual nature of the epidemic in Africa, there has also been a growing recognition of the importance of sexual transmission between men. The very high levels of homophobia found in many communities had pushed these activities underground (Paparini et al. 2008; Long 2003). However a recent review of the literature concluded that MSM in the region were about eight times more likely than other men to be HIV positive (Smith et al. 2009). There is also evidence of growing numbers of infected IDUs, especially in the countries in the south and south-east of the region (van Griensven et al. 2009).

The epidemic in the Caribbean is usually classified with those in Central and South America because of their geographical proximity. However the pattern of HIV and AIDS is much more like that in the African region, reflecting their historical connections. Hence they will be considered together here.[11] At 1 per cent the prevalence rate in the Caribbean is the second highest in the world, with transmission being mainly through unprotected sex between women and men. As a result just over half of HIV positive people in the Caribbean are female. But again recent evidence suggests that the rate of transmission through sex between men may be greater than had been assumed, with high levels of homophobia having distorted perceptions of who is infected (Caceres 2002; Caceres et al. 2006).

This brief overview has highlighted the diversity of the various epidemics. We have seen that each is made up of different combinations of men and women with different sexual practices and different patterns of injecting drug use. Most discussions of these differences have explored their implications for prevention. But for our purposes here we need to shift the focus to assess how they interact with a range of other influences to shape the lives and deaths of those already infected. This is especially important in light of the fact that, as we have seen, the number of people living with HIV is increasing markedly in most parts of the world

Diversity *within* Positive Populations: Developing an Eco-Social Approach

Most statistical accounts give only a very limited picture of the characteristics of HIV positive populations.[12] This is because the focus on routes of transmission

---

11   Farmer (2010) draws important historical analogies between the role of slavery and other forms of oppression in Haiti and in Africa and explores their impact on HIV.

12   The main exception to this is the United States, where the data produced by the Centers for Disease Control and Prevention (CDC) is very detailed and contains information

creates social groups based on very narrow biological criteria. If we are to make sense of the realities of living with HIV and AIDS then we will need to map these onto the standard categories used by most social science researchers: socio-economic status, sex and gender and 'race' and ethnicity. Because of the nature of the pandemic itself we will also need to include different sexual identities and patterns of injecting drug use as analytical categories.

These different indicators are usually presented as 'scientific' representations of the relationship between individuals and social structures. But, as we shall see, they are complex social and cultural constructions that cannot be taken at face value. Hence we will need to 'deconstruct' them to explore their implications in the context of HIV and AIDS. This analysis will be based upon what Nancy Krieger has called an 'eco-social' approach. As she describes it: 'the way we develop, grow, age, ail and die necessarily reflects a constant interplay within our bodies, of our intertwined and inseparable social and biological history' (Krieger 1999 p.296).

Socio-Economic Status and HIV: Making the Links

The concept of 'socio-economic status' (SES) is normally used to measure the location of an individual within the broader economic and social structure of the country in which they live. Because of the global distribution of HIV and AIDS between countries it is widely assumed that there is a consistent negative correlation between the SES of individuals and households and their risk of HIV infection. However, this is difficult to confirm or deny since the relationship between SES and HIV is rarely included in national statistics and attempts to measure it face significant methodological challenges (Braveman et al. 2005; Krieger et al. 1997).

What little evidence we do have suggests that the relationship between the two variables is often bi-directional (Barnighausen et al. 2007). That is to say, SES may shape vulnerability to HIV; but conversely HIV infection itself may have an impact on SES. This complex interaction has led to what may sometimes appear to be contradictory research findings. In the African context in particular evidence on the relationship between HIV and SES has been difficult to interpret (Parkhurst 2010). Some population-based surveys have indicated that HIV prevalence is higher in those households that are relatively better off, while others have shown the poor to be more affected (Mishra et al. 2007; Shelton et al. 2005).

In a survey of socio-economic status and HIV among cohabiting couples in eight African countries, HIV prevalence was generally found to be higher among wealthier and better educated groups (Mishra et al. 2007). By contrast a longitudinal study carried out in a poor rural community in KwaZulu-Natal, South Africa found that the likelihood of becoming infected with HIV was greater among those with lower SES (Barnighausen et al. 2007).

---

rarely found in other national or international statistics.

It appears therefore that in the African region at least, both high and low SES may be associated with greater vulnerability to HIV. The positive relationship found in some settings has been attributed to the fact that relatively greater wealth is associated with better education and hence with a higher likelihood of living in an urban area where HIV itself is more prevalent. Moreover wealthier men (but not necessarily women) also appear to be more likely to have earlier sexual debuts and to be able to afford more lifetime sexual partners (Mishra et al. 2007).[13]

Where the relationship between HIV and SES is negative, very different factors appear to be involved. The biological vulnerability of lower status individuals may be greater as a result of poor nutrition over lengthy periods as well as untreated illness, especially sexually transmitted infections and tuberculosis (Sawers et al. 2008). At the same time, low SES may mean that women in particular have few survival strategies and hence may feel pressure to engage in transactional sex and/ or to agree to sex without a condom (Wojcicki 2005).

In light of these findings it has been suggested that the relationship between SES and HIV will vary between settings and may even change over time in the same epidemic (Parkhurst 2010). It appears, for example, that those with the highest SES (especially those with the most education) are likely to be the first to benefit from information about safer sexual practices. Conversely the progress of the epidemic may worsen the poverty in the wider community, thereby increasing the relative risk to lower status groups (Gillespie et al. 2007a, 2007b; Parkhurst 2010).

Moving 'downstream' to the period after infection, the relationship between socio-economic status and the effects of HIV will of course be more consistent. By definition those with lower SES will have fewer resources to meet their needs during their illness. As their condition worsens, many will be unable to work in paid employment or on domestic tasks.[14] Low levels of access to medical treatment may result in a diminished quality of life, an inability to control opportunistic infections and the more rapid development of AIDS.[15]

Since HIV often clusters within families, both parents may fall sick, meaning that entire households may find survival extremely difficult. Children may be left isolated when they have lost both parents and access to most forms of social support. Poor nutrition may lead to poor health in adulthood and these children are likely to carry their low socio-economic status over their lifetimes and into future generations.

Overall then, we can conclude that most (but by no means all) of those living with HIV and dying from AIDS are disadvantaged through their unequal access to necessary resources. Those who live in rich countries will often belong to marginalised groups who are entitled to fewer benefits than most of

---

13   It would be possible to compare this with the situation of (mostly white) gay men in the US.

14   For more discussion of these issues see Chapter 5 on livelihoods.

15   For more discussion of these issues see Chapter 4 on health care.

their compatriots. But, most importantly, the vast majority of positive people are disadvantaged by the fact they have low incomes and live in settings where public sector provision is scarce and often of poor quality. Hence their socio-economic status can be said to be unequal not just by comparison with their compatriots but also when measured in a wider global context.

Sex and Gender: Nature or Nurture?

As we have seen, most descriptions of the various epidemics do refer to the different rates of HIV and AIDS in women and men. However these are rarely accompanied by clarification of the mix of biological and social factors underlying them. Historically, discussions about the differences in health between women and men were focussed mainly on the biological sphere of sex organs and reproductive capacities.[16] However the 1960s saw the emergence of the concept of 'gender' to describe the ways in which femaleness was socially as well as biologically constructed.

Feminist academics and activists of the period argued that many of the supposedly 'natural' differences between women and men were in fact the result of the ways in which societies were organised. Thus 'gender' was a new expression designed to counter biological determinism. As one writer has briefly summarised it: 'we are born biologically sexed but society en-genders us' (Dowsett 2003 p.23).

Despite this clarification, the terms 'sex' and 'gender' are still too often used interchangeably (Annandale and Riska 2009; Doyal 2001; Krieger 2003b). Moreover the concept of 'gender' is frequently used to apply only to women despite the fact that men's lives are also gendered. These mistakes will need to be avoided if we are to make sense of how male and female biological sex interacts with masculine and feminine gender to influence vulnerability to HIV infection and to shape experiences of the illness itself (Belden and Squires 2008).

As we saw in the previous chapter, women are biologically more vulnerable than men to infection with HIV during episodes of heterosex. This derives mainly from the fact that potentially infectious semen is left for some time on the woman's vaginal membranes. This is especially dangerous in the presence of traumatic injury or existing genital infections (Abrahams et al. 2004; McNamara 2003).[17]

---

16   The last decade has seen an extension of this concept to 'sex-related biology', which explores a broader range of hormonal and metabolic variations between women and men. There has also been growing recognition of the differences between males and females in their experiences of diseases that affect both sexes: heart disease in particular (Wizeman and Pardue 2001).

17   This is an important point since it links gender violence to the spread of HIV, especially when it is combined with the fact that many women in poor countries experience high rates of untreated sexually transmitted infections.

Female gender may also increase women's vulnerability through placing arbitrary limits on their access to the resources necessary for health (Annandale and Riske 2010; Doyal 1995; Doyal and Payne 2011; Payne 2006; Krieger 2003b). These will include many of the 'intermediate need satisfiers' identified in the previous chapter – with physical and emotional security, a nutritious diet and educational opportunities being especially notable. As regards the basic need for autonomy, women are also more likely than men to be constrained in their capacity to make informed choices about their lives, especially in the context of sex and reproduction (Gupta 2002). This may result in harm that they have little chance of preventing.

Obviously, men too may be exposed to HIV through sexual transmission. As we have seen unprotected anal sex is significantly more dangerous than vaginal sex posing particular risks for MSM (Baggaley et al. 2010). Those men engaged in heterosex are less physiological vulnerable than women. However the social construction of heterosexual male gender may still lead men to harm their health (Barker and Ricardo 2005; Connell and Messerschmidt 2005; Courtney 2000). This can take many different forms but will usually include the social expectation that 'real' men will 'perform' their masculinity through having frequent (often unprotected) sex with different women. This is clearly a gendered risk factor for HIV, yet very few studies have explored the sexual subjectivities and practices of heterosexual men (Bowleg 2004; Doyal 2009b; Doyal et al. 2009; Raj and Bowleg 2011).

The interaction between biological sex and social gender is therefore of central importance in shaping vulnerabilities to HIV in both women and men. And of course it continues to have a major influence on individual lives after infection. Inequalities in access to resources will affect the capacities of women and men to manage their illness. This will usually cause greater harm to women, but in the context of health care in particular men may be disadvantaged by their 'masculine' reluctance to admit weakness and to seek help.[18]

'Race' and Ethnicity: Biological or Social?

The categories of 'race' and 'ethnicity' are frequently used as variables in both medical and social research. But again we need to look very carefully at how they are operationalised and what they can be taken to signify (Gravlee and Sweet 2008; Gravlee 2009). As in the case of sex and gender, they have frequently been deployed interchangeably and often inappropriately. Moreover each has its own problems from the standpoint of methodological clarity (Bhopal 2008; Krieger 2003a).

The term 'race' has traditionally been used with reference to the notion of a group biological 'heritage' that affects individual health. However this concept

---

18   For further discussion of this point see Chapter 4 on health care.

has been widely criticised in recent years. A few single gene disorders such as sickle cell anaemia or Tay-Sachs disease do occur more often among particular population groups. However the current consensus is that the concept of 'race' adds little or nothing to our understanding of such phenomena.

Recognising this reality, both biomedical and social scientists have increasingly preferred to use the social concept of 'ethnicity' rather than the biological concept of 'race'. This usually refers to an individual's membership of a (minority) group which is defined in terms of what is perceived to be its cultural homogeneity. In some settings there has been a move towards allowing individuals to define their own 'ethnicity'. But either strategy raises a variety of problems.

Many individuals come from mixed social and cultural backgrounds and their location is often in flux. Moreover it is very difficult to place clear boundaries around what are to be called separate 'ethnic groups'. Most importantly, it is hard to trace relationships between particular 'ethnicities' and specific health issues. Given these difficulties, many researchers have resorted to the composite term 'race/ethnicity', but again this usually adds little to our understanding of the health problem in question.

An alternative strategy for framing these issues has been to focus on the negative experiences of people who have been discriminated against on grounds of their 'race' (usually defined in terms of skin colour). This has the disadvantage of aggregating people from countries and regions with very different histories solely on the basis of their (not quite white) skin colour (Agyemang et al. 2005). However it does highlight the ways in which people from a range of subordinated and racialised groups share common experiences of discrimination.

Again, this will often involve constraints on their access to the resources required to satisfy their intermediate (and therefore their basic) needs. Thus there may be significant overlap in practice between 'race/ethnicity' and socio-economic status. But such discrimination will also be experienced in more existential ways. Indeed it has been argued that experiences of racism may themselves act as stressors, damaging health through mechanisms such as elevated blood pressure and impaired immune responses. Thus biologically mediated harm may increase those risks that are socially produced (Krieger 2003a).

It is of course after infection that issues relating to discrimination on the grounds of skin colour will be most clearly identifiable. As we have seen, data from the USA show marked racial differences in access to services, and hence in morbidity and mortality. Outside the developed countries data on HIV are rarely collected by either 'race' or 'ethnicity'. However we have already seen that the epidemic is at its most severe where populations are living with forms of structural violence that may (or may not) include racist and ethnic discrimination.

Hence it will be important to be aware of the complexity of these issues and to review their potential significance in the context of particular epidemics. As one commentator has put it:

Race and ethnicity are poorly defined terms that serve as flawed surrogates for multiple environmental and genetic factors in disease causation, including geographic origins, socio-economic status, education and access to care. Research must move beyond these weak and imperfect proxy relationships to define the more proximate factors that influence health. (Collins 2004 p.S13)

Sexuality and Sexual Identity: Making the Connections

Sexuality and sexual identity were rarely used as descriptive categories in research before the pandemic of HIV and AIDS. However this had to change as sexual practices came to be seen as central to the transmission of the virus. As we have seen, estimates are now routinely produced of the proportion of individuals infected through heterosex and through sex between men. This does represent a step forward, but much work is still needed to explore the wider implications of different sexual activities for individuals in terms of their vulnerability to infection as well as their lives with HIV.

We need to start by recognising that individuals (as opposed to their sexual practices) cannot be divided into two separate groups as researchers so often assume. Sexual identities and desires must be seen as a continuum along which individuals may move at different points in their lives. This will include men and women attracted to the opposite sex, those attracted to their own sex, those who are bisexual and those who are transgender[19] (Caceres et al. 2006; Saavedra et al. 2008; Dowsett 2003). At any point on the continuum the relationship between private and public identity and between desires and practices may be very complex.

As we have seen, the most common context for the transmission of the virus is unprotected vaginal sex between men and women or anal sex between men. This may occur in a variety of ways across many different settings and in the context of a wide range of relationships. All of these factors will be important in making sense of the dynamics of the lives of individuals caught up in the different epidemics (Boyce et al. 2007; Dowsett 2003).

Thus far the major focus of researchers has been on men who have sex with men. Indeed there has been a tendency to treat sex between men and women as though it was 'normal' rather than just one choice among many. Sexual

---

19   These may be either male to female or female to male individuals whose gender identity, expression or behaviour is not traditionally associated with their birth sex. Some of these may seek some degree of sex reassignment surgery and/or hormone therapy, while others may pursue gender expression through external self-presentation and behaviour. There has been a growing recognition that transgender people may have an especially high risk of HIV. No national data are available on this largely invisible group. However a recent review of small-scale studies in the USA showed very high rates of HIV, at around 11.8 per cent self-reported and 27.2 per cent after testing (Herbst et al. 2008). Transgender sex workers seem to be especially vulnerable (Operario et al. 2008).

relationships between men on the other hand are seen to be 'different' enough to need special attention and interrogation. This has of course been encouraged by the many same-sex identified men who (understandably) see this as an important strategy for ensuring that their needs are properly recognised.

The term 'men who have sex with men' (MSM) continues to be widely used in the arenas of HIV policy and research even though it has been extensively criticised (Young and Meyer 2005; Aggleton 2009). This is because statistics based on this definition do provide information on a key risk factor in the pandemic: unprotected anal sex.[20] However they are based on a narrow conception of decontextualised men unified by their same-sex physical relations. In fact men aggregated by epidemiologists (and many other researchers) into this apparently homogeneous group will vary markedly. Some will be 'out' and identify themselves as gay, bisexual or transgender in both their social and their sexual lives. Others will have same-sex desires but will not be open members of a 'gay community'. Many who have sex with other men in constrained circumstances (such as prisoners or male sex workers) will not consider themselves (or wish others to consider them) as homosexual or bisexual at all.

Not surprisingly it is those who openly share their sexual identity with others who have received the greatest attention from researchers. Most studies of these HIV positive 'gay' men have been carried out in the USA, with the majority focussing on sexual activities following diagnosis.[21] Other researchers have explored the shame so many report as a result of their doubly stigmatised status as both gay and HIV positive (Wolitski and Fenton 2011).

In many parts of the world advocacy and equality legislation have led to a diminution in discriminatory behaviour towards HIV positive same-sex identified men. However in too many, sex between men remains illegal.[22] Indeed homophobia has been actively encouraged by some governments as part of nationalist discourses (Doyal et al. 2008; Rispel and Metcalf 2009; Long 2003). Even where laws have been liberalised there is often continuing hostility towards lesbian, gay, bisexual and transgender (LGBT) people and as a result they may be isolated and especially reluctant to seek medical care.

The first meta-analysis of the risk of HIV infection among MSM across all low and middle income countries found that the odds of having HIV infection

---

20   Most (but not all) sex between men involves anal penetration. It will of course also occur between women and men but we have no way of knowing the contribution of this to the epidemic.

21   The term 'gay' is usually deployed as more 'politically correct' in studies that do not use the category of MSM. This may or may not be appropriate in terms of the self-perceptions of the individuals involved or their lifestyles. Peter Aggleton has recently argued instead for the use of the term 'same-sex sexuality' (Aggleton 2009).

22   For an excellent summary of sex-related legislation around the world see http://en.wikipedia.org/wiki/LGBT_rights_by_country_or_territory. For more detail of the implications of these laws see Chapter 9.

are markedly and consistently higher among this group than among the general population of adults of reproductive age (Baral et al. 2007; Smith et al. 2009). A recent report from the International Gay and Lesbian Human Rights Coalition provided a detailed account of what they call this 'invisibilization' of African men who have sex with men (IGLHRC 2007). As the authors point out, this neglect has fuelled the HIV epidemic and continues to play a significant role in many thousands of deaths from AIDS.

It is evident that women are much less likely than men to acquire HIV infection as a result of same-sex relationships. It is not impossible for bodily fluids to be shared during sex between women but very few cases have been identified. Women who identify as lesbian can, of course, become infected as a result of sex with a man or through injecting drug use (Deol and Heath-Toby 2009).[23] However we know virtually nothing about those lesbian or bisexual women who are living with HIV, especially those in extremely homophobic settings (Dworkin 2005).

IDUs and HIV in a Social Context

Recent years have seen a growing recognition of the role of injecting drug use in the global pandemic (Mathers et al. 2008). The most recent estimate suggests that worldwide there are around 3 million HIV positive IDUs, accounting for around 30 per cent of HIV infections outside sub-Saharan Africa (Nieburg and Carty 2011). As we have seen, the highest rates of infections related to IDU are found in Eastern Europe and Central Asia, while there is also evidence of a recent rise in some countries of sub-Saharan Africa (Nieburg and Carty 2011). This needs to be viewed in the context of the stigmatising attitudes still directed at users in most parts of the world.

The act of injecting drugs cannot in itself lead to the transmission of HIV. This occurs only when the injecting equipment is shared with others who are themselves positive. This sharing of potentially contaminated needles is rarely a deliberate choice. Rather it reflects the refusal of many governments to provide needle exchanges which can prevent this risk entirely. At an even more basic level it results from the criminalisation of drug use which forces many addicts to live their lives in ways that make harm reduction extremely difficult to achieve.

Due to their social invisibility very little is known about the particular disadvantages experienced by of IDUs who are also HIV positive. However it is clear that despite the recent rise in their numbers they have been left behind in the provision of preventive services and in access to therapies (Mathers et al. 2008; Persson et al. 2011). This is especially true for women, who are estimated to make up some 40 per cent of injecting drug users in the US and some parts of Europe and 20 per cent in Eastern Europe, Central Asia and Latin America (Pinkham and Malinowska-Sempruch 2008).

---

23 Indeed there is evidence from South Africa in particular of lesbian women and transgender men undergoing 'corrective rape'. See Human Rights Watch (2011).

A Brief Note about Ageing

Because of the link with sexual activity, one of the main characteristics of the HIV pandemic has been the age distribution of those infected. This in turn has meant that most research and service delivery has been focussed on young and middle-aged adults. However the combination of the ageing of the pandemic itself as well as the effectiveness of ART has meant that the age distribution in the HIV positive population has begun to change.

UNAIDS estimates that 2.8 million HIV positive people are 50 plus, making up 7 per cent of those infected.[24] In sub-Saharan Africa about 3 million people over 50 are thought to be positive, making up some 14 per cent of the total, while in the US this figure is now approaching 30 per cent (Mills et al. 2012). Yet few studies have explored the particular physical and psychological challenges facing those who are HIV positive outside what is seen as the 'normal' age range (Schmid et al. 2009; Negin and Cumming 2011).

Studies have now begun to explore the more qualitative aspects of ageing with HIV. Recent work in the UK for example has highlighted the loneliness and the financial worries that are often involved (JRF, Terrence Higgins Trust and Age UK 2010; Elford et al. 2008). While these problems are commonly associated with ageing in the general population, there is evidence that they may be especially challenging among those who have been infected for many years and have lost most of their friends (Owen and Catalan 2012). For many positive people these problems are exacerbated by what appears to be an increased and earlier incidence of what are usually age-related illnesses: coronary heart disease, cancer and diabetes in particular, as well as dementia. The reasons for this are uncertain but much research is currently exploring the links between HIV infection, effects of treatment and the ageing process itself.

Putting the Pieces Together: Introducing Intersectionality

Despite their conceptual limitations, the categories of socio-economic status, sex/gender, sexual identities and practices, 'race/ethnicity' and injecting drug use as well as age provide a framework for a preliminary mapping of the characteristics of individuals affected by different epidemics. At a micro-level this can then be used to assess which individuals in a given population are more likely to be infected and to identify the major influences on how they will live and die (Dworkin 2005; Doyal 2009a).

However it is important to be aware that these characteristics will be of limited explanatory value when viewed in isolation. As we have seen, research

---

24   In a global context 50 is taken as the age at which individuals are defined as 'old'. This is because so many are living in societies with a relatively low life expectancy (Mills et al. 2012).

findings are usually analysed using binary categories such as gay versus heterosexual, men versus women or black versus white. This will sometimes be useful in testing particular hypotheses. But of course different influences do not operate independently in the real world. Hence we will also need to consider the importance of what has come to be called 'intersectionality' in the analysis of human behaviour.

The foundations for this approach were laid by a group of writers often referred to as 'critical race feminists' (Collins 2000; Crenshaw 1994). They began with the argument that, for most purposes, all 'women' could not be treated as a single group.[25] Nor was it appropriate to simply add 'black' and 'women' together to create a homogeneous category of 'black women'. Variables such as sex/gender and race/ethnicity were therefore described as 'multiplicative' rather than 'summative'. That is to say they were biological and/or social influences interacting with each other rather than separate and static characteristics of individuals.

A particular woman will not just be HIV positive. She will also come from a particular part of the world; be employed (or not employed); prefer sex with women (and/or men); be a parent (or not). Similarly a positive man may be white or black, rich or poor, open or closed about his sexuality and injecting drugs or not. As Olena Hankivsky has described it: 'Intersectionality challenges practices that privilege any specific axis of inequality such as race, class or gender and emphasizes the potential of varied and fluid configurations of social locations and interacting social processes in the production of inequities' (Hankivsky 2012 p.1712). Thus it is their (constantly changing) positions at these 'intersections' of social, economic and cultural structures which will shape the opportunities and constraints within which all individuals must manage their lives (Doyal 2009a; Hancock 2007; Bowleg 2008; Bredstrom 2006; Hankivsky 2012).

In the chapters that follow, this framework will provide the conceptual foundation for exploring the narratives of those who are HIV positive. Few of the studies to be cited will be explicitly intersectional in their methodology. However their findings will be combined in ways that offer an intersectional perspective on the strategies HIV positive individuals adopt in dynamic (re)negotiation of their lives (and deaths) in local settings within a global context.[26]

Conclusion

This chapter has provided a preliminary overview of the diverse patterns of advantage and disadvantage that characterise the various epidemics that constitute

---

25   These ideas were developed as part of a critique of 'white feminists' who were said to be prioritising gender over race in their analysis.

26   For excellent empirical studies using explicitly intersectional frameworks see Logie et al. (2011) and Berger (2004). Olena Hankivsky (2012) offers a valuable review of the development and utilisation of intersectionality as well as its methodological challenges.

the global pandemic. It is evident from these patterns that complex economic and social processes are interacting with the biological constitutions of individuals to shape not only their vulnerability to HIV but also their capacity to 'manage' their condition. International inequalities in access to the necessary resources stand out, as do those between disadvantaged groups and their compatriots. We have begun to identify the range of variables shaping these inequalities, with particular reference to socio-economic status, sex/gender, race/ethnicity, sexuality and injecting drug use. The following chapters will explore in greater detail how these influences impact upon different dimensions of daily life.

Chapter 3
A Biographical Overview

This chapter will provide an introduction to the diversity of life (and death) with HIV and AIDS. It will draw on the wider literature on chronic illness while at the same time highlighting the characteristics of HIV and AIDS that differentiate them from most other long-term health problems (Pierret 2000).[1]

The last few years have been marked by a significant 'roll out' of antiretroviral therapy (ART) in many countries around the world. However we need to beware of assuming that HIV has been transformed into a 'manageable disease' in every setting. Official estimates indicate that around 1.8 million people died from AIDS in 2009. Despite the development of new therapies, most suffered in very similar ways to those described by gay men during the early phase of the pandemic in the USA (Shilts 1987). Indeed their experiences were usually even worse since they faced the same severe and unpredictable episodes of illness leading to a painful death while living in situations of extreme poverty with little or no health care.

The following sections will provide a broad overview of what is known of the lives of those diagnosed as HIV positive at this stage of the pandemic. It will outline the experiences of individuals in different settings, at different stages of illness and with varying access to therapy. Some may fit the category of 'physically healthy' as access to therapy keeps HIV and AIDS at bay. Some will be in a terminal decline, while others will be in an indeterminate illness zone with intermittent periods of distress and debility that severely limit their social interaction.

The main focus here will be on the experiences of adults, but of course it is important to remember that some 3.4 million children worldwide were living with HIV in 2011 (UNAIDS 2012a). Most acquired their infection from their mothers before birth or from breastfeeding. In 2010 only about 23 per cent of those under 15 were able to access ART and an estimated 250,000 died from AIDS-related causes (WHO, UNICEF and UNAIDS 2011). Those who are now living to adulthood face significant challenges but there has been little research on how these can most appropriately be tackled (Persson and Newman 2012; Hazra et al. 2010).

Mind and Body: Symptoms and Constraints

The symptoms of HIV and ultimately of AIDS are many and varied, and largely unpredictable. While ART can significantly improve an individual's well-being,

---

1   Pierret (2000) provides an excellent discussion of the methodological problems in undertaking qualitative research in the context of HIV and AIDS.

those living with HIV (or AIDS) can still expect a range of symptoms at different stages, with pain being one of the most common. The drugs themselves are also likely to bring their own 'side effects'.

As yet, accounts of these physical problems are largely confined to the biomedical literature, with few attempts to integrate them into the broader analysis of daily life (Kelly and Field 1996). The significance of this invisibility can be highlighted by a recent study carried out in South Africa which illustrated the multiple HIV and AIDS symptoms affecting a group of 607 patients in the Eastern Cape Province (Peltzer and Phaswana-Mafuya 2008).

Almost half of the respondents were on ART while the rest were not. On the day of the interview they reported an average of 26.1 symptoms.[2] Headaches, fever, thirst, fatigue, weakness, painful joints, nausea, muscle aches, fears and worries and dizziness were the top 10 reported. Numbness and tingling of hands and fingers, weight gain in the stomach area, loose stools and skinny arms and legs were more frequently reported by those on ART, while diarrhoea, sore throat, painful swallowing and sore/bleeding gums were mentioned by many of those not in receipt of drugs.

The overlap between HIV and TB in many low income countries is also important here. The risk of developing tuberculosis is estimated to be between 20 and 37 times greater in people living with HIV than among those who test negative. In 2009 1.2 million (13 per cent) of the 9.4 million new cases of TB worldwide were among people living with HIV. Of the 1.7 million people who died from TB in that same year 24 per cent were HIV positive (WHO 2011). Hence many people will have to cope with the symptoms of both diseases and the side effects of two groups of drugs. They may also have to deal with the additional stigma associated with TB (Bond and Nyblade 2006; Daftary 2012). This will pose major challenges to both mind and body, as a woman in Cameroon explained:

> It was too much for me. Just in a matter of two weeks everything was going wrong in my life. First I came here thinking that it was a simple cough and was told it was TB. The next thing I was doing an HIV test. I just couldn't handle it all at once. (Barnabas et al. 2010 p.28)

Not surprisingly many are reluctant to test for both diseases: a situation often exacerbated by the lack of integration between HIV and TB services (Reid et al. 2006). As one community health worker put it: 'TB patients only come to the clinic when they are extremely ill and they don't want to be counselled or spoken to about HIV, as they fear having both diseases' (Heunis et al. 2011 p.5). A study of a small group of co-infected people in Zambia gives a glimpse of the stresses involved. Many reported 'rejection, isolation and name calling' (Chileshe and

---

2   This is from a possible total of 64 on the Revised Sign and Symptom Checklist for Persons with HIV Disease (Holzemer et al. 2001).

Bond 2001) as well as practical difficulties attending two separate clinics (Abdool Karim et al. 2004).

Recent reviews of research on the relationship between mental health and HIV in the African region found few relevant studies (Brandt 2009a; Breuer et al. 2011; Shin et al. 2011). However the general conclusion was that around half of those who were HIV positive were also experiencing mental health problems. This figure was considerably higher than that of comparable negative populations. The most common problem that emerged was depression, with the highest levels of morbidity usually found among the poorest women with least support. The scarcity of mental health care for populations in low and middle income countries has received considerable attention in recent years (Prince et al. 2007). Three-quarters of those in need go untreated, while 40 per cent of African states have no budget dedicated to mental health services (Skeen et al. 2010). This will obviously have a particular resonance for those who are HIV positive (Collins et al. 2006).[3]

Making Sense of Long-Term Illness: Changing Identities

The concept of 'biographical disruption' provides a useful starting point for making sense of narratives of chronic or long-term illness (Bury 1982).[4] Bury defines this moment as a fundamental shift from 'a perceived normal trajectory … to one fundamentally abnormal and inwardly damaging' (p.171). In other words it can be seen as a 'before and after' dividing line (Pierret 2001). For many this will be the first time their lives have strayed from an anticipated path. For others it will be an additional challenge in what are already difficult circumstances.

The diagnosis of HIV may portend a debilitating, lengthy illness and a shortened life expectancy. As a result those involved will need to confront what Burchardt (2010) has called 'biographical uncertainty' and the fragmentation of a coherent sense of self. This is likely to be especially brutal for the majority who are still young and have lost the 'bright future' of work and parenthood many were envisaging. How people respond to the diagnosis will of course be influenced by many factors. Some of these will relate to the individual's particular psychological and emotional characteristics, while others will reflect the social support and the financial resources they have at their disposal. The stage of their illness as well as the range of symptoms they are experiencing will also be crucial.

The single most important resource potentially available to them will be access to medical care. If they cannot access therapy their lives are likely to be brutish

---

3   Not surprisingly, much more attention is paid to psychological needs of people in the rich world. For one example, see British Psychological Society et al. (2011).

4   For a valuable account of the emergence of this concept and its subsequent development in medical sociology see the editorial in the virtual issue of *Sociology of Health and Illness* by Judith Lawton (2009). See also Ciambrone (2001), who uses the same concept to analyse the lives of a group of HIV positive women in the north-eastern USA.

and short. Since many of those living in resource-poor settings will be diagnosed (if at all) when their disease is already well advanced, they may have little time to mend the emotional and psychological tears in the fabric of their lives or to come to terms with their situation.

Most people think they know exactly 'who' they are and do not expect this to change across the span of their lives. However the 'self' is not fixed over time and space. Rather it is fluid and responsive to changing circumstances, with radical changes requiring the active (if often unrecognised) involvement of individuals in the reconstruction of their 'fractured selves' (Ciambrone 2001). As the physical and psychological changes associated with illness constrain their capacity to continue their 'normal' lives this will inevitably affect the way they see themselves as well as the way others see them. In an attempt to come to terms with these internal and external changes, individuals will begin to reshape the 'biographies' or 'narratives' with which they make sense of their situation and through which they present themselves to others (Burchardt 2010; Levy and Storeng 2007; Pierret 2001; Radley and Billig 1996).

These personal reconfigurations are central to individual experiences of all long-term or chronic illness. But, as we shall see, they are of particular importance within the context of the highly charged symbolism of stigma associated with HIV and AIDS. The author of a recent study in South Africa summarised the situation facing many people:

> With the diagnosis the perspective on the future is doomed to shrink. According to most studies, particularly during the first phase of confronting the diagnosis people inevitably find themselves thrown into a precarious and emotionally painful present in which subjective uncertainty even about short term survival is radically disrupting all connections to an envisaged future. (Burchardt 2010 p.3)

Deconstructing Stigma

A number of diseases have historically been defined as more stigmatising than others: epilepsy and leprosy for example. However, as Susan Sontag argued, HIV has emerged as 'a disease whose charge of stigmatisation (and) whose capacity to create 'spoiled identity' is far greater than any other' (Sontag 1991 p.101). As we shall see, this can create major obstacles to the maintenance of physical and emotional well-being, social interaction, economic security and even physical survival.

The original notion of stigma was popularised by the Canadian sociologist Erving Goffman as part of his work on the sociology of deviance. Based on the experiences of people with mental health problems, physical disabilities or other 'socially undesirable' characteristics he described the 'stigmatised' individual as someone who is 'different', whose identity is 'spoiled' and who is 'negatively valued in society' (Goffman 1963). In the early years of the pandemic, this same term was widely used to describe the negative experiences of those suffering from symptoms later found to be associated with HIV infection. Not surprisingly, the concentration of the illness among gay men and other marginalised groups exacerbated the hostility directed towards those dying from this mysterious new condition.

The early recognition of the reality of this 'stigmatisation' was of great importance since it placed social factors alongside medical ones in HIV and AIDS discourse and advocacy. However, in too many instances 'stigma' came to be used as a general explanation for all the negative experiences of HIV positive people. One commentator has used the notion of 'conceptual inflation' to describe this increasingly unclear and inappropriate usage of the term: 'Stigma is creaking under the burden of explaining a series of disparate, complex and unrelated processes to such an extent that use of the term is in danger of obscuring as much as it enlightens' (Prior et al. 2003 p.2192, quoted in Deacon 2006 p.419).

Recognising this danger, recent debates have attempted to deconstruct and clarify the meanings of stigma in the wider context of the HIV pandemic (Parker and Aggleton 2003; Steward et al. 2008; Mahajan et al. 2008; Scambler 2009). Individuals may be allocated a 'stigmatised identity' either by other individuals or by groups or institutions. This in turn may (or may not) lead to active discrimination: the denial of jobs on grounds of seropositivity for example.

The term 'enacted stigma' describes those unjust acts of hostility directed by one individual towards another whom they perceive as deserving a stigmatised status. 'Perceived stigma' on the other hand refers to the subjective awareness (or fear) of such actions by HIV positive people who may try to conceal their status in order to avoid being judged. This in turn may lead to 'internalised stigma', where a positive individual has come to believe in the negative definition projected upon them. Not surprisingly a number of studies have shown clear links between depression and this internalisation of a devalued status (Simbayi et al. 2007).

All these aspects of stigmatisation will emerge in context as the different dimensions of life with HIV and AIDS are explored in subsequent chapters. But before moving on we need to examine in more detail the origins of stigma and the varying forms it takes in different societies and communities.

Social Origins of Stigma and HIV

It is usually assumed that HIV and AIDS have been stigmatised because of their links with infection, sex and death. In the early stages their untreatability clearly added to these attitudes of social exclusion.[5] However there are many other factors shaping the intensity, the texture and the content of discourses of stigma as they

---

5 While there have been some signs that treatability might reduce stigma, the evidence is difficult to interpret (Campbell et al. 2011). For a good discussion of the methodological problems in evaluating this see Maughan-Brown (2010). For an excellent account of continuing stigma in the UK see (Elford et al 2008a).

have been enacted across a range of political and economic settings (Castro and Farmer 2005; Parker and Aggleton 2003).

Stigmatisation does not emerge from nowhere, but can be seen as defensive and self-justifying behaviour 'following the existing fault lines of society' (Castro and Farmer 2005). Thus, in societies characterised by profound racism, HIV positive 'people of colour' will be among the most likely to experience stigma. Similarly, high levels of gender inequality are likely to generate particular forms of stigma against HIV positive women (Rohleder and Gibson 2005; Shamos et al. 2009). On the other hand, heterosexual men may be stigmatised because illness makes it difficult for them to conform to what has been termed 'hegemonic masculinity' (Connell and Messerschmidt 2005).

An illustration of the importance of gender in shaping patterns of stigma can be found in an excellent study from Peru (Valencia-Garcia et al. 2008). The authors show how the dominant models of *marianismo* and *machismo* cannot easily be combined with an HIV positive status. *Marianismo* constructs a social role that values women for being faithful wives and devoted mothers who are sexually naive and passive in their relationships. However those who become infected with HIV (often through their husband's extramarital sexual activity) will be unable to sustain this position as a good *mariana*. Stigmatising discourse will leave them 'no place to create or maintain a socially sanctioned identity with its incumbent social power and rewards' (Valencia-Garcia et al. 2008 p.412). Instead they are too often seen as promiscuous or even a *puta* or whore.

Positive men who have sex with men (MSM) are likely to be doubly disadvantaged in the (many) settings where heteronormativity is dominant.[6] A number of studies have explored the experiences of these men in Jamaica (or in the Jamaican diaspora), where levels of homophobia are especially high (Human Rights Watch 2004; Norman et al. 2006; Anderson et al. 2008, 2009). One Jamaican man described his experiences of health care:

> About two years ago I went to get a test for genital warts. There was a male nurse ... he told me to pull down my pants and press hands against the wall. He said 'Open your ass. I am going to test you.' ... So I did as he said and he shined the light ... and the nurse decides to say 'Why are you doing it with a man?! That is so wrong ... That's why you get this thing now because you are not supposed to be buggering you ass.' (Rutledge et al. 2009 p.21)

Thus different communities show diverse patterns of intersectional stigmatisation and discrimination against people with HIV. As yet, there appear to be no communities in which stigma does not exist at all. But the extent and form will

---

6   Heteronormativity holds that heterosexuality is the normal sexual orientation and that sexual relations are only fitting between a man and a woman. Consequently, a heteronormative view is one that involves alignment of biological sex, sexuality, gender identity and gender roles. For a good discussion see Persson (2012 pp.315–17).

vary with both the past history and the present circumstances of the group itself. In many settings it has been historically linked with different types of what has been called 'disordered development' (Stadler 2003). We can illustrate these links with brief examples from Africa and China, both of which are experiencing epidemics of HIV and AIDS while also undergoing rapid social and economic transition.[7]

HIV and Stigma in an African Context: Mediating Moral Panics

Much has been written about the causes of stigma or hostility against HIV positive people in different parts of Africa. Though South Africa has received most attention, broadly similar patterns have emerged in other countries. In many settings, shifts in local economies from agricultural to wage labour have had profound effects not only on living standards but also on 'neighbourly, gender and generational relationships and sexual relations' (Dilger 2008; Peters et al. 2010; Stadler 2003).

A recent study of five African communities highlighted the significance of material poverty and access to local health and social care in shaping hostility towards HIV positive people (Maman et al. 2009a). Most of those who cannot support themselves as a result of HIV or AIDS have only their families to fall back on. Under these circumstances some family members will be willing to provide whatever support they can, but others may be hostile and stigmatising. The findings from this study showed that in settings where services and resources were more easily available families felt less pressure and were less likely to blame those who were infected and to treat them badly. This illustrates an important link between enacted stigma and poverty.

As one respondent in Zimbabwe pointed out, those who cannot make a contribution to a poor household may simply be treated as a drain on scarce resources: 'They are already declared dead and regarded as useless as a grave. That is how they are treated ... This means that these people are no longer able to do anything useful. They say they are waiting for the day of their death' (Maman et al. 2009a p.2275). Thus some aspects of hostile behaviour may need to be understood in immediate and pragmatic terms.

However broader analysis reveals other elements contributing to the discourses of HIV stigma and associated discrimination. Research in a number of African settings has noted that the current outbreak of HIV and AIDS is often linked to what is seen as the decline of traditional values and practices (Dilger 2008). Thus infected individuals are blamed for failing to behave in morally appropriate ways. This was reflected in a recent analysis of the particular rhetoric of HIV stigma in the Caprivi region of Namibia (Thomas 2008). Four main themes were identified in the context of broader socio-economic change in recent decades. These can be summarised as: declining access to resources; pollution and disorder; religious interpretations; and witchcraft narratives.

---

7   For a systematic review of similar issues in India see Bharat (2012).

Narratives relating to resource use refer back to earlier times when people from the region had much greater access to land and were able to eat a greater range of animals, fish and plants. Younger people were now said to eat badly and to be weaker and therefore more vulnerable to HIV and other illnesses. Increased ritual pollution is also blamed primarily on younger people on the grounds that that they pay too little attention to the rules surrounding contact with bodily fluids and with death. This is blamed as a frequent cause of illness that can be spread to others through intimate contact. Significantly it is women and girls who are most often blamed for such pollution (Campbell et al. 2005).

In the Caprivi context, Christian churches wield considerable power in relation to issues of morality and sexuality. Again those who have 'sinned' or broken rules (usually in a sexual context) are blamed for their illness. This reflects similar findings in a study of AIDS rumours in the Lowveld in South Africa (Stadler 2003). Here too, elders explained the severity of the AIDS epidemic through the widespread failure of the young to observe the rules of sexual behaviour or *milawu*.

Even though most Caprivi people regard themselves as Christians, many still draw on ideas of witchcraft to explain illness such as HIV (Campbell et al. 2007). In many parts of Africa there is evidence that such claims are increasing with social disruption and with the rise in illness and death rates among the economically productive. These trends have been linked to increasing social heterogeneity and to the envy created as traditional hierarchies are distorted.

In many parts of Africa the benefits expected from independence or democracy have not been realised by the masses, and existing elites are afraid of losing their power. It is in this period of economic and social crisis that we can make sense of the ways in which older people are trying to maintain their real and their symbolic status through stigmatising those (usually younger and frequently female) who are infected.

Posel et al. take this analysis a stage further in the South African context. Describing the relationship between the social body and the individual (female) body in the context of the local world view, they claim that:

> In the case of HIV/AIDS the physical illness is read as a symptom of the cultural damage inflicted by the country's transition to democracy – principally through the allocation of new found rights and freedom to women and children that are seen as flouting patriarchal 'traditions' and undermining the cornerstones of moral order in the community. (Posel et al. 2007 p.144)

HIV and Stigma in a Chinese Context: Family Shame in a Time of Transition

China is also going through a period of rapid change with the shift from state control to a market economy. This in turn has been linked to a demographic transition, with some 8.5 million surplus men as a result of the one child policy and a huge increase in rural to urban migration (Tucker et al. 2005).

Very few researchers have explored the experiences of HIV positive people themselves in China. However one recent study gives a broad indication of the general pattern. Central to the response of most people to their diagnosis of *ai zi bang* (or HIV) was shame and guilt towards their relatives and dependants. Given the continuing centrality of the family in Chinese society, they saw it as inevitable that their situation would cause emotional and material damage to those for whom they felt love and responsibility (Li et al. 2006).

A study in Yunnan Province found that if families were told, most were willing to provide financial support as well as physical care (Li et al. 2006). However, very strict secrecy was usually maintained to avoid family 'loss of face'. Interestingly, a number of positive respondents reported that even though they knew HIV and AIDS were not contagious, they always ate with separate chopsticks to avoid alarming those around them.

Though it is difficult to compare rates between societies, studies have indicated that levels of enacted stigma are very high in many Chinese communities (Li et al. 2006; Zhou 2007). A recent study of market workers in an eastern coastal city found that half believed that punishment was an appropriate response to people living with HIV and that over half (56 per cent) were unwilling to be friends with them, while 73 per cent thought they should be isolated (Lee et al. 2005).[8]

Most positive people reported that those who knew their status asked how they had been infected. Those infected by blood transfusions were generally regarded as innocent, but others were thought to be promiscuous – with drug users and sex workers at the bottom of a highly visible hierarchy of stigma (Zhou 2007). Not surprisingly, many of those who were 'innocent' were anxious to make this known as widely as possible. Minqin, who received infected blood as a haemophiliac, said: 'People like me are different from others. ... Why? I am innocent! I was not infected because of drug use, sex or homosexuality. I am innocent! So why shouldn't I stand up and speak?' (Zhou 2007 p.290).

By contrast the internalised stigma of those deemed 'guilty' is dramatically reflected in the words of Guoqiang:

> Though we are all people with HIV/AIDS I feel I am inferior. People infected through blood transfusion are better than me, even those infected through drug use are better than me, and those infected through heterosexual behaviour are better than me. It's so hard for people infected through same sex behaviours to come out! (Zhou 2007 p.290)

Many 'culpable' respondents reported how much pressure they were under to keep their status secret for the sake of themselves and their families. Terms like

---

8   In Yunnan a very high proportion of health professionals were reluctant to treat an HIV-infected patient, with stigmatising attitudes higher among the most senior clinicians (Li et al. 2006).

'having two faces' or 'living a double life' were frequently used. Yu described the difficulties this could produce at work:

> In my previous company I felt like a half-human and a half-devil … because of my health status I was unable to work very hard. My colleagues would wonder 'Why is this person always sick …?' Sometimes they joked with me saying 'Do you have HIV?' They were joking – which would be OK if I didn't (have HIV) but I did. So it was very hard for me to pretend that I didn't (have it) and to joke back with a laugh. It was very hard! (Zhou 2007 p.291)

Comparing experiences of HIV with those of other serious diseases, Guo pointed out: 'If I had cancer I could tell people about that, but if you get AIDS you cannot tell anyone about it. You have to endure it alone' (Zhou 2007 p.292).

The result of this stigmatisation and discrimination is that many people are forced into isolation either within or outside their families. In recent years there has been a more progressive turn in central policy towards HIV and AIDS in China. However there are still few organisations offering support to positive individuals. Moreover, continuing restrictions on civil society and free expression and association mean that HIV-related non-governmental organisations (NGOs) and AIDS activists often face repression and harassment from the authorities, especially in local settings.[9]

Stigma and Intersectionality

Thus far we have talked about patterns of stigma in different social settings and among different social groups. However we need to be very clear that experiences of stigma will be shaped not by just one aspect of an individual's identity but by several, and can operate in many different dimensions of their lives. A recent Canadian study of female sex workers in Ontario has illustrated this point especially well, highlighting the intersectional impact of 'HIV-related stigma, sexism and gender discrimination, racism, homophobia and transphobia and sex work stigma' on their everyday lives (Logie et al. 2011 p.5).

All were experiencing some degree of discrimination related to their status as HIV positive and as sex workers. However they also described the additional hostility associated with other aspects of their identity. One Aboriginal participant described her feelings: 'We are suppressed as natives in our own nation' (Logie et al. 2011 p.7). A number of women also talked about what they perceived to be institutionally racist attitudes in health care and pregnancy planning. One African Caribbean woman said: 'Because you are black, if you go to the clinic and you say you want to have a baby, they say, "Why do you wanna have a baby when you

---

9   For an interesting discussion of similar experiences with diabetes activism in China see Bunkenborg (2003).

know your situation?" Well they don't say that to the white people' (Logie et al. 2011 p.7).

Some participants also reported experiences of homophobia and transphobia in a number of different contexts. One said: 'I think the stigma is double – it's stigma because you're HIV, stigma that you are not straight. The pressure is just too much to carry. It's just too much to handle' (Logie et al. 2011 p.7). The perception of HIV as a gay disease was cited by many as a cause of hostility, with one woman saying 'they see you being queer as being demonic or evil' (Logie et al. 2011 p.7).

This brief review of discourses of HIV stigma and discrimination has highlighted the ways in which they are shaped by pre-existing social traditions, by the impact of rapid social change and by current patterns of inequality, disadvantage and discrimination. The remaining part of this chapter will explore how the narratives of HIV positive individuals emerge from the interweaving of their physical condition, their access to care and their changing sense of self.

Diagnosis, Disruption and Disclosure

Individuals diagnosed with HIV usually find themselves in a state of extreme 'biographical uncertainty', with most reporting shame and despair. It is a time of 'threat to the self where the individual is faced with incorporating the bad identity which is attached to the disease' (Rohleder and Gibson 2005 p.5). One South African woman explained:

> When I found out I was HIV positive I thought of killing myself. I never told anyone as I did not want people to gossip about me, as it was evident in my neighbourhood that those that are positive are spoken of as being promiscuous women who deserve to have this disease as it is a punishment for their sins. (Gilbert and Walker 2010 p.142)

Stigmatisation, hostility and discrimination will all pose major challenges – as Cynthia, an African American woman from Detroit, described it: 'We began fighting for our dignity the day we found out we were HIV positive' (Berger 2004 p.87).

It is only recently that studies in different parts of the world have begun to focus on the diverse (and non-linear) transitions through which HIV positive people move from their initial diagnosis to a different sense of themselves. These include the construction of new strategies for carrying out their social responsibilities and for interacting effectively with others (Burchardt 2010; Baumgartner 2007; Shamos et al. 2009; Medley et al. 2009). A young man from northern China explained what this had meant to him:

> My previous life road was extremely smooth. ... But suddenly I was struck by a lightning bolt [i.e. HIV infection] from nowhere. ... But it might not be a bad

thing – it woke me up, and then I knew that life is not always so smooth and
there are many challenges to confront. … That kind of feeling is like falling
into an abyss; when you get out, you just find that the sky and the world look
completely different than before. (Zhou 2010 p.319)

Many of those to whom ART is available will try to restore their lives to what
used to be 'normal' – with or without disclosing their HIV status. But for others
the illness can offer an opportunity to learn new things and maybe to lead to what
they perceive as a better life. Some will go even further to become HIV activists
(Russell and Seeley 2010; Seeley and Russell 2010; Berger 2004).

Whatever their survival strategies, decisions about whether or not to disclose
their status, when and to whom, will be central concerns (Bond 2010). Some may
disclose immediately, usually to family members and sometimes to partners. Others
may focus their efforts on keeping their status secret. The factors influencing these
choices will be varied and will change over time as 'cost benefit' calculations and
states of health shift.

The responses of those to whom disclosures are made will also be diverse. A
number of studies have indicated that the *fear* of being stigmatised is often worse
than the reality (Medley et al. 2009). However this is by no means always the case
and hostility from family can be especially distressing, as reported by one South
African woman: 'All my family know my status … families don't treat you well.
They won't share spoons, bathroom … they watch you closely … nobody wants
you to come when you are ill, especially my mother, they avoid you' (Gilbert and
Walker 2010 p.1127).

In many situations individual decisions to disclose their status will be
influenced by the biophysical trajectory of the illness itself. As it becomes more
serious, many are forced to seek treatment, which usually means engaging with
others both inside and outside the health care system. Thus there is often a close
connection in time between disclosure and treatment initiation (Burchardt 2010;
Medley et al. 2009): 'I could not manage any further. I felt very sick all the time. I
was tired and coughing and I was finding it very hard to work' (Gilbert and Walker
2009 p.142). One woman in a Kenyan study described how her need for treatment
left her few options for secrecy: 'And with the adherence you have to disclose
because you have to be very strict with the time of taking the drugs. … if I have
not disclosed to you (husband) what will I do? Am I going under the bed? Or going
out for the loo? (Gillett and Parr 2011 p.340).

Moving on from the Diagnosis

As they move further away from the moment of initial diagnosis some individuals
will find themselves on a downward slope towards an early death. Others will
be engaged to a greater or lesser extent in the 'mending of their fractured selves'
(Ciambrone 2001). Access to antiretrovirals will be central to any long-term

improvement in physical health. Many report feeling 'stronger' after treatment, making it possible for them to return (for a longer or shorter period) to paid work, domestic labour, care work and/or subsistence agriculture. This in turn will play a major part in facilitating their transition to a 'normalised' self and a positive (if changed) identity within the wider society.[10]

However, most of those living with HIV (with or without drugs) will also need 'social support' if they are to optimise their well-being. In some parts of the world this will be available from paid carers. But most of those in impoverished settings will need to turn to partners and/or family. Other sources of support include faith-based organisations and community groups involving other HIV positive people.

Religion and Spirituality as Sources of Support

The relationship between organised religion and HIV is a complex and sometimes contradictory one. Early research focussed mainly on its negative effects in creating and reinforcing stigma through the discourse of 'sin' (Burchardt 2010; Zou et al. 2009). A woman in Swaziland described her experience in the following terms: 'Discrimination is high, especially in the church. Since I disclosed I am no longer allowed to cook at weddings for fear I will contaminate the food. The "hug and kiss-kiss" – that business in the church has stopped. You are made to feel dirty' (Shamos et al. 2009 p.1685).

However the last decade has seen a more nuanced approach to the analysis of HIV and religion (Dilger et al. 2010; Keikelamem et al. 2010; Munoz-Laboy et al. 2011). More attention is now being paid to the importance of religion and spirituality for HIV positive people as well as the role of the pandemic itself in changing aspects of theology and religious practices (Munoz-Laboy et al. 2011). Faith-based organisations have become extensively involved in caring and support services: worldwide they now provide about one-fifth of these for HIV positive people (Munoz-Laboy et al. 2011). In the Democratic Republic of the Congo (DRC) the proportion is as high as 70 per cent (Haddad et al. 2008).[11]

The majority of people living with HIV in the USA report the value of both spirituality and religion in coping with their illness (Cotton et al. 2006). This may include prayers and meditation, spending time with fellow believers and being actively involved in formal church and other religious activities. A recent study highlighted the value of prayer among a number of different groups living in the UK (Ridge et al. 2008). Being diagnosed with HIV often appears to strengthen individual faith, and some studies have even suggested that it may slow disease progression (Ironson et al. 2006). An ex-crack addict interviewed in Detroit

---

10   This is discussed in more detail in Chapter 5.

11   Indeed Dilger has suggested that this could be seen a 'redemptive moment' when religion and HIV come together through the rhetoric of hope embedded in ARTs combined with the theological discourse of redemption (Dilger et al. 2010).

described the emergence of her new religious beliefs as she came to terms with HIV and began to work with others:

> It is the glue that holds me together. Not everyone needs this type of glue so to speak. I do. My faith is what helps me to get through the day. All the things I am telling you that I do on behalf of people with HIV right? All that stuff is possible because I am comfortable being known to God. (Berger 2004 p.112)

Studies of women in the DRC (Maman et al. 2009b), Tanzania (Watt et al. 2009; Zou et al. 2009) and Uganda (Hodge and Roby 2010) have all shown that personal faith (or lack of it) plays a major part in determining how individuals come to terms with their situation. In one group of Ugandan women 85 per cent reported that spirituality or religion were important coping strategies, while 43 per cent highlighted this as their main resource (Hodge and Roby 2010). A man in northern China stressed the value of religion in a very different setting:

> I think it's better for one to have a religious affiliation, a spiritual support, especially when he or she is psychologically challenged. No matter what the problems are, [guided by Buddha] I can find answers. ... Simply speaking, the Buddha teaches us how to be a person, like one should be open-minded and tolerant when she or he encounters difficulty. That is also the way that I comfort myself, so my psychological status is always good. (Zhou 2010 p.320)

Growing Together: Sharing Problems and Solutions

For many individuals the 'normalisation' process is greatly facilitated by membership of some kind of HIV-related organisation (Ciambrone 2002).[12] These groups can be compared with the traditional 'self-help' groups for those with chronic illnesses. Membership of a community of one's 'own' will usually be beneficial in dealing with stigma and hostility (Alonzo and Reynolds 1995). However the origins and the goals of these groups will differ between communities. Some will be ad hoc and 'grassroots' in their approach, growing informally so that members can offer each other emotional and practical support. Relatively few studies have examined the functioning of these groups but we can get a brief glimpse through examples from Thailand, Vietnam, Uganda and South Africa.

In Thailand, as in most other parts of the world, participants in community-based HIV support groups are predominantly female (Lyttleton 2004; Liamputtong et al. 2009). Women are expected to provide home-based care for the HIV positive men in their families, who usually die first. Most have been infected by their husbands, but despite this it is women who tend to experience more discrimination, or *Rang*

---

12   Of course some do not want to have their lives revolve around their HIV status and prefer to rebuild a new reality free of the label.

kiat as HIV stigma is known. Hence the majority are left as positive widows with few resources.

The main aim of the women who join these groups is to 'realign' themselves and to restore their sense of balance through the performance of appropriate behaviour. In the largely Buddhist culture of Thailand, HIV infection is associated with disruption of harmony and order. Hence the groups offer individuals a publically condoned way of reworking their subjective sense of self through contributing to the wider society.[13] As one woman described it: 'When I learned I was positive others looked on me as if my life had no worth. Now I have regained a sense of self worth (mi khu'n khan) from doing things for others (tham peua khon un)' (Lyttleton 2004 p.20).

The last few years have seen the emergence of a number of support groups for HIV positive mothers in Vietnam (Oosterhoff et al. 2008a). 'Sunflowers' was set up by and for mothers who lived with drug users and were often isolated as a result. As the group progressed they were gradually able to reshape their identities from the double stigma associated with HIV and drug use to becoming 'good mothers' and involving themselves in service delivery and wider educational activities. Members began by developing their confidence and supporting each other, as a woman in Hanoi explained:

> I felt alone and weak. I used to keep my feelings to myself because I was afraid
> I would not be accepted if I spoke about my problems. I am confident in myself
> now that I have been able to share with so many women like me and they have
> told me they feel better listening to me. (Oosterhoff et al. 2008a p.164)

Despite the general predominance of women in these activities, a few groups are now being organised by and for men (Wyrod 2011). One of the best known of these is Khululeka, set up by Xhosa men in Gugulethu township in Cape Town (Colvin et al. 2010). The declared aim of members is to reshape their masculinity and regain their dignity through overcoming the dependency of illness and taking responsibility for themselves and their families (Colvin and Robins 2009; Colvin et al. 2010).

Groups that begin on a small scale can of course expand into something much bigger. One example of this is the AIDS Support Organisation (TASO) set up in Uganda in 1987 by Noerine Kaleeba and 15 other women, most of whom were HIV positive.[14] Begun as an informal local support group, it gradually extended to include the provision of counselling and the mobilisation of neighbourhood care for people with HIV and AIDS and their families.

---

13   For an account of a comparable group of widows in Zanzibar (AWITA) see Beckmann and Bujra (2010).

14   For an excellent account of the emergence of the group in an interview with Noerine Kaleeba go to http://www.pbs.org/wgbh/pages/frontline/aids/interviews/kaleeba.html.

Positive Activism

The example of TASO highlights what is often a narrow dividing line between the activities of HIV positive people in support groups on the one hand and in advocacy on the other.[15] For many, more active involvement demonstrates the desire to tackle the disease itself as part of the process of reshaping their sense of themselves.

In the USA the early years of the pandemic were marked by intensive campaigning on the part of gay men and their supporters. These campaigns focussed mainly on the issue of stigma and on the need for more research to produce effective treatment and to widen access. Of course many HIV positive men were too ill to be active. However those gay and lesbian communities in the USA already involved in campaigning for sexual rights moved quickly into the political arena when HIV and AIDS were identified.

By the late 1990s a multifocal AIDS activism movement had developed in the USA, with many groups coming from previously marginalised populations. Few attempts have been made to explore these activities from the perspective of positive participants themselves. However a notable exception is Michele Tracy Berger's study of politically active HIV positive women in Detroit (Berger 2004).[16]

The participants were mostly 'women of colour' who began as sex workers, drug users and lawbreakers of various kinds.[17] Hence before their diagnosis they were already 'intersectionally stigmatised'. According to Berger the diagnosis of HIV offered them an interruption to this destructive cycle, creating a dramatic shift in their lives. What she calls their 'life reconstruction' gave them new capacities which were initially derived from substance abuse treatment and therapy on early sexual abuse. They were then enabled to undertake HIVand AIDS-related work in a community context, as advocates, activists and helpers.

For most, these activities began with what they perceived to be the inhumane and neglectful way they were treated after diagnosis both by health workers and sometimes by families. This in turn led many to reflect on the other inequalities and disadvantages – 'narratives of injustice' – that had shaped their lives. Of course all moved at a different pace and some eventually relapsed. But Berger provides an important illustration of the radical potential of HIV activism for positive individuals.

---

15   In identity politics there is often an overlap between movements making claims for justice from the larger society and support groups for people sharing common problems. For a good discussion of this see Reynolds Whyte (2009).

16   For an interesting comparison with a similar group of women see Ciambrone (2001).

17   Berger selected this particular group from a larger sample with the same origins but more diverse narratives. Hence they are not representative of the sample as a whole but give important insights into the potential for positive activism among particularly disadvantaged women.

In Africa the best-known political project by HIV positive people (and their supporters) is probably the Treatment Action Campaign (TAC), which has played a major part in reshaping attitudes and policies towards AIDS in post-apartheid South Africa. In the early days of the epidemic campaigning was similar to that in the USA, involving a relatively small group of gay white men and lesbian women. However by the period of transition to democracy the activist movement was growing in size and diversity.

TAC was founded in 1998 by Zackie Achmat, an HIV positive gay activist, and formed the basis for a widespread campaign that included many who had also been involved in the struggle against apartheid.[18] Not surprisingly, the harm caused by stigma was a major focus of the early years of campaigning. This reflected the extreme violence and hostility towards both homosexuality and HIV and AIDS that characterised the South African scene. For many this meant fighting for the right to privacy, with confidentiality high on the list of priorities.[19]

While these campaigns highlighted the right of HIV positive people to keep their status to themselves, it did little to tackle the basic issue of stigma. Hence large-scale demonstrations were organised, with thousands of both positive and negative activists wearing T-shirts proclaiming 'HIV POSITIVE'. Positive individuals also began to speak out at public meetings to ensure that the epidemic was visible and that their voices were heard. During this period effective drugs were becoming available in the global north but were denied by South African government policy under the leadership of President Thabo Mbeki. As a result the main demands of TAC shifted towards affordable and effective treatment for all those in need, with its campaigns playing a significant role in the creation of a South African National AIDS Plan in 2007.

The Shadow of Death

Thus far we have talked about living with HIV and the diversity of strategies for physical and psychological survival. But of course many have already died of AIDS and millions more will tread the same path. Hence we need to conclude this chapter with a note on the reality of these deaths in marginalised and deprived settings: situations like that of Simon whom we met in chapter one

Until recently the social process of dying had received relatively little attention from researchers in any part of the world. This has now begun to change as the taboo of death starts to lift (Exley 2004; Seale 2000). However most studies have explored hospital or hospice based deaths from cancer. Much less interest has been

---

18   The stoning to death of HIV positive activist Gugu Dlamini for revealing her status also led many to become involved.

19   For a personal account of these developments see Judge Edwin Cameron's excellent autobiography (Cameron and Sherratt 2005).

shown in the so-called 'disadvantaged dying' who end their lives in the shadows as a result of chronic disease (Exley 2004).

We still know very little indeed about deaths from AIDS, especially those in low income countries. However it is clear that the vast majority occur in very poor conditions with little access to medical support. A recent review reported that only 26 out of 47 countries in the African region have formal end of life care programmes (Gysels et al. 2011). Even South Africa has only about 70 hospices, mostly run on a voluntary basis and often with limited access to morphine for pain relief (Demmer 2007).[20]

There is evidence from many parts of the world that those in the last stages of their life would prefer to die at home. However the poorer the setting the more challenging such a death is likely to be both for the person who is dying and for the carers (Akintola 2008; Thomas 2006).[21] Community and home care services are being developed in areas of high prevalence, but their effectiveness is inevitably limited by lack of resources and poor domestic circumstances (Schneider et al. 2008).

For some, the experience is likely to be made worse by the attitudes surrounding AIDS-related mortality. In most African communities, for example, deaths are seen not as the end of existence but as the gateway to an afterlife. However, dying from AIDS is often believed to block an individual's passage to the next phase of their existence. A 'good death' in old age is seen as 'natural' and dignified, making the regeneration of the social group unproblematic. However the 'bad death' of a young person can be seen as a moral threat to the social order (Dilger 2008). This will inevitably add to the distress and existential anxiety of those who know they are dying such a 'bad death' (Nzioka 2000; Posel et al. 2007).

People known to be HIV positive may be perceived to be in a 'waiting room for death'. Indeed in the later stages of AIDS many sick people are kept from view (Dilger 2008). In Niehaus's study in the South African Lowveld these terminally ill people were often referred to as 'noisy ancestors' (*bakwale badimo*) who were disturbing the natural order of things. Corpses were not feared, but dying people were. As one man explained:

> I can tolerate a corpse but not a person who is dying. When I look at such a person his agony will be transferred to me and I will feel his pain. ... I will be traumatised. I will also think about those who have to care for me when I am in such a situation. (Niehaus 2007 p.856)

Many of those dying from AIDS will therefore experience a social death before their biological end. As they are increasingly unable to play a part in the survival strategies of their household and community, they have to face not only pain and

---

20   For an interesting review of gender issues in pain in HIV and AIDS see Gray and Berger (2007).
21   For a more detailed discussion of the experience of carers see Chapter 5.

physical disintegration but also loss of personal relationships which in turn leads to loss of self (Lavery et al. 2001). And very few resources are available to help them through this process. It is in this context that inequality and disadvantage reach their most extreme.

One of the most moving accounts of an AIDS death (without access to ART) comes from Didier Fassin's account of the circumstances of a young South African woman who died in the township of Alexandria in 2002:

> Puleng lived in a cellar dug out beneath a shack made of wood and sheet metal, reached through narrow winding alleys lined with houses and criss-crossed with laundry lines ... In the bedroom, devoid of natural light, stood only one piece of furniture, the big bed she shared with her daughter and to which she was now nearly confined. (Fassin 2007 p.18)

Puleng herself was anxious to narrate the story of her life as it ebbed away, one of great hope and strength but without access to the resources to realise her potential:

> So this is my life. A life of misery. We've been suffering so much. But I was talented. I used to write stories when I was a child. The first one, it was after reading a book about Florence Nightingale. And I liked to write poems. I even got a scholarship to study abroad. ... Now my life is sinking but I'm very strong, very, very strong. And I'll live until God decides I should pass away ... I told my family 'On my funeral day I don't want you to prepare a meal.' ... It costs a lot of money ... But I don't think of that all the time. I thank God to have brought me into this world. (Fassin 2007 p.19)

Conclusion

This chapter has given an overview of the central themes emerging in the literature on living with HIV in different parts of the world. It has highlighted the diversity of individual experiences, with many managing a return to something like 'normality' with the help of ART; some creating radically new lives as HIV positive activists; but others dying of AIDS, often in the worst of circumstances. The many different factors shaping these narratives have been introduced, with structural inequalities interlinked in complex ways to create varying levels of basic need satisfaction and (dis)advantage. We have seen how these impact on social identities and individual cognitive and emotional characteristics. The fear and the reality of social stigma have also been shown to be of continuing significance. The following chapters will build upon these brief observations through exploring these various themes in greater detail.

Chapter 4

Depending on Health Care for Survival

During the early stages of the pandemic, a positive diagnosis of HIV was assumed to be the harbinger of an early death from a painful illness. But, as we have seen, dramatic changes occurred with the arrival of antiretroviral therapy (ART) in the mid-1990s. Though not offering a cure, it did lead to a new 'discourse of hope' with major improvements in well-being and life expectancy.

Some commentators expressed doubt about the possibility of 'rolling out' ART from richer countries into resource-poor settings. They warned of what they called 'antiretroviral anarchy' as drugs increasingly developed resistance due to poor adherence (Harries et al. 2001). However others campaigned against this 'double standard', calling for a more equal distribution of drugs (Moatti et al. 2004; Coetzee et al. 2004; Farmer et al. 2001). As a result of initiatives such as WHO's '3 by 5' significant progress has been made in opening up access: 47 per cent of those 14.2 million eligible people in low and middle income countries were receiving treatment at the end of 2010 compared with 39 per cent at the end of 2009 (UNAIDS 2012c).

Until recently there had been no population-based evidence of the impact of these developments. However the first sign of their potential effectiveness came with a study from rural KwaZulu-Natal in South Africa. A cohort of positive people was followed between 2000 and 2011. In the absence of treatment life expectancy fell from 59 to 52 years between 2000 and 2003 but by 2011 there was a gain of 8.2 years as a result of the roll-out of ART (Bor et al. 2012). However many challenges still remain.

First, it is clear that for millions of people ART is still difficult to access and/ or unaffordable. Many remain undiagnosed and untreated, while others are unable to take the drugs as prescribed (Gill et al. 2005). If services are available, they may be delivered inappropriately, unreliably and with little sensitivity, inevitably reducing their effectiveness. Second, access to ART can only be a partial answer to meeting the health care needs of positive people since they will need not just drugs but also a range of other medical resources. And here too there is evidence of major differences in availability both within and between countries.

Finally, as we shall see, the effectiveness of ART in improving quality of life and increasing longevity also depends on the circumstances in which infected individuals are living. The potential of drugs to optimise health will be either enhanced or limited by the strength of those consuming them and by the demands made on their minds and bodies in the wider struggle for survival.

This chapter will explore these issues in more detail. It will trace the 'therapeutic itinerary' through which each potentially positive individual goes:

testing (or not), seeking care (or not) if the test is positive, negotiating life with ART (if it is accessible) and fighting for life if it is not. We begin with an overview of differences in current levels of access to HIV therapies.

Who Gets Access to ART?

The most visible inequalities in the numbers of HIV positive people benefiting from ART are found between rich countries and poorer countries, creating obvious disadvantages for many. By 2009 access was assumed to be universal for those living in the global north.[1] But, as we saw in Chapter 2, the comparable figure for those in the transitional societies of Eastern Europe and Central Asia was only about 15 per cent (WHO, UNICEF and UNAIDS 2011). In most low and middle income countries those in need also tend to access care at a much later stage, often worsening their prognosis significantly (Bekker et al. 2007). These inequalities in access are usually explained in terms of different levels of health service provision, which in turn are related to the overall wealth of individual countries (Natrass 2006b).

However the political priorities of governments will also play a major part. In some parts of Eastern Europe, as we have seen, the epidemic is mainly among injecting drug users (IDUs). Since they represent an especially stigmatised social group this appears to have been an important factor in limiting the resources spent on their care (Cohen 2010; Mimiaga et al. 2010; Rhodes et al. 2009). Similarly the 'AIDS denialism' of the South African government is calculated to have cost some 330,000 lives (Chigwedere et al. 2008; Forsyth et al. 2008; Natrass 2006b).

In the early years the cost of drugs was an important element in limiting access to therapy in many of the poorest countries. However new initiatives have led in some places to the provision of cheaper or free drugs via a range of partners and donors (Posse et al. 2008). The cost of first-line drugs in particular has fallen dramatically since around 2000.[2] But despite these reductions, the weakness of health care systems continues to create inequalities in access between countries. In Mozambique, for example, a study showed the limited absorptive capacity of HIV services where less than 30 per cent of funds earmarked for the Ministry of Health for 2006 were able to be spent. Only 14 per cent of those in need had been treated but the rest of the money had to be returned to donors (Posse et al. 2008).

Within this context, the scarcity of skilled and motivated health workers is recognised as one of the key barriers to progress (Schneider et al. 2006). ART is not easy to manage, necessitating lifelong treatment as well as frequent and careful monitoring (Barnighausen 2010; Bloom and Humair 2010). Yet the longstanding

---

1   'Universal' is taken to be more than 80 per cent coverage of those in clinical need, which under WHO guidelines of 2010 is indicated by a CD4 cell count of 350 or less.

2   Though the cost of second and third line drugs remains high. These are used when cheaper options fail but are often unavailable.

brain drain of health workers from Africa and Asia has accelerated in recent years (Médecins Sans Frontières 2007, 2010). Nearly 500 doctors and 1,000 nurses from South Africa register annually with the regulatory agencies in the UK (Schneider et al. 2006).[3] These human resource problems are often exacerbated as health workers leave the public sector and rural areas to earn more in private practice in the cities. At the same time HIV infection among staff is a major cause of attrition in many health systems. Estimates from South Africa have suggested that more than 16 per cent of health workers were themselves HIV positive (Schneider et al. 2006).

Unfairness in access to care is also found *within* countries, with members of marginalised groups being disadvantaged compared with their HIV positive compatriots.[4] In the USA, for example, recent studies have highlighted the unequal access of some minority ethnic groups to testing and appropriate therapy (Henry J. Kaiser Family Foundation 2012). One of the few studies of the access of men who have sex with men (MSM) to services in Africa found that they too were significantly disadvantaged (Rispel et al. 2011). A multilingual global online survey of 5,000 MSM found that only 36 per cent were able to easily access treatment (Global Commission on HIV and the Law 2012).

Evidence from both the USA and Western Europe indicates that IDUs too are less likely to access highly active antiretroviral therapy (HAART) than the majority of the HIV positive population (Lert and Kazatchkine 2007; Wolfe et al. 2010; Wood et al. 2003) and they are likely to face even greater challenges in developing and transitional countries (Aceijas et al. 2006; Rispel and Metcalfe 2009). Lesbian, bisexual, queer and transgender women have also reported major challenges in accessing services (Logie et al. 2012).

Similar problems have been found in many countries among both male and female sex workers (Chakrapani et al. 2009; Scambler and Paoli 2008; Stadler and Delaney 2006). In Vancouver's Downtown Eastside, a study found that only about 9 per cent of HIV positive sex workers were receiving HAART despite its easy availability in the wider community. The authors explained this in terms of a range of factors, including high rates of injecting drug use and the fact that the group included a significant percentage of Aboriginal women (Shannon et al. 2005).[5] Similar discrimination was reported recently from Uganda, where sex workers were having difficulty accessing life-prolonging drugs. As human rights activist and sex worker Maclean Kamya described it: 'When we visit health centres some health workers say, "But why you are a sex worker and we are just wasting our

---

3   The number of enrolled nurses in South Africa fell from 60 to 52 per 100,000 population between 2000 and 2005, while the equivalent number of professional nurses fell from 120 to 109 (MSF 2007).

4   Access is of course most equitable in those countries with effective national health systems free at source (Souteyrand et al. 2008).

5   For a comparison with lack of health care for Indian sex workers see Gangoli (1999).

ARV's. Why should we give you our treatment? We just have to give it to someone who needs it." That is total discrimination' (Kiapi 2010 p.1).

In most parts of the world there are also marked gender differences in access to services. As the pandemic became increasingly 'feminised' it was widely assumed that women were missing out on treatment compared with men. However recent studies have shown that that in many settings it is actually (heterosexual) men who have least access to services relative to their needs (Natrass 2006a; Muula et al. 2007; Cornell et al. 2009).[6] Significantly a recent study in Canada highlighted the problems of the many heterosexual men who saw HIV services as 'gay territory' (Antoniou et al. 2012).

Research in Europe has highlighted the particular difficulties often faced by African migrants (Fakoya et al. 2008). There are many reasons for this but among the most significant are restrictive immigration policies and complex regulations governing access to free care (Burns and Fenton 2006; Doyal 2009). Similar patterns have been found among African migrants in the USA (Foley 2005).

This overview of the evidence has shown that that there are still marked inequalities between populations and social groups in their opportunities for accessing ART. But the factors behind these patterns of disadvantage are not straightforward. The next sections will look in more detail at the complex ways in which such differences are produced at various stages of individual journeys through illness and care.

Beginning the Journey: Who Tests?

The availability of testing facilities worldwide has increased markedly in recent years, from 78,000 in 2007 to 107,000 in 2009 (WHO, UNICEF and UNAIDS 2011). However these services remain unevenly distributed. In low and middle income countries the average number of centres is only 5.5 per 100, 000 population. One estimate has indicated that in the most affected African countries only about 10 per cent of women and 12 per cent of men have been tested for HIV and know their results (Obermeyer and Osborn 2007). Even in more developed countries such as the USA at least one-third of those who are positive are thought to be ignorant of their status (MMWR/CDC 2008). The global median percentage of positive people who know their status is estimated to be less than 40 per cent (WHO, UNICEF and UNAIDS 2011).

This ignorance is of course extremely significant since neither preventive nor care strategies can be effective if individuals are not aware of their status.

---

6   It is interesting, however, that in a recent study of injecting drug users in Canada the situation was reversed, with women having less access to ART (Tapp et al. 2011). This appears to be common among the IDU population in other settings but more research is needed.

Increasing the scale of regular testing has therefore been identified as a major policy goal (de Cock et al. 2006; Obermeyer and Osborn 2007).[7] But symptom-free individuals (or even those with symptoms) will often put this low on their list of immediate priorities.

Reluctance to test may sometimes reflect a misunderstanding of the disease itself. Individuals may not believe they are at risk despite their own histories, or may think that HIV is not a 'real' disease.[8] On the other hand some will fear that a positive diagnosis would herald both social and biological death (Frank 2009). On the basis of past experience they may assume that there is little chance of successful treatment and hence no point in discovering their fate. These concerns will often be exacerbated by practical problems in accessing facilities.

Gender Differences in Testing Behaviour

In most settings men appear to be more reluctant to test than women.[9] A partial explanation for this is that women are more likely to be tested in the context of antenatal care. But recent studies have gone further in exploring the reasons for these differences (Beck 2004; Fitzgerald et al. 2010; Skovdal et al. 2011). They have highlighted the ways in which 'doing masculinity' requires men to avoid any signs of the apprehension usually associated with testing. A nurse in rural Zimbabwe described how men were not supposed to show emotion or anxiety about their own welfare: 'Men as I see them don't want to know their about their status when they are fit and strong, they do not want to appear afraid I think. Not wanting to know what their status is, is like saying 'I'm strong, I'm strong' (Skovdal et al. 2011 p.5).

This is reinforced by their tendency to distance themselves from all medical facilities. As one South African man explained:

> Clinics are women's places and HIV is a women's disease. [The clinics are] ... more female dominated, like, nurses, so men don't like to be [laughs] exposed to, er, to succumb to women. So that is why they are less likely to go to the health facilities, like, because they are more likely to be attended by women. (Beck 2004 p.16)[10]

---

7   For an excellent overview of methodological and ethical issues relating to testing see Obermeyer and Osborn (2007).

8   A recent study of men who have sex with men in Beijing found that 82 per cent had never tested for HIV even though facilities were easily available. The majority (72 per cent) believed they were not at risk (Choi et al. 2006). See also Zhou (2008).

9   Most studies have focussed on 'men' without taking any account of sexual identities or practices. For a recent overview of qualitative studies of testing among MSM in developed countries see Lorenc et al. (2011).

10   The examples given in this study are from Xhosa men but other studies of masculinities and health have shown similar findings. See Chapter 3 on masculinities and stigma.

Even when symptoms have already begun to appear, many men still have to be persuaded by their partner to seek help. Indeed there is evidence from South Africa that some are even willing to accept the woman's diagnosis as their own in order to avoid connecting with the health care system itself: 'The stories that we get here, the man says to the woman, no ok, if you are HIV positive it means I am HIV positive, so I don't need to go and test, I'm ok, I don't want to, I don't want anything to do with it' (Beck 2004 p.9).

As a result of this reluctance to test, men are likely to be diagnosed at a later stage in the development of their illness. In a recent study in Zimbabwe a nurse pointed out that some men only came to hospital when they were too sick to avoid it: 'Men will only come to us when they are bedridden and brought to us in a wheelbarrow' (Skovdal et al. 2011 p.9).

A number of health workers in the same study commented on their frustration with men who would not take their own or their partner's health seriously:

> I am very unsatisfied and I feel pulled down when I am dealing with a female patient whose male counterpart refuses to come for an HIV test. You see this means your efforts are in vain because you treat her and she goes to be reinfected at home because the husband disregards condom use. (Skovdal et al. 2011 p.6)

A recent study in India broke new ground in making a direct comparison between testing behaviour in women and men. The women almost always tested not because their own behaviour had been risky but because their husband had already been diagnosed HIV positive.[11] Moreover the testing process was frequently initiated by their family rather than by the women themselves.[12] The authors commented that: 'Women's lack of agency in HIV testing was strikingly evident: women were found to be generally unaware of the risk of infection through their husbands and of the importance of testing' (Joseph et al. 2010 p.292).

Fear of Ill-Treatment in Counselling and Treatment Centres

In many settings both women and men report being reluctant to test in case they are treated badly. This stems in part from their anticipation of being actively stigmatised if they are found to be positive. However it also reflects the fact that staff in many clinics are overworked, with numbers of patients increasing dramatically (Dieleman et al. 2007; Obermeyer and Osborn 2007). Many workers may also be worried about their own health (Namakhoma et al. 2010). Hence clinics are often highly stressed institutions with harmful effects on care (Jones 2010).

---

11   As we saw in Chapter 2 some 90 per cent of married women in India were infected by their husbands.

12   This example highlights the importance of making sense of illness behaviour and treatment in relation to wider patterns of gender inequality. For an excellent article on the relationship between gender and HIV services in India see Sinha et al. (2008).

What goes on in health care settings is of course largely invisible. However a few studies have highlighted some of the difficulties that may arise in following the principles of 'western' counselling in different social contexts (Angotti 2010). Studies in India, for example, have shown that many women testing in private hospitals are not even told their own diagnosis on the grounds that they will not be able to understand or cope with a positive result (Datye et al. 2006; Joseph et al. 2010).[13] Living in a small community will also make anonymity and confidentiality very difficult. One Malawian counsellor explained how it 'broke his heart' when he saw that a neighbour he had found to be positive was still having what he presumed to be unsafe sex with women other than his wife (Angotti 2010).

Similar problems have been identified in other settings and especially among marginalised populations. A recent study in Eastern Indonesia provides an excellent illustration of the problems faced by both service users and health workers (Butt 2011). The isolated and inferior status of the study population within the wider Indonesian context means that ethical practice is almost non-existent. The author summarises the situation as follows: 'The gap between the ideal – constant, complete confidentiality – and the practice – constant, almost complete lack of confidentiality – is not a gap of omission but a gap of commission' (Butt 2011 p.232).

There is also anecdotal evidence of physical abuse within the privatised setting of the counselling room, where there is usually an imbalance of power between health workers and service users and also between women and men. Such abuse is rarely visible but in a recent study in Nairobi a female counsellor revealed what may be the tip of an iceberg:

> One of the most difficult experiences I had was when a client phoned me. She said she has been raped within one of our counselling rooms … she told me she had come to VCT with a friend and she was called for her finger prick … and then she was told … 'You know there is another test which has to be done with my penis.' So then the counsellor put a condom on and penetrated her and he came. (Hamilton et al. 2008 p.393)

This is clearly an extreme case but highlights what may happen (or be feared) in what is effectively an unregulated environment.

ART: Patterns of Acceptance and Retention

Among those who test positive and are deemed (either immediately or subsequently) to be in need of ART, significant numbers will still not be able to access them. Among those who are given drugs there are marked variations in the degree to which they conform to medical protocols (Nachega et al. 2010;

---

13   These hospitals are not held to the same ethical codes as public institutions. For more discussion of these issues in a maternity context see Chapter 6.

Reynolds 2004). 'Adherence' of this kind is a complex process which is hard to monitor, especially in a comparative context. As a result the simpler measure of 'retention' or continuing contact with services is often used as a proxy (if limited) indicator for the appropriate use of health care.[14]

An analysis of recent studies in sub-Saharan Africa indicated an average retention rate of about 70 per cent at three years (Fox and Rosen 2010). Surprisingly perhaps, studies indicate that average continuation rates are broadly similar in the USA. However there is also great diversity between settings and between social groups in both rich and poor countries (Horstmann et al. 2010; Mills et al. 2006; Nguyen et al. 2007).

Two broad conclusions can be drawn from this data. The first is that there are many problems in retaining some groups of HIV positive people on ART even in those countries where services are widely available. And second, it demonstrates that better results can be obtained in resource-poor settings than was initially expected.[15] However this evidence needs to be read against the fact that, in Africa, only about one-third of those known to be in need of ART are receiving it. Moreover this third are likely to be among the most educated and motivated in the population and hence are more likely to continue with the medication.[16] If these rates are to be sustained in the future more clarity will be needed about the ways in which patterns of drug use are shaped in different settings.[17]

It has frequently been assumed that failure to conform to protocols or loss to follow-up can be explained by individual ignorance and 'irrationality'. However this ignores the fact that external factors will also have a major influence on the therapeutic 'choices' individuals are able to make (Hirsch 2007; Bangsberg et al. 2006; Gill et al. 2005; Grant et al. 2008; Merten et al. 2010; Thomas et al.2009). Hirsch says accordingly: 'Our understanding of uptake and adherence would be considerably enriched by attending more closely to how culturally variable ideologies intertwine with socially structured inequalities to shape both what individuals want out of their lives and what they can hope to achieve' (Hirsch 2007 p.22).

---

14   For a discussion of the challenges of measuring adherence see Ross-Degnan et al. (2010), Gerver et al. (2010) and Horstmann et al. (2010).

15   Most studies of retention in resource-poor settings have been in Africa so we cannot easily generalise to other low and middle income countries.

16   A recent review of adherence in low and middle income countries (Nguyen et al. 2007) suggests two other reasons why adherence might be overestimated in these countries. The first is that potentially non-adherent patients may be more likely to be excluded from treatment, either actively or passively. It is also likely that the pilot programmes reported in the literature may be benefiting from exceptional financial, human and technical resources (Nguyen et al. 2007).

17   As the roll-out is extended, more marginalised people are likely to enter the programmes, leading to increased rates of adherence difficulties (Hardon et al. 2007; Mills et al. 2006).

Most early studies of retention and adherence were done in developed countries and focussed mainly on the impact of unwanted biological effects of treatment. But, as we shall see, there are also significant economic, social and cultural 'side effects' that need to be taken into account, especially in resource-poor settings (Hardon et al. 2007; Kumarasamy et al. 2005; Ruanjahn et al. 2010; Rosen et al. 2007; Russell et al. 2010).[18]

The major reason why HIV positive people turn to ART is self-evident: a belief that this may be the only way to ensure a longer life of better quality. Those who have seen or heard about what are often near-miraculous effects on others will wish to obtain the same benefits for themselves. And once they have seen their own condition improve, they clearly have a very strong incentive to maintain these changes. One Tanzanian woman described her feelings in the following way:

> I have no such idea of stopping to take them for sure, because I was too much tortured before. I was sick for a very long time. I was just sleeping in bed. But now I am not. Therefore it's not easy for me to stop them because they are the ones that made me better. (Watt et al. 2009 p.1795)

However individuals may be encouraged to take on a medical regimen for reasons more complex than simply ensuring their own survival. Hence such choices can only be understood within the context of 'local moral worlds'. In many low and middle income countries in particular, respondents frequently talk about their duty to ensure that they are able to look after dependants who may have no other source of support:

> I was feeling very stressed and thought of killing myself but I had to think about my children and be strong. I'm happy taking the medication as long as it helps me – I want to see my kids grow up. 'What example would I set for my daughter' ... if I die what will happen to my children? (Gilbert and Walker 2009 p.1127)

A recent study carried out in Nigeria, Tanzania and Uganda took this analysis a stage further. The authors found that many HIV positive people have to resort to 'begging and borrowing' funds from friends and family to obtain ART (Ware et al. 2010). In return for any help they are given they feel a moral obligation to take the drugs appropriately. This in turn ensures that they retain the 'social capital' they have invested in these essential relationships. For many, such feelings of personal responsibility also extend to those health workers who have supported them in their efforts to survive (Watt et al. 2009; Gilbert and Walker 2009). But however much they want to succeed there may be significant constraints on their capacity to do so.

---

18   For a valuable collection of recent articles on the policy implications of ART roll-out see the special edition of *AIDS Care* edited by Russell, Seeley and Whiteside (2010).

Constraints on Successful Treatment

The challenges of adherence face those in marginalised groups in rich countries and many more in low and middle income settings (Russell et al. 2010). Indeed, as Vinh-Kim Nguyen has suggested, in many settings the key question we should be asking is not why so many fall by the wayside but how so many manage to adhere to treatment (Nguyen et al. 2007). Recent US studies have indicated that those at particular risk of dropping out are in the younger age groups, have less education, lack health insurance, have low household income and are more likely to be black or Latino (Horstmann et al. 2010). Injecting drug users have also been found to be at particular risk of not having the capacity to continue with therapy in both rich and poor countries (Bergenstrom and Abdul-Quader 2010; Lert and Kazatchkine 2007).

As we have seen earlier, the experience of being stigmatised is a constant theme in accounts of the use of health services, especially for those who are already marginalised. A Serbian injecting drug user felt unable to continue with treatment because of the hostility and discrimination he experienced: 'I don't want to go to Belgrade again. I don't want to because they treated me so like an animal. They know me and my characteristics (an injector). It's very, very, very bad. ... I won't even go! I don't care!' (Rhodes et al. 2009 p.1056).

Thus the 'double discrimination' many face may play a significant role in preventing them from obtaining the potential benefits offered by ART. However for many it is material deprivation that presents the single most important obstacle to successful treatment (Boyer et al. 2009).

Practical Obstacles: Poverty and Hunger

Antiretroviral drugs themselves may be unaffordable. And even when they are free there may be charges for blood tests or for other treatments needed for opportunistic infections (International Treatment Preparedness Coalition 2007). A 42-year-old man in south-west China explained:

> If I get side-effects I have to spend my own money to go to the doctor. My biggest problem now is that my parents are both in their sixties and seventies. ... Their retirement wages together only add up to 500 RMB [about $65] a month. It's used for four people. (Sabin et al. 2008 p.1246)

There have also been a number of reports of corruption in settings where drugs are supposed to be free but patients are forced to pay bribes, usually to health workers. A recent study in Zimbabwe found that 57 per cent of HIV positive people had been asked to pay in this way for drugs and 24 per cent for diagnostic tests (Zimbabwe Lawyers for Human Rights 2010). Most were living on less than $100 a month and hence many had to go without. The authors of the study comment:

The research findings reinforced the view that corruption in health care discourages treatment, testing and other health seeking behaviour. In these circumstances the general attitude has been observed to shift towards resentment and resignation (among those who are living with HIV) who then give up on accessing essential medicines and diagnostic tests. (ZLHR p.9)

Alongside the cost of treatment itself, the expenses of transportation are the most frequently mentioned problem. Interviews with 41 people living with HIV/AIDS in Mbarara, Uganda identified the cost of the monthly clinic visit as a constant source of stress and anxiety (Tuller et al. 2010). Participants struggled with competing demands between transport costs and other necessities such as food, housing and school fees. A 38-year-old woman with seven children explained how she missed a visit when she could not work, and the family's retail business also failed:

> It was about the time I fell sick, and I didn't have strength to do some gardening, and it was around the same time that the store collapsed, so there was no money for transport ... I was feeling very weak and I was sleeping most of the time, and I would feel that since I was missing medicine that I was supposed to be taking, I would be dying any minute. (Tuller et al. p.780)

The cost or unavailability of food is also cited as an obstacle to appropriate drug use across a range of settings (Franke et al. 2010). The links between hunger and HIV are complex. Lack of food may exacerbate side effects for those established on ART as well as increasing their appetite and making them feel hungrier.[19] For some this may put their therapy at risk: 'I want to eat all the time and fear the hunger will eat into my stomach, since I have ulcers already. Sometimes I wake up in the night to eat food. This is a difficult situation for me' (Hardon et al. 2007 p.661).

In a recent study in Zambia a man came into the examining room demanding food because the treatment made him so hungry (Frank 2009). The doctor explained that this was normal but the man was not satisfied. Frank continues: 'He demanded to know where he was going to find food as he did not have work. He was desperate. He complained that the claws of hunger were scratching out his insides' (Frank 2009 p.523).

In some countries those in the advanced stages of HIV and AIDS are sometimes eligible for disability grants (usually assessed on the basis of a CD4 count of less than 200). These grants are relatively high in the context of poverty-stricken communities and may be a major element in the family's budget. However they can create a double bind for recipients who need to be very sick to get the funds in the first place (Hardy and Richter 2006; Leclerc-Madlala 2006; Natrass 2005):

---

19   See Anema et al. (2009) for an overview of the complex links between food insecurity and HIV, including a summary of antiretroviral pharmacokinetics and immunological and virological outcomes. See also further discussion of hunger in Chapter 5.

'That's the problem when they say your CD4 count is still high and you are still strong. Too strong for how long? My stomach is hungry now. If I don't eat now I'll be sick. That's what they want, for us to be sick' (Leclerc-Madlala 2006 p.251).

Paradoxically, the grant may be withdrawn as their CD4 count improves since they are no longer perceived to be in need. As a result many people face impossible choices that may severely inhibit their use of ART. As a recipient in South Africa's East Rand explained:

> I am worried to hear that the grants are being reviewed because I don't think I qualify any more. My health has improved since I started ARVs. I am very worried, because my grant is my only means of support. I think I am only alive today because of the grant. (Hardy and Richter 2006 p.85)

As a result of these financial pressures, a negative HIV test result may even produce a reaction of disappointment rather than relief (Nattrass 2005). In the impoverished Eastern Cape region of South Africa, testing positive is said to sometimes be referred to as 'having won the lotto' (Leclerc-Madlala 2006; Uys et al. 2005).[20] Not surprisingly perhaps, there are also reports of a trade in positive blood, where someone known to be positive will stand in for the test for a negative person who needs the grant (Leclerc-Madlala 2006). These extremes of poverty and hunger are more commonly found among patients in low income countries. However research in Downtown Eastside Vancouver found that 71.5 per cent of HIV positive people on ART were food insecure: a rate seven times higher than the rest of the Canadian population (Anema et al. 2011).

Making Sense of Medicines and their Effects

Many service users know very little about biomedicine in general and HIV therapy in particular (Chopra et al. 2006; Reynolds et al. 2006). This lack of knowledge has emerged in many settings as a barrier to successful continuation. Health workers may not provide enough information, especially if they are overworked. At the same time patients may resist what they experience as being treated like children, as one study in rural Zimbabwe showed:

> He will be shouting different kind of instructions for example 'make sure you are in line' and 'may everyone sit down, I won't serve anyone standing up.' The benches will be full so some will sit on the floor … if you try to complain he might even shout at you. (Campbell et al. 2011 p.179)

---

20   For excellent accounts of the complexities of setting up equitable social security systems in the context of HIV and extreme poverty see Natrass (2005) and Hardy and Richter (2006).

The regimen of treatment for HIV and AIDS is especially difficult to understand since many aspects of it are counter-intuitive – the fact that there will be no cure for example. One young man in Tanzania asked: 'Now, tell me, what is the use in having someone use drugs, or anything that does not cure? What it (ART) does is simply make the *virus* drunk … yes you may prolong your life a little bit … and that's all!' (Ezekiel et al. 2009 p.960).[21]

Because medicines have traditionally been thought of as curative (as in the case of antibiotics for example) their use is assumed to be short term. As a result there are many examples of patients using the drugs then stopping when they feel better (Murray et al. 2009; Sanjobo et al. 2008; Schumaker and Bond 2008). Such decisions may be encouraged by the negative physical effects many experience with ART – including lipodystrophy (or visible changes in fat distribution), peripheral neuropathy, diarrhoea and tiredness (Persson 2005).

Lack of trust in western medicine itself may also be a factor militating against the continuation of ART. It is sometimes said to be unsuitable for Africans for example, or even to be deliberately poisoned. As an elderly healer in Zambia put it:

> Medicine that comes from out (side) the country, if it was me I would not be ordering the medicine because I don't trust the white people … What they want is to finish us all completely – maybe even this disease (AIDS) came from them it's only that Zambia does not have powers to do something … maybe they add disease in the medicine because they don't like us. (Schumaker and Bond 2008 p.2132)

Not surprisingly, studies have shown that that these attitudes to ART can be rooted in experiences of biomedicine that reach back to the colonial period.[22]

Around the world there is also evidence of high levels of use of 'complementary' or 'alternative' (CAM) or 'traditional' medicines in most settings (Babb et al. 2007; Peltzer et al. 2008).[23] In the USA for example research has indicated that between 60 per cent and 90 per cent of HIV positive people are using CAM therapies. In a recent study in the UK 45 per cent of African migrants interviewed said they were using some form of non-biomedical treatment (Thomas et al. 2009). However the

---

21 Ezekiel et al. (2009) provide a valuable account of the interaction between biomedical and indigenous discourses in making sense of perceptions of ART among a group of young people in Tanzania.

22 In South Africa these feelings were exacerbated during the earliest years of the epidemic by government rhetoric which denied the reality of HIV itself and denounced related treatments as 'western' (Forsyth et al. 2008).

23 As Thomas et al. (2009) point out, terms such as 'alternative' and 'traditional' can be seen as problematic since they normalise biomedicine. While recognising the heterogeneous, fluctuating and overlapping nature of these categories, they are used here in line with the terminology of the research findings being quoted.

authors point out that this is likely to be an underestimate since there is evidence that many did not want to 'confess' in a hospital setting.

Some will use these remedies alone but they are usually consumed in combination with ART or other biomedical interventions. In most cases they are not taken as treatment for HIV itself but to help with fertility and to boost the immune system as well as helping with the side effects of drugs. In both Africa and Asia there has also been a dramatic growth in new treatments referred to as neo-traditional or neo-phytotherapeutic products (Hardon et al. 2008). These consist mainly of herbs and nutritional substances and are usually packaged like modern medicine.

Little is known about the pharmacological interaction between these different types of 'alternative' therapies and ART but there is some evidence of potentially hazardous effects (Dahab et al. 2008; Liu 2007; Mills et al. 2005). The continuing promotion of unproven AIDS 'cures' as well as the distribution of counterfeit pills is also causing concern (Amon 2008). These are often seen as the last hope by desperate people but few governments have put in place appropriate legislative and regulatory protection (Peltzer et al. 2008).

Managing Hope and Insecurity

As we have seen, HIV itself engenders much insecurity among those who are positive. Many are constantly wondering what symptoms they will develop, and when will they move on to AIDS and ultimately to death. For those in treatment these concerns are exacerbated by insecurities about the availability of drugs. Supplies may be intermittent, as a result of inefficiency or even corruption, or because of natural events, social conflicts or other emergencies that are more common in resource poor settings.

A recent review of these problems highlighted the 2008 floods in Mozambique, the ongoing political crises in Zimbabwe and the 2007 public sector health strikes in South Africa as examples of situations where access to ART was threatened (Veenstra et al. 2010). A UNICEF report described the situation of a Haitian woman who was unable to continue her therapy in the midst of the 2010 earthquake:

> One patient wore a turquoise flower in her hair, and twisted her beaded necklace as she spoke in a soft sing-song. She had walked three hours to the clinic from her tent city in the sprawling slum of Cité Soleil. Having missed an appointment the day after the earthquake, she had run out of pills and found herself racked by diarrhoea and vomiting – on the streets, no less. Further, she added, patting her very small belly, she was eight months pregnant and the father of her baby had been killed during the earthquake. (Sontag and Thompson 2010)

One of the most sophisticated accounts of the problems of institutionalised insecurity in treatment comes from a study carried out in Serbia (Bernays and

Rhodes 2009; Bernays et al. 2007; Rhodes et al. 2009). The analysis highlights the 'narrative of hope' that was engendered in individuals by the emergence of HAART (Bernays et al. 2010). But it also shows how for them HIV treatment often falls short of these expectations. Drug shortages and cycles of unwanted changes in treatment and testing strategies create conditions of major uncertainty which individuals experience as highly stressful. As one woman expressed it: 'We all need to know that there won't be a shortage. ... I need to know so that I am not scared, so I am calm. I want to be calm. I don't want there to be a shortage and I know there will be' (Rhodes et al. 2009 p.1053).

Lack of drugs and also of the equipment and reagents needed for monitoring CD4 levels and polymerase chain reaction (PCR) may lead to a 'compromised knowledge of illness state'. Under such circumstance individuals will not be able to make sense of their symptoms and health workers will also be working largely in the dark. Such experiences have been described as a 'blind date' (Bernays et al. 2007).

> The doctor says, opens my files and says, 'You know you should get CD4 and PCR.' and I'm like great and he says 'only we don't have.' ... And then you say 'Alright, thanks when it's available we'll do it.' And then, I don't know I come the following month and then it turns out 'Oh you know it was available from the 1st to the 20th' and I went there on the 21st and they've used it all. (Rhodes et al. 2009 p.1054)

Not surprisingly, patients find it especially difficult to deal with unexplained changes of treatment that seem to have no medical rationale. New combinations are often difficult to get used to and may produce side effects that generate increasing doubt about the medicines themselves. This was reported by a woman in the same study: 'They (treatment medicines) make me ill because they cause these complications during treatment. It's probably my body protesting. It's disgusting. ... Before it was like "Oh I just want to survive." Now it's not just to survive. I want to have quality of life' (Rhodes et al. 2009 p.1057).

Many talk about the huge effort involved in trying to keep up with therapy. While lack of money may not be the immediate cause of their insecurity, they nevertheless describe 'chasing medicines' as taking up a greater part of their lives. Indeed for some it simply becomes one stress too many and may lead to temporary or permanent cessation of therapy. For one injecting drug user the difficulties he faces have led him to disengage from treatment, but he has not given up on ART altogether. He simply plans to play a 'waiting game' and hopes he is still alive when a promised new clinic opens: 'I'll try to get treatment, start therapy again. I'll try it with the medicines. Well fuck it what can I do?' (Rhodes et al. 2009 p.1056).

As the authors point out, this insecurity and the stresses it engenders need to be read in the context of the transitional status of Serbia itself. Just as people are waiting for the drugs, so they are waiting for Serbia to catch up with the rest of

Europe where 'fancy combinations' or more advanced drugs are assumed to be easily available. Thus the promise held out by western medicine in the form of HAART can be double edged when what is optimally possible from a technical point of view is not delivered to the rest of the world: 'HIV treatment experience feeds a cycle of risk production with the consequence that some patients fluctuate between hope and hopelessness, between managing their HIV as a chronic condition and as a terminal illness' (Bernays et al. 2007 p.S9).

'Therapeutic and Bio-Political Citizenship': Tensions and Contradictions

In many parts of the world ART is increasingly provided through partnerships between national governments, non-governmental organisations (NGOs) and a range of international donors. As a result the relationships between local and global stakeholders have become ever more complex, with the needs and desires of service users too often being lost in the tumult.

The rhetoric underpinning many of these new initiatives is that individuals derive the right to HIV treatment not from the resource-poor states in which they often reside but from the 'international community' – or more accurately the richer countries of the world. Thus it is argued that their biological status as sick people gives them membership of a group with moral claims to be met. Based on detailed studies of service delivery in a number of West African countries, Vinh-Kim Nguyen coined the phrase 'therapeutic citizenship' to describe this situation (Nguyen et al. 2007; Nguyen 2008):

> Therapeutic citizenship is emerging as a salient force in the local African settings … where widespread poverty means that neither kinship nor a hollowed out state can offer guarantees against the vicissitudes of life. It has also emerged as a rallying point for transnational activism in a neoliberal world in which illness claims carry more weight than those based on poverty, injustice or structural violence. (Nguyen 2008 p.143)

However it is clear that these so-called 'bio-political rights' do not come without duties. In return for their treatment, individuals are expected to 'live positively'. This may involve using 'confessional technologies' to publically disclose their status, adhering properly to treatment protocols, regularly attending support groups, and giving up alcohol and other forms of consumption deemed unhealthy. By this means they can hope to be viewed as 'responsiblised HIV positive citizens' entitled to leverage treatment, food and other resources: 'Bluntly put, skill at telling the right stories gets activists drugs and keeps them alive' (Nguyen et al. 2007 p.34).

But the rhetoric of therapeutic citizenship can be evangelical in tone and harmful in effect. .While the concept may offer HIV positive individuals a new base from which to make moral claims (though there is no certainty they will be met) and provide sound information about how to optimise well-being, it may also prevent individuals from 'normalising' their situation or recreating their social identities on their own terms. Indeed, they may have to pay for survival through adopting particular lifestyles as directed by funders. The tensions arising from these developments have been observed in a number of different settings, including Brazil (Biehl 2007; Cataldo 2008), South Africa (Colvin and Robins 2009; Colvin et al. 2010; Mfecane 2011; Richey 2006; Levy and Storeng 2007), Zambia (Frank 2009), Tanzania (Beckmann and Bujra 2010; Mattes 2011) and Gambia (Cassidy and Leach 2009). These studies have highlighted two key points.

On the one hand 'living positively' may be very difficult if not impossible for individuals to achieve, given the structural, financial and knowledge constraints they face. On the other the highly 'rational' and individualistic behaviour implied by the positive therapeutic model is rarely an option in real lives that are constituted by relationships, emotions, duties and responsibilities towards others.[24] Cassidy and Leach have summarised this complexity in the context of Gambia:

> We find that people's adoption of biomedically shaped HIV positive identities and AIDS-related 'sick roles' is contingent and fragile, negotiated with other forms of knowledge, subject-positions and worries of disclosure. ... Rather than the image of active treatment-rights claiming therapeutic citizens, what we see is a less-empowered conformity to global discourses and procedures as a route to particular sorts of 'getting by'. (Cassidy and Leach 2009 p.10)

As we have seen, the most fundamental challenge that many positive people have to face is to make a public disclosure of their status. Many have spent much of their time and energy trying to conceal their status, yet this is what is required of them in the context of 'positive living'. Telling partners can be especially difficult. As one Zambian woman explained, she has to hide her packet of pills from her husband:

> I put it on a plate, add mealie meal, so when he takes the lid off he [does not find ART]. [When] I take the medicine. I have to make sure that he is outside. That is why I forgot to take medicine four times since I started treatment. (Human Rights Watch 2007 p.28)

Men too have reported fear of unwanted disclosure, talking of hiding their medications, disguising them, lying about them and delaying taking them. Again, discovery by partners was especially feared. One man interviewed in South Africa said:

---

24   The incoherence of imposing moral duties in return for human rights in circumstances where lack of basic need satisfaction makes compliance impossible will be explored in depth in Chapter 8.

Some are scared to disclose … If a person does not disclose to his partner he will have a problem in taking his medication, because he will have to hide … and if they have to hide medication … one day you are not going to take it because you'll be scared. Oh is she going to see me? Let me not take it today. I'll take it when she has gone. (Dahab et al. 2008 p.32)

A Nigerian man living in London described how his nightmare came to pass when his wife abandoned him after discovering he was HIV positive: 'My marriage just crashed after my diagnosis. I came home and told my wife and she stopped talking to me, my children too were made to stop talking to me so it was total isolation and I realised that I was in a different world' (Doyal et al. 2009 p.1903).

The contradictions inherent in these 'positive living' situations have recently been explored through the experiences of groups of Xhosa men in Mpumulanga, South Africa (Mfecane 2011) and of Shona men in Zimbabwe (Skovdal et al. 2011). In both settings the concept of being a 'real man' is focussed on economic and emotional independence and on playing the role of 'breadwinner' (Mfecane 2011; Morrell 2001). Associated with this are what are usually 'male' habits – including drinking alcohol, smoking cigarettes and having frequent sex without condoms.

Before beginning ART, most of the men in the study (implicitly) modelled their existence on these local versions of what Connell has called 'hegemonic masculinity' (Connell and Messerschmidt 2005). As a result many were anxious about adhering to the 'positive living' approach while also retaining what they perceived as their 'manliness'. As one Xhosa man put it: 'If I have to stop drinking then I don't need them (ARVs) Amanye ama auty a busy ayarhasa and mina ngihleli! (Other guys are busy drinking and I am just watching! No these ARVs are not for me) … Kungcono ngife (I would rather die)' (Mfecane 2011 p.133).

Compulsory attendance at support groups with women was also seen as alien by many, especially when they were run in a top-down way by leaders or facilitators. A few joined in and accepted the benefits offered, some even becoming peer educators. However for most there was a continuing tension between doing 'men's things' and acting as what was defined as a 'responsible positive person'.

For women too, conforming to the expectations of 'positive living' could be difficult, especially in the context of a culture of almost universal childbearing (Richey 2005, 2006). For them to become pregnant will require unprotected sex, which others may define as non-adherence to a 'positive living' regimen. Yet such actions are easy to understand in a context where a woman without a child is to be pitied and perhaps even abandoned. Hence many women of reproductive age have to negotiate between the global expectation of 'good therapeutic citizenship' and their own sexual and reproductive desires (Richey 2006).

Thus the strategy of 'positive living', as currently practised, can have complex and contradictory effects which may or may not be in the interests of those it is apparently intended to empower. As we have seen, progress is being made in opening up access to the relevant medications. But many are still being denied them. And even for those in receipt of ART, there is often a significant (but rarely acknowledged) price to pay in terms of loss of autonomy. As one group of authors neatly summarised it: 'Many have to face conflicting demands of patienthood and personhood' (Hirsch et al. 2007 p.S2).

Conclusion

This chapter has highlighted the complex processes by which inequalities in receipt of ART are created. While some disadvantages arise directly from the limitations of supply in poor and marginalised communities, others reflect much wider aspects of the lives of those affected. This highlights the fact that access to health care alone will not be enough to meet individual needs when material and other resources are limited. Indeed it is clear that terrible choices will have to be made when the need for health care may seem to 'trump' the need for food or for other basic necessities not just for those who are positive but also for those around them. Many will have to pay for their treatment not just in money terms but also in terms of severe threats to their capacity to exercise their autonomy in situations where their physical health or even their survival may be at stake.

Chapter 5
Challenging Livelihoods

The role of poverty in the promotion of HIV infection has been widely discussed. However less attention has been paid to the economic aspects of living with HIV or dying with AIDS. The majority of adults are at least partially dependent on their own paid and unpaid labour to ensure their survival and that of their dependants. Hence one of the most serious effects of any long-term illness is the harm it does to an individual's capacity to work. HIV and AIDS are clearly no exception and these effects are likely to be exacerbated in the context of current economic crises and austerity policies.

Working in 'Welfare' States

In the early years of the pandemic it was assumed that work and HIV were incompatible except in the very early stages. However this was transformed for some with the advent of effective therapies. As highly active antiretroviral therapy (HAART) became more widely available, researchers in the global north began to explore changes in individual experiences of working life (Bernell and Shinogle 2005; Douglas 2009; Nixon and Renwick 2003).[1]

For most of those using HAART, improved treatment meant a reduction in physical symptoms and improvements in psychological well-being, helping many to remain in employment or to take on voluntary work. Among those who remain active most report a range of benefits, including improved economic status, greater independence, a more positive sense of self and increased capacity for social interaction (Conyers et al. 2005; Douglas 2009). However the option of continuing paid work is not equally available to all. Some are too ill to work, while socio-economic status, gender, age and race/ethnicity will all be significant in shaping individual work options (Dray-Spira et al. 2008). Drug use may also be important, with a number of studies reporting that HIV positive injecting drug users (IDUs) are among those least likely to gain employment (DiClementi et al. 2005).[2]

---

1   A recent review showed that most of this research originated in the USA, with a few papers from Canada or Australia. There have been few studies originating in Europe, with the notable exceptions of those from France (Dray-Spira et al. 2008) and Italy (Alcano 2009).

2   A study in Spain found that HIV positive women were less likely than positive men to be employed, and more work is needed to explore the significance of this (Oliva 2009).

An interesting study carried out among construction workers in Milan highlighted the difficulties caused by the physical weakness so many feel as a result of antiretroviral therapy (ART) as well as the illness itself (Alcano 2009). Heavy labour was very difficult to combine with an intensive drug regimen. Though they had frequent access to medical care their 'life world' had changed dramatically. As Paolo described it:

> You can try to make your life more comfortable as you go along man, but you cannot change it altogether. Like I said, I live like this because of who I am, because of where I am from. That's the way the world goes. We all know men like me cannot leave their jobs just like that. (Alcano 2009 p.127)

Despite the introduction of equality legislation, studies have also shown that occupational discrimination – or fear of it – is still a major challenge for many HIV positive people. A recent UK study found that 62 per cent of those questioned had disclosed their status at work (Douglas 2009). However those who identified as gay men felt that the addition of HIV increased their chances of experiencing discrimination in the workplace (Douglas 2009). Similar fears of being penalised twice over were expressed by men who were African migrants (Douglas 2009; Doyal et al. 2009).[3]

It is clear that the availability of effective treatment has enabled many more HIV positive people to participate actively in working life. However others still face difficulties in supporting themselves, especially if loss of work means loss of health insurance – as it often does in the USA. Under these circumstances most developed countries have witnessed the extension of state and other charitable services to provide a basic income for those without private means.[4]

Working in the Global South

For those individuals who face the inequality and disadvantage of resource-poor settings the situation is often much more difficult because of their limited capacity to support themselves. On the one hand, paid work will often be hard to find even in the absence of an HIV diagnosis. On the other hand, millions who are positive still do not have access to regular supplies of ART and associated health care.

---

3   Neither study identified respondents who were both men who have sex with men (MSM) and African and hence potentially at a triple disadvantage. There have been relatively few studies of discrimination against positive employees and almost none have been comparative in their approach. One important exception is a comparison between workplaces in Beijing, Hong Kong and Chicago (Rao et al. 2008). This showed much higher rates of discrimination in Beijing and Hong Kong, though stigmatising attitudes were evident in all three.

4   In the US the Ryan White Care Act has been one of the most important examples.

Hence they are unlikely to be able to maintain their health and strength in what are often physically demanding jobs. Many will have been unemployed even before the 'shock' of illness and few public services will be available to help them. Their livelihood choices will be severely limited and the impact on those around them may be very damaging.

The remainder of this chapter will explore the effects of HIV on the working lives of the (relatively few) in formal employment as well as the huge numbers attempting to survive in the informal sector. It will also explore the wider impact of HIV on households responsible for the care of (one or more) members who have become economically dependent as a result of their illness.

HIV and Formal Employment

Despite the central importance of work for human survival, a recent review found only 11 studies exploring the impact of HIV on employment in low income countries (Beard et al. 2009). Moreover most of these were concerned not with the quality of life of the individuals involved or their financial circumstances but with the economic implications for employers. As we have seen, research in North America and Europe focussed mainly on individual choices about working life and the impact of these decisions on well-being. Studies in southern countries, on the other hand, have been concerned mainly with labour productivity and absenteeism. In other words they have emerged in the context of a concern not about the needs of HIV positive people themselves but about the maintenance of a skilled and reliable labour force.

There can be little doubt that for those who are able to access it ART does significantly reduce absenteeism from work – at least in the short term. A study at the Electricity Company of Cote d'Ivoire found a 94 per cent drop in days of work missed over three years (Eholie et al. 2003). On a Kenyan tea plantation, HIV positive male workers produced about 27 per cent less than a control group of negative colleagues in the final month before initiating ART. However levels equalised after only about seven months of medication (Larson et al. 2009).[5]

Results of this kind have encouraged some employers to provide testing and treatment for skilled workers, especially in settings where ART is otherwise difficult to access (Setswe 2009). However such services remain rare (Mahajan et al. 2007). In a recent study of large firms in 'developing' countries, only 6 per cent of those who responded had formal HIV policies, while 14 per cent were said to have informal ones (Bloom et al. 2006). Only in regions where HIV prevalence exceeded 20 per cent had the majority of firms made any provision. And most of

---

5   Significantly this study showed that female employees benefitted less from ART than men. More research is needed to make sense of the social and/or biological reasons for this. More generally a recent study highlighted the need for greater gender sensitivity in HIV workplace programmes (Sprague 2008).

these services were focussed on prevention, with only about one-quarter offering treatment.[6]

Hence few workers in low income countries are able to access services either in the wider community or in their workplace. And those who do will still face significant problems. Most importantly the services are precarious since they depend on workers maintaining their jobs. Loss of work is likely to mean not just loss of income but also withdrawal of access to ART, with many migrant workers in particular (like Simon in Chapter 1) simply being sent home to die.

There are also frequent accounts of discriminatory practices that discourage workers from taking advantage of what little is available to them. In South Africa, for example, it is estimated that around 30 per cent of gold miners working underground are HIV positive (World Bank 2011). The mines also have among the highest rates of tuberculosis (TB) in the world (Rees et al. 2010). Most employers have been providing voluntary counselling and testing (VCT) and ART since around 2001 but many workers are still reluctant to use them. This is because they believe they will be stigmatised if their status is known.

One of the few qualitative studies carried out among South African mine workers highlighted the fact that many were reluctant to take the test at all because of fears about confidentiality. One mine worker said:

> They say that the results are confidential but it's worrying me. In the testing there is only two people, the counsellor and the patient, but next time you hear people talking about the status of another person when he goes past … One day I was just with some guys at the shopping mall. When I was standing there I overheard them telling each other saying that, 'Do you see that guy who is passing there, he is HIV positive.' (Bhagwanjee et al. 2008 p.274)

And another mine worker expressed the same feelings:

> The problem is when we do the testing there are people who take long and there are those who take a short time. Those who take long are suspected (of being) infected and (that) they are trying to console them. And you can see those people who take long … are so stressed and no longer the same as before.' (Bhagwanjee et al. 2008 p.274)

For those who do test positive there is not only the shock of diagnosis but also the fear of losing their job. Hence many will go without treatment or seek it elsewhere in order to keep their status secret. Those who are treated may still find it difficult to work in what are often very strenuous settings. In Lesotho, for example, the clothing industry now employs some 46,000 workers, of whom 85 per cent are

---

6   For a detailed discussion of workplace programmes in southern Africa and priorities for research see Mahajan et al. (2007) and Fultz and Frances (2011) and for South Africa in particular see Connelly and Rosen (2006).

women. A community survey undertaken by the group Apparel Lesotho Alliance to Fight AIDS (ALAFA) found that 43 per cent of those who agreed to be tested anonymously were HIV positive and most were unaware of their status (AEGIS-IRIN 2009).

HIV services have now been set up in the largest factory in the capital, Maseru, and by 2009, 800 women were receiving treatment. But for many the situation remained very hard:

> 'The job we're engaged in is too heavy' said Manthabiseng, whose husband resigned from his job at the factory after complaining of shoulder pain. 'We're given masks, but the pieces of thread are everywhere and we still feel we're breathing them; there are many TB cases. I'd take any kind of job as long as it's not in the factory.' (AEGIS-IRIN 2009 p.2)

Mary's husband is also unemployed, except for occasional piece-jobs, and her monthly salary of 741 maloti ($75) is barely enough to support her family: '"There are days when I feel sick but I have to come to work anyway," she told IRIN.[7] Only after she has worked at the factory for more than a year will she be eligible for paid sick leave' (AEGIS-IRIN 2009 p.2).

The International Community of Women Living with HIV/AIDS (ICW) explored the daily lives of working women in several different countries and found widespread discrimination in a number of settings. One woman from Thailand said:

> At the same time that I got AIDS I had my job and they wanted to drive me out. I knew but I did not accept it because I did not want to quit my job. They forced me to have blood taken. Eventually they drove me to live in this house for AIDS people. (Participant in Thailand Voices and Choices quoted in ICW 2004 p.2)

Another from Mexico explained:

> I felt like I was falling into a huge abyss because I knew what was going to happen at work. They sacked me as soon as they found out and most of my so-called friends turned their back on me. ... My dream, what I was – a nurse known by all, with prestige, loved by everyone – had gone. I fell into a depression and forgot everyone in the world. (Participant in Voces Positivas quoted in ICW 2004 p.2)

---

7   IRIN is the humanitarian news and analysis service of the UN Office for the Coordination of Humanitarian Affairs.

Fighting for Survival in the Informal Sector

Life can be even tougher for the millions working to survive in the informal sector of economies in the global south.[8] Cooks, shop assistants, barbers, hairdressers, fruit-sellers, agricultural labourers and sex workers are among the many who have to survive on the most precarious of livings. And it is women who make up 80 per cent of these workers, often combining their labours with child care.

Their public entitlements are very limited, with little access to health services or any form of income supplement. Indeed many are invisible to the wider society, especially those working in their own homes. If they have a period when they are too sick to work it may be difficult for them to return as their piece of pavement or market stall may have been taken over by others. Those (usually female) workers involved in food preparation or in personal services are especially liable to be victims of discrimination.

The work of May Chazan and colleagues in Durban has shown the vulnerabilities of street traders who are both infected and affected by HIV (Chazan and Whiteside 2007). There are an estimated half a million of these workers in South Africa and their numbers are growing throughout the region. HIV in her family has left this Zulu seamstress from Durban to support 18 people on her small income:

> My niece was sick and died last year. I looked after her because nobody else was interested ... She didn't say that she had AIDS, but I knew and she knew ... My main worry is that I won't be able to work, and then what will happen? I tell my kids that one day we will have a problem: I will die and they need jobs. But they have stopped looking. (Chazan 2008 p.940)

HIV positive people may be forced into a downward spiral when their poor health means they are no longer physically able to carry on their normal work. This will affect both them and those around them, as a study in a Kenyan fishing community on Lake Victoria showed. The prevalence of HIV among the men in the group was estimated to be as high as 70 per cent. Few services were available and for many the work became too hard:

> ... an inability to withstand the physical rigours of deep-water fishing is resulting in some men withdrawing from fishing and remaining onshore. As a consequence they are taking over traditionally female activities such fish processing. ... the repercussions for women displaced from this activity are far more serious particularly as employment opportunities for women in fishing communities tend to be very limited and associated with high levels of commercial sex work. (Allison and Seeley 2004 p.225)

---

8   Very little has been written about the experiences of living with HIV in the informal sector, especially from a gendered perspective. For exceptions to this see recent work from the Health Economics Research Unit, University of KwaZulu-Natal (HEARD).

The gendered implications of this are obvious. On the one hand women may be forced to find employment to make up for the loss of income, and this may put them at a high risk of infection or re-infection.[9] On the other hand men who have to give up their work may experience psychological as well as economic harm. Few studies have explored the loss of status and respect often involved in male unemployment, especially when it is linked with illness. However it is clear that many face a crisis in their sense of their 'manliness' (Tersbol 2006). One man described the experiences of his fellow migrants living with HIV in London: 'Most of the African men, just because they're failing to find jobs here, they just become depressed and stressed out and compounded with the HIV it just leaves them hiding under their mattress' (Doyal et al. 2009 p.1903).

This in turn can cause serious harm to both physical and mental well-being. A Namibian man described his feelings in this way:

> When I grew up I was a very good person physically and mentally. If I compare myself now, my body disappears ... I do not understand this. I worry a lot and I can't sleep ... I cannot find an income. ... I worry about support to family members. To think about these things gives me chest pain and the heart. ... it feels like someone stabs me in the heart. (Tersbol 2006 p.407)

HIV positive women working in traditionally female jobs may also face gender-related problems. Domestic workers are especially vulnerable to contracting HIV through sexual abuse and may then lose their employment. A number of South African studies have highlighted the challenges they face in these circumstances (Peberdy and Dinat 2007). Women in many parts of the world have to go abroad to find domestic work. However a number of countries have mandatory health checks at points of entry and those who are HIV positive are barred. A Filipina described her experience in the following way:

> I was about to leave for Malaysia as a domestic worker when my medical test results showed that I was positive for HIV. When I was diagnosed it felt like the moon exploded in my face ... I kept asking myself, what will I do? I was so shocked. I couldn't accept it. I didn't want to go home. I wanted to be alone ... One of the worst impacts of HIV infection is that I can no longer work abroad. (Remoto 2009 p.1)

A number of the Gulf countries in particular also require annual testing of domestic workers. There are no proper counselling procedures and women found to be positive are placed in a holding centre in a hospital until they are deported. They are unable to pack their belongings or collect wages. Back home they are likely to

---

9   For excellent discussions of the role of transactional sex in the fishing community and its particular implications for women see Westaway et al. (2007) and Bene and Merten (2008).

face discrimination and social isolation and to have difficulty in finding alternative jobs (UNDP 2008).

Both male and female sex workers who are HIV positive will also be at risk of infection through work itself. A recent meta-analysis estimated that overall HIV prevalence among female sex workers in low and middle income countries stood at about 12 per cent, making them around 13 times more likely to be infected than other women of reproductive age (Baral et al. 2012). There is also evidence of HIV-related harassment of sex workers in a number of different countries.[10] The most widely publicised recent example is that of sex workers in Athens who were arrested and forcibly tested. Those who were found positive were charged with 'intentional gross bodily harm' and then had their photographs and personal details published in the newspapers.[11]

We can see from this analysis that the impact of HIV infection on an individual's working life can be severe. They may have to struggle on in jobs that are too demanding for them, often taking further risks with their health. Many will not be able to sell their labour at all. In the absence of public services they are then forced into greater dependence on others. The household in which they live is likely to be pushed further into poverty and the pressure on those who are sick as well as those who are supporting them will be intensified.

Measuring the Impact on Livelihoods: The Broader Context

In most communities in the global south, family and household groups are still the main sources of personal care and social security. Hence the majority of HIV positive people are cared for within these walls. The recognition of this reality has fuelled the emergence of a growing literature on the economic implications of HIV and AIDS for households across a range of resource-poor settings (Barnett et al. 2001; Barnett and Whiteside 2002; Nkurunziza and Rakodi 2005; White and Robinson 2000; Seeley and Pringle 2001).

The shapes and sizes of households vary around the world. However the basic configuration is a group of people who live together and share a range of assets and resources as well as responsibility for daily activities, including the care of

---

10   See discussion of male sex workers in Chennai, India in Chapter 6. See also Scott et al. (2005) on violence in the male sex industry.

11   It is important to point out that this occurred in the context of the severe austerity policies recently imposed in Greece, which included cutbacks in the public provision of condoms. The justification for the harassment was said to be a 60 per cent increase in rates of HIV infection between 2010 and 2012, but this has been mostly among IDUs as a result of reductions in the provision of clean needles (Paraskevis et al. 2012). For details see http://www.unaids.org/en/resources/presscentre/pressreleaseandstatementarchive/2012/may/20120510psgreece.

dependants.[12] Most are also bound by complex sets of reciprocal obligations to groups or individuals living elsewhere. These include the so-called 'stretched' households which are based on circular migration, with some members leaving to earn a living but returning at periodic intervals.

The notion of 'livelihoods' was first used to explore these survival strategies during periods of famine in Africa in the 1970s. It is now being used by a growing number of researchers to explore how families 'cope' in the context of HIV/AIDS (Seeley 2002). Thus far this concept has been applied mainly in the context of rural southern Africa but it clearly has wider applicability in other settings where the burden of HIV is high.[13]

Illness will not only limit the capacity of women and men to do paid work but will also place severe constraints on their ability to carry out the many unpaid tasks that play a major part in sustaining all households. At the same time more labour and more financial resources will be required to provide care for those who become sick and dependent. Even the finality of death will usually be costly, with the expenses of burial and associated rites impoverishing those left behind (Case and Menendez 2009). This may lead to productive assets such as land and tools being sold, often intensifying the poverty. Studies have also shown that the division of labour within the household may be reshaped in line with the state of health of individual members. These changes will reflect existing gender divisions and will usually involve a transfer of work between generations (Mutagandura 2005) [14] Increased demands may also be made on those outside the immediate family who owe the household a duty of care. However in the context of a generalised HIV epidemic this wider social capital is likely to have diminished significantly.

The analysis that follows will explore these issues in more detail. However two cautionary notes are needed about the scope of available studies. First, most research has treated the household as a single unit of analysis in order to explore its collective capacity to sustain itself over time. But household groups are not internally homogeneous. Individuals have varied responsibilities as well as unequal status, power and access to resources and these are allocated mainly with reference to gender and age (Masanjala 2007). Hence we cannot assume that members of the family will be treated fairly with reference to their needs in tackling the challenges that have to be faced.[15]

---

12   This very broad typology is based mainly on the situation in rural areas in low income countries.

13   For comparative material in an Indian context see Pradha and Sunda (2006) and Pallikadavath et al. (2005).

14   For a useful annotated bibliography on household care in the context of HIV and AIDS see Gibbs and Smith (2010).

15   The problem of analyses based on households has been extensively discussed in the wider context of gender and development. The 'black box' of the family or household has been shown to conceal some of the most significant aspects of gender inequalities (Seeley et al. 2004).

Second, little attention has so far been paid to the emotional narratives either of those being cared for or those who are doing the caring (Thomas 2006; Mathambo and Gibbs 2008; Evans and Thomas 2009). In the case of the sick we can only guess at the damage caused to them by their inability to look after dependants, as well as the loss of personal autonomy. For those who have to take on extra work and lose the care they might otherwise have received from others, the emotional response is also likely to be complex. Using the little qualitative evidence so far available, the remainder of this chapter will begin to explore these issues in the context of a broader economic analysis of the livelihoods of HIV-affected households.

Sustaining Social Reproduction: Gender Divisions and Intergenerational Bargains

Domestic labour or 'social reproduction' is essential if households are to survive. This work is especially onerous in the deprived communities where the majority of HIV positive people live. This is partly because many of the tasks have to be undertaken through direct physical activity rather than the monetary exchange underlying the sustainability of most households in richer communities. It also reflects the scarcity of public institutions such as universal health care and education.

The jobs associated with maintaining a household and family will vary between urban and rural settings but are likely to include constitutive activities related to basic need satisfaction such as food acquisition and preparation, fuel and water collection, cleaning, washing clothes, childbearing and rearing and providing emotional support as well as informal education. In many rural areas, social reproduction also includes heavy agricultural work. This may be done to provide food for the household and/or to earn money to meet other needs.

Thus a central element of domestic work will always be caring for others as well as caring 'about' them. In most circumstances the major burden of this physical and emotional labour will involve adult women caring for children, for partners and for the older generation. However the advent of HIV and AIDS has changed this dramatically. Now younger (previously active) adults will also need to be cared for, sometimes over lengthy periods of time. Care of a family member (or members) with HIV and especially AIDS generates an enormous burden of work. The majority of those living in rich countries will not be so disadvantaged. They will usually be able to access services even if they are not themselves wealthy. They can expect to mitigate the worst of their symptoms through ART as well as other curative or palliative therapies. And if intensive nursing care is needed, formal institutions often exist to take over.

But in many poorer countries few drugs will be available and care will usually have to be provided informally and at great personal cost. While most carers 'strive for normalcy' this can be extremely hard to achieve (Peters et al. 2008). A recent study in the Balaka District of Malawi highlighted the attempts of caregivers to create moral sense out of what was often a desperate situation:

> Most caregivers had few possessions: some patients were lying on mats because they had no bed or mattress. Like almost all rural residents they used pit latrines and their homes had neither electricity nor running water. The cheapest bar of soap cost K 6.5 but caretakers did not regularly have soap with which to wash sheets soiled by diarrhoea or vomit, or to buy the sodas (K 15) which their patients craved. (Chimwaza and Watkins 2004 p.798)

In households where someone is seriously ill with AIDS, the amount of water needed increases substantially: those who are sick may experience continuous episodes of diarrhoea each day. Bedding and clothes need to be washed, as well as the patients themselves. Clean drinking water is also essential for rehydration. In remote rural areas this can mean walking long distances and head-carrying a heavy load back home (Urdang 2006). In order for this work to be undertaken alongside paid employment, a reallocation of both paid and unpaid labour will be required. This may involve a radical restructuring of the household itself, which will have both psychological and physical effects on its members. As we shall see, it is likely to involve the renegotiating of both gendered divisions of labour and intergenerational 'contracts' (van Blerk and Ansell 2007).

Reshaping the Gendered Division of Labour?

In most parts of the world it is women and girls who are assumed to be responsible for domestic work while men earn money outside the home (Ogden et al. 2006; Akintola 2008; Mutangadura 2005). However this 'patriarchal bargain' rarely conforms to reality (Kandiyoti 1998). Increasing numbers of women are now supporting their households alone[16] while many of those who are living with men still have to take on paid work in addition to domestic responsibilities (UN 2005).

For many, these gender inequalities in workloads have been intensified by the HIV pandemic. It is estimated that some 90 per cent of care for HIV positive people takes place in the home, and the vast majority of this is done by women and girls. The allocation of a disproportionate amount of caring to females is, of course, deeply embedded in prevailing cultural norms. Indeed 'homecare' forms the underpinning of HIV care services in most high-prevalence settings (Akintola 2008).

---

16 Recent evidence from South Africa highlights the significance of 'absent fathers', especially in the context of the HIV epidemic. In one recent study in KwaZulu-Natal three-quarters of the biological fathers had not sustained contact with their children despite the fact that the family was affected by HIV and/or AIDS (Denis and Ntsimane 2006). For interesting comparative material on Latin America and the Caribbean see Barker and Veroni (2008).

Under these circumstances most women will do what is expected of them. They may (or may not) gain emotional satisfaction from doing so but this will usually be accompanied by much more complex and ambivalent feelings (Urdang 2006; Evans and Thomas 2009; Baylies 2002):

> There is the risk that the use of the term 'care' will mystify the relationship between the provider and the receiver. It must be recognised that care may be given unwillingly, extracted by psychological and social pressure or even physical violence, from women who can see no alternative but to provide care, even to those who oppress them. (Urdang 2006, quoting Elson 2003 p.23)[17]

One Tanzanian woman spoke succinctly about her experience of caring for her male partner: 'A husband with AIDS is worse than a lazy husband, because you can't divorce him – it's not his fault' (Appleton 2000 p.22).

The predominance of female caregiving in families affected by HIV and AIDS is widely documented. However evidence is also beginning to emerge that some boys and men are now playing a greater role in the provision of care both in their own households and in wider communities. Studies in South Africa have highlighted these changes (Montgomery et al. 2006; Bray and Brandt 2007; Morell 2011), while the same trend has been observed in Tanzania (Evans and Thomas 2009).

The significance of these developments needs to be understood within the wider context of gendered patterns of work. It is, of course, common for women to cross the boundaries between domestic labour and waged work without transgressing gender norms. Indeed it is often essential that they do so in order for the household to survive. For men, however, the boundaries are usually much less permeable. They are expected to be 'proper' men and will run the risk of being stigmatised if they do what is seen as 'women's work'. In many African contexts in particular there is 'little social space for competing forms of masculinity' (Montgomery et al. 2006). Nor is there an appropriate language to talk about men who do get involved in caring; evidence from one recent study indicated that even when men did take on 'women's work' it often seemed to be invisible to those around them (Montgomery et al. 2006).

It would seem therefore that in some settings, HIV and AIDS are at the root of complex changes beginning to take place in the gendered division of labour. Inequalities have certainly been intensified by the greater need for caring within households. However the demographic effects of HIV combined with changing economic and social circumstances have created new options for 'doing' masculinity. The practical implications of this were described in the following way by one Kenyan woman:

---

17   For excellent illustrations of carers' feelings in a Malawian setting see Chimwaza and Watkins (2004).

It was against Luo culture for a boy to cook but today it has changed, they cook and do domestic duties. If the first born are boys and the parent is sick it will be the boys who cook not the younger girls … If you don't teach him to cook, his first wife may die leaving him with the children. Today you cannot know who will die first. (Skovdal et al. 2009 p.590)

Breaking the Intergenerational Contract?

Alongside these changes in the gender division of labour there is also evidence of shifts in the balance of work between generations. As adults become too ill to work, it is the oldest and youngest in the household who must take on an increased burden. For children, this means that they may not get as much care as they would have done in the past. Similarly, older people may miss out on support they would have expected in their later years (Juma et al. 2004; Ssengonzi 2007; Moore and Henry 2005; Schatz and Ogunmefun 2007; Schatz 2007).

The crucial part played by 'grannies' in household survival during the era of HIV is now being more widely recognised (Orbach 2007). The extent of these responsibilities can be seen from a study of market traders in Durban (Chazan 2008). Two-thirds of older women had either cared for someone who was HIV positive in the past or were doing so now. This compares with one-third of younger women, one-third of younger men and no older men (Chazan and Whiteside 2007). However, as Chazan points out, most of these women are in their forties or fifties rather than being the frail, elderly women portrayed in much of the literature (Chazan 2008). While they often act as primary caregivers and as homemakers they may also be required to earn money. The implications of this were spelled out in bleak terms in a recent study of fishing communities in Tanzania: 'Some elderly women go to the seashore to buy fish directly from the fishermen. In the days when they have no money one has to offer sex to the fishermen in order to get fish to feed the grandchildren' (Bene and Merten 2008 p.875).

Those who are old enough to get a pension will usually be expected to share it (Sienaert 2008). Many of these women experience severe stress on a daily basis. Lifelong economic pressures continue as they struggle to support themselves and those who depend on them. This is often intensified by the sadness of the untimely and 'unnatural' loss of their own children and sometimes grandchildren. The economic marginality faced by many is illustrated by this account from one Zambian grandmother:

We rely on my nephews for assistance; they have informal jobs so I use the little money they give me to buy the food we need. I send my grandchildren to fetch water in small containers, they bring it back and I boil it to avoid diseases. If the owner of the well is there they come back with empty buckets because I cannot afford to pay. The money I would spend on water could buy maize flour and charcoal to prepare a meal. (Hunger Watch 2008 p.40)

Studies in South Africa (Clark et al. 2007) and Thailand (Knodel and van Landingham 2003) have shown that many seriously ill migrant workers return to their family homes in rural areas to die as their condition deteriorates. This reflects the strongly held belief in many communities that it is the mother and not the wife who should care for dying men (Clark et al. 2007; Hosegood et al. 2007a, 2007b). Thus 'homeland' populations are now supporting a growing burden of sickness and death among 'the brightest and the best' who had formerly worked in the metropolitan, mining and large-scale agricultural areas (Clark et al. 2007).

A recent study in Thailand found that two-thirds of all adults died in their parents' home (Knodel and van Landingham 2003). Half died within three months of returning and one-fifth within one month. To see adult children become ill, and to care for them as they die, inevitably leaves most older adults with 'a burden of sadness' that pervades the rest of their lives (Williams and Tumwekwase 2001). A Thai woman expressed her feelings in the following way:

> I was so sorry at the time when I found out because he was my only son and usually according to our culture, the son is supposed to look after the parents when they grow old but in my case my son couldn't do that for me … Even now, when I see other boys or men, it makes me sad and reminds me of him. (Orbach 2007 p.8)

Older carers in a number of studies have reported the problems they experience with their own health. Headaches, joint and back pain are common (Amoateng et al. 2004). Many feel exhausted as a result of their responsibilities, and this Vietnamese woman reported fatigue due to lack of sleep and constant worry:

> Few people knew about our situation because my son didn't talk about or reveal his status, so there was no support for me … I had to do all the work myself. Even though I knew he would die, I spent a lot of money on medicine and bought him whatever he wanted. (Orbach 2007 p.7)

Many experience substantial weight loss as a result of stress, and sometimes a reduction in food intake. A declining physical state may increase their vulnerability to illness and many are reluctant to seek medical treatment due to the cost. They may also be at risk from exposure to the opportunistic infections (including TB) experienced by other family members, particularly those living with AIDS (Orbach 2007). Because it takes a toll on their own health and denies them the support they might have expected at the end of their lives many older carers report feeling frustration as well as sadness. As one woman in Lusaka ruefully commented: 'Patients can be difficult, fussy about their needs and irritable with their carers' (Baylies 2002 p.367). Another complained that: 'they want to eat expensive "white man's dishes" which we parents cannot afford' (Baylies 2002 p.367).

At the other end of the age spectrum, children too may receive less care as more attention and resources are directed towards the needs of sick parents. They may also have to assume adult roles in the attempt to secure household livelihoods (Becker 2007; Mathambo and Gibbs 2008). Many children (especially girls) are pulled out of school either because there is no money for the fees or because their labour is needed in the home or as wage earners. These patterns have been reported not just in African communities but also in Thailand (Singhanetra-Renard et al. 2001), India (Krishna et al. 2005) and China (Zhang et al. 2009).

Child migration has always existed in parts of Africa, with young people brought up by relatives.[18] However it has increased with the HIV epidemics (Young and Ansell 2003; Haour-Knipe 2009; Madhavan and Schatz 2007). Children are sometimes required to migrate to earn money, with many employed as domestic workers (Young and Ansell 2003; Mathambo and Gibbs 2008). Others may be sent away to provide care for sick relatives, as studies from Malawi and Lesotho have shown (Ansell and van Blerk 2004; Bray and Brandt 2007).

To date, few researchers have explored the experiences of children living in HIV-affected families across Asia. However one recent study of a poor village in central China presented a very similar picture to those found in African settings (Zhang et al. 2009).[19] Forty seven children were interviewed, of whom 34 were double orphans, while the rest had lost one parent. These children were often making major contributions to household survival, reflecting the spirit of filial piety enshrined in Buddhist religious beliefs

One 11-year-old girl had lived with her grandparents before being relocated to an AIDS orphanage. Her father died when she was seven years old, and her mother when she was nine. Pin Yin recalled her life at home prior to her parents' death·

> Sometimes my mum didn't have time to cook because she had to ask me to have some instant noodles before I went to school. … I washed clothes for my brother and sister. My sister didn't go to school at that time. She wanted to learn some knowledge, so she asked some questions. I taught her to learn math, e.g. what is one plus one, and I helped her learn some letters. (Zhang et al. 2009 p.545)

Inevitably many children around the world have to undertake the very difficult task of caring for their own parents. As well as the physical stresses there are also psychological challenges, with some even having to help a parent die (Evans and Becker 2009). As Stephen Lewis has pointed out: 'Kids become orphans while their parents are dying. … The little boy or the little girl [who] actually sees the parent in the throes of death and then dying it is a trauma that haunts that child for life' (Lewis quoted in Bell 2004 online).

---

18   This was especially true in South Africa during the apartheid period when many were cared for by their grandparents.

19   The families involved had mainly been affected by unhygienic blood transfusion practices.

There can be no doubt that many aspects of the lives of these children are difficult and distressing. However recent studies have also highlighted the creativity and competence so many show in mobilising support, generating income and constructing positive identities in conditions of poverty and stigma (Evans and Becker 2009; Skovdal and Ogutu 2009; Skovdal et al. 2009; Robson 2004; Robson et al. 2006; Zhang et al. 2009).

A 15-year-old Chinese boy lost his father when he was eight years old and his mother when he was 13. Prior to his mother's death he provided daily care, including an intravenous injection. He recalled:

> There was no one else to do the treatment [injection] for my mother at night. I bought a bike. I went to the hospital to buy the medicine, which was not easy to find; sometimes I had to go to several hospitals ... When I got the medicine and came back, it was already dark. I injected for mum wearing once-used gloves. I gave her the injection when she was asleep. (Zhang et al. 2009 p.545)

Coping or Not?

As families regroup and try to meet the challenges of daily life, poverty continues to limit their ability to meet their basic needs. Of course some are able to maintain themselves despite the disadvantages they face. However for others such inequalities are too great. The survival capacity of each household will depend on its access to resources and on the age and gender composition of its members. A recent review showed, for example, that women-headed households were usually among the poorest overall but those headed by an adult male were more likely to report food insecurity (Lemke 2003).[20]

Recent studies have focussed on particular aspects of intermediate need satisfaction. For example, food insecurity and hunger are key features of family impoverishment (Hunter et al. 2007; Loevinsohn and Gillespie 2003). This may result both from the inability to grow food and from lack of income to purchase it. There is still considerable debate about the overall effects of HIV epidemics on local and national food production.[21] But for individuals, lack of access is usually the central issue.

---

20   This was explained in part by the fact that in male-headed households the available resources were less likely to be spent on immediate household needs. Indeed in some settings a migrant father might also have another family to support in the town.

21   Much of this debate has centred on the notion of 'new variant famine' (NVF) proposed by de Waal and Whiteside (2003).This model puts HIV and AIDS forward as key factors promoting the current food crises experienced in many southern African countries. While the epidemics have clearly affected food production as well as patterns of consumption, others have argued that many other factors are involved and call for more context-specific analyses (Ansell et al. 2009; Murphy et al. 2005; Hunter 2007).

Food may be available but the household may not have enough money to acquire it and there is unlikely to be charitable or state provision. Moreover family members will have varying levels of entitlement, with women and children often coming off worst despite what may be their greater needs (Ansell et al. 2009). Lack of food will be especially difficult for those who are HIV positive (Samuels and Rutenberg 2008). Some studies have shown people taking their medication only once a day in the evening (instead of twice daily) because that is the only time they have any food (Hardon et al. 2007).

As we saw in Chapter 4, these problems related to nutritional insecurity raise the wider question of how effective ART can be in rebuilding the lives of those in resource-poor settings. While the availability of HAART in the US and other rich countries has led many of those who are HIV positive to be 'born again', it is clear that this will not be so simple for those who are still struggling for survival in the context of poverty, deprivation and inequality.

Their 'new lives' will have to be constructed within what remains for most a fragile and potentially unhealthy environment. Survival was often challenging even before their HIV diagnosis and will not be changed simply by pills. This was highlighted by a recent study exploring the experiences of those seeking to rebuild their lives in what the authors call 'the harsh realities of poverty and vulnerability' in Uganda (Russell et al. 2007). For the majority of participants, their most important project was dealing with a devastated household economy. As their condition improved, men and women embarked on a range of productive activities, talking of 'working hard' and 'digging again'. This was significant not just for economic survival but also for the achievement of greater well-being and enhanced autonomy:

> The appearance of a well-tended and successful garden, with crops in the field or laid out to dry in the compound, was a visible demonstration of a return to order. The mud on participants' feet and shins and sweat on their faces from digging were common observations by interviewers as they arrived at participants' homes in the mid-morning. These scenes provided neighbours and the community with images of normalcy. (Russell and Seeley 2010 p.379)

Thus access to ART can give many a period of renewed vitality. But both individuals and households may still face major problems over which they can have little control. It is this reality which has led a number of commentators to caution against the over-use of the term 'coping' in this context (Rugalema 2000). Such language is clearly of value in emphasising the resilience and creativity with which many people tackle huge challenges. However, as Gabriel Rugulema points out, these problems may sometimes be insurmountable. In this context what he calls 'euphoria over coping strategies' may obscure the real suffering of individuals, households and communities. And, worst of all, those who do not survive may be blamed for having failed to 'cope' effectively (Rugulema 2000).

Finally it is important to be clear that deaths from AIDS are likely to harm those members of the household who remain behind as well as future generations. Widows in particular are likely to be seriously disadvantaged after the death of their partners (Luginaah et al. 2005; Pallikadavath et al. 2005). Their lack of inheritance rights combined in some settings with the rights of male relatives over their bodies can make their lives extremely hard. Many are of course infected with HIV themselves and may be highly stigmatised.

Yet very little attention has been paid to other circumstances of these women as they grapple with their own illness after what may be a lengthy period of looking after their partner. For example, a recent study in Indonesia highlighted not only the poverty but also the distressing and debilitating emotionality experienced by many. Within a short period of time, all of the participants experienced at least three traumatic life events in a row: they learned that their husbands were HIV-positive; they discovered that they themselves were living with HIV, and they lost their husbands to AIDS-related illness. Not surprisingly, their feelings were complex and often contradictory as they struggled to ensure their own survival as HIV positive single parents: 'When I think of him, the first thing that comes to mind is that I'm positive. I don't really blame him but when I think of him I think about HIV/AIDS. That's the most important legacy he left me with' (Dannar and du Plessis 2010 p.427).

Conclusion

This chapter has shown that in most settings HIV and/or AIDS will limit the capabilities of women and men to earn a living and to carry out domestic labour. This in turn will prevent them from meeting their basic needs for survival/physical health and autonomy thus limiting their capacity for the social interaction required for protecting their critical interests. Constitutive activities such as providing and caring for others as well as being and feeling creative will all be heavily constrained, often leading to a loss of self-respect as well as respect from others.[22] The greater the poverty and lack of relevant resources the more intense these effects will be, increasing the harm experienced by those who become infected in what are already the most unequal and disadvantaged settings. Hence the effects of HIV and AIDS spread far in both time and space as the 'long wave' continues to threaten not just individual lives but collective livelihoods.

22　See the discussion on this point in Chapter 1.

Chapter 6
Changing Sexual Lives

The reshaping of human sexual activities has been the major goal of prevention strategies during the HIV pandemic. In the early days, epidemiological studies of sex and its relationship with HIV transmission expanded rapidly. Surveys mapped the frequency of different types of sex acts, the numbers and types of partners, and patterns of condom use in different populations (Boyce et al. 2007; Crepaz and Marks 2002). This work provided the basis for educational programmes targeted mostly at HIV negative individuals and couples.

The main message promoted across diverse settings was 'abstinence, be faithful and condomise' (ABC). Not surprisingly these policies proved to be limited in their effectiveness. And this in turn raised questions about the knowledge base upon which they had been developed. There was, of course, no doubt about the role of the sexual exchange of bodily fluids in the spread of the virus. However it gradually became clear that the 'sexual intercourse' through which this most commonly occurs is a complex and highly symbolic form of human behaviour. Hence it could not easily be changed through what was usually a simple message presented in a didactic form (Barnett and Parkhurst 2005).

The main aim of policy initiatives in these early years was to prevent the further spread of HIV. This meant that there was little or no concern about the sexual needs of those who were already known to be infected. Indeed they were frequently assumed to be 'desexualised' as they waited for death. But as the numbers of positive people living longer increased, many saw the revival of sexual activity as part of their new existence. In some settings this was reflected in a rise in the rate of HIV and other sexually transmitted infections, especially among gay men (Elam et al. 2008; Bunnell et al. 2006; Chen et al. 2002). Hence the sexual activities of those who were already infected could no longer be ignored (Fisher et al. 2010; Relf et al. 2009; King et al. 2008). At the same time, HIV positive people themselves had come out of the shadows to talk about the challenges they faced in practising safer sex. This reinforced the need for new understandings of the social and cultural construction of human sexualities and their relationship with HIV (Aggleton 2009; Higgins et al. 2010; Schiltz and Sandfort 2000; Sandfort and Dodge 2005).

Within the context of HIV we need to ask many questions about how a positive diagnosis changes sex lives. Under what circumstances do people continue (or not) to have sex and why? How do they find/choose partners? What influences their decisions to tell (or not tell) others their status? What social, emotional and physical challenges do they face in having sex in ways that will both satisfy and protect themselves and their partners? The answers to these questions are obviously of importance from the perspective of prevention. But they can also fill gaps in our very scant knowledge of the sexual needs and desires of people who are already positive.

Broader Perspectives on Sex

The 'western scientific' model of penetrative sex or 'intercourse' has been widely accepted as the starting point for much HIV-related research. But it is usually treated in an overly simplistic way which ignores some of the most fundamental aspects of sexual behaviours as they are practised in the real world (Adams and Pigg 2005; Obermeyer 2005). 'The details of the sexual terrain remain simultaneously murky, unquestioned and over determined' (Gorna 1996 quoted in Gurevich et al. 2007 p.15).

The standard model assumes that the anatomical sex of an individual provides the basis for the ascription of gender. In the context of what is defined as 'normal' heterosexuality, individuals are attracted to those from the other sex/gender. Those women and men who are sexually attracted to individuals of the same sex/gender as themselves have traditionally been referred to as 'homosexual',[1] or more recently as men who have sex with men (MSM) or WSW in the case of women.[2]

Most current research on HIV and sexual behaviour is based on the simple division between MSM on the one hand and those engaged in heterosexual relationships on the other. It rarely recognises that some individuals could belong to both groups.[3] Moreover it usually involves either one group or the other, with few attempts to make formal comparisons of experiences between the two.[4] This chapter will attempt to bring them together and to assess the impact of HIV on relationships across a range of sexual and cultural contexts (Vance 1991; Weeks 2009).

HIV and Sex between Men: Difference and Diversity

The most visible 'characters' in mainstream HIV research are probably those gay-identified men whose lives centre on their sexuality. Many live in actual or

---

1   This is of course a highly contested term which is rarely used today. In this chapter a wider range of terms will be used as appropriate to describe the sexual activities being referred to in particular sources. Where this is unclear or ambiguous we will revert to the more technical term MSM introduced in Chapter 2.

2   As we saw earlier, lesbian women or women who have sex with women (WSW) hardly figure at all in HIV and AIDS research since they have rarely been infected through lesbian sex itself.

3   It has also paid very little attention to the sexual lives of HIV positive transgender people, who are known to be at particularly high risk of harm (http://www.cdc.gov/hiv/transgender).

4   For two of the very few exceptions see Kerrigan et al. (2006), comparing different groups in Brazil and the work of Courtenay-Quirk et al. (2006) and Gil (2007).

virtual 'gay communities' in urban areas, mostly in the global north. Those who frequently engage in casual sexual encounters are seen by others as especially emblematic of the pandemic.

However by no means all men engaged in same-sex relationships live in this way. They may prefer sex and/or emotional closeness with other men (and sometimes women too). But their personal friendship networks and leisure activities are not same-sex based (Holt 2011). Many will be open about their preferences but others will prefer to keep them private.

Some men will have sex with both men and women (MSMW). They may identify as 'bisexual', being equally attracted to both. Others are basically same-sex identified but live in particularly homophobic settings. Their sexual encounters with other men usually have to be casual and often anonymous in order to ensure their own physical safety and social identity (Malebranche 2008). They may also have to hide their range of desires through engaging in sex and/or marriage with women (Ford et al. 2007; Siegel et al. 2008; Padilla et al. 2008).

It is clear from what has now become a very extensive body of research that an HIV diagnosis has a profound impact on men who have sex with men, often altering their sexual repertoires and emotions in quite profound ways. The varying degrees of stigma already attached to their sexuality are likely to be worsened by the addition of a label of HIV positive. And this will be especially challenging for those who view sexuality as the central aspect of their social identity.

HIV and Heterosex: The Power of Gender

The literature on HIV and sex between women and men is much sparser than that on sex between men despite the predominance of heterosexual transmission (Parker and Gagnon 1995). Thus far, this research has focussed mainly on the inequality of gender relations from the perspective of women, highlighting how it can lead to their engaging in unsafe sexual practices which they may not desire or even consent to. However we know relatively little about the impact that a positive diagnosis will have on their sexual practices or on the quality of their sex lives (Higgins et al. 2010).

The sexual lives of heterosexual men have received even less attention than those of women despite the fact that they make up the largest single group of people living with HIV (Doyal 2009b). It is clear that gendered pressures to 'act out' their masculinity may render sexual encounters problematic for positive men as well as for women (Higgins et al. 2010). But we know very little about the physical or experiential impact of HIV on these activities (Persson 2012).

Whatever the setting or social group, we need to look at sexual strategies as resources for building and strengthening relationships, creating social reputations, asserting power, experiencing pleasure and advancing towards other socially valued goals. In the case of heterosexual relationships in particular this will often include the formation of a family.

Most long-term partnerships between women and men are deeply embedded in the wider social context of their lives. In many settings they may have little to do with individual choice and/or mutual passion. Instead they can more appropriately be seen as 'life projects' shaped (or even mandated) by kinship expectations, economic necessity and local sexual geographies (Coates et al. 2008; Hirsch 2007). Hence a diagnosis of HIV will have especially profound effects. Some positive women may be too ill or too afraid to have children because of the potential harm to themselves, their partner or the child. Many men too will have parental desires and will inevitably be entangled in these moral and practical complexities.

The remainder of this chapter will illustrate the ways in which some of these themes are played out in different types of sexual relationships in the current state of post-antiretroviral therapy (ART) epidemics.

Constraints of Poor Mental and Physical Health on Sexual Activity

Studies consistently report lowered sexual activity, interest and satisfaction in the majority of HIV positive people, whatever their sexual preferences (Siegel et al. 2006; Gurevich et al. 2007). A recent study in the UK found that the majority of women (72 per cent) had resumed sexual activity with men after diagnosis, but more than half stated that it had impaired their enjoyment or even destroyed it (Lambert et al. 2005).

For many this will be linked to the psychological problems associated with HIV itself. Depression and anxiety are common among those who are positive, and both are likely to limit or eliminate sexual desire and/or pleasure. A number of studies suggest that women are more likely than men to experience such 'hypoactive sexual disorder' (Gurevich et al. 2007).[5] The physical signs and symptoms that often accompany life on ART can also have a negative impact on sexual activities. Symptoms such as fatigue, headache, stomach ache and diarrhoea were all reported by gay men in Amsterdam as inhibiting their sex lives (van Kesteren et al. 2005).

A number of studies have also identified the importance of body dysmorphia as an aspect of sexual dysfunction (Luzi et al. 2009; Siegel et al. 2006). When a positive white American woman was asked how she felt she replied:

> Ugly! You know, like I'm not a woman anymore. To him (the husband) anyway. You know, it's so hard. You know, I try to do things that I used to do that, you know ... in a second would get him running. And it's like, you know it doesn't faze him anymore. (Siegel et al. 2006 p.446)

---

5   Dyspareunia (pain) and vaginismus are also frequently reported (Gurevich et al. 2007).

Men too have talked about the deterioration in their sexual satisfaction due to the impact of bodily changes – especially the lipodystrophy that often accompanies the use of ART. Studies suggest that this is especially problematic for gay men (van Kesteren 2005; Gil 2007). Among this group, additional health burdens stem from the recent increase in sexually transmitted infections, including syphilis and hepatitis C. In some settings the latter is now said to be even more stigmatising than HIV itself (Owen 2008; Wolitski and Fenton 2011; Urbanus et al. 2009). High rates of sexual dysfunction, including erectile problems, are also reported – especially among positive gay men (Wolitski and Fenton 2011).

A very common theme in accounts from heterosexual men is bodily weakness. In a study in Kenya a number of men reported loss of sexual capacity until they were able to access treatment. But even when ART was available their physical ability to 'satisfactorily complete' sexual intercourse remained limited (Sarna et al. 2009). They talked about needing to regain their strength after any sexual activity. As one 62-year-old Ugandan man put it:

> If I slept with a woman for two consecutive days I would feel the heart beating strongly. So when they told me you could abstain for two days, I said I could. So I started reducing. We even stopped having sex and I regained my strength and the heart stopped beating strongly. (Allen et al. 2011 p.535)

This weakness seems to reflect not only loss of physical strength but also a more symbolic challenge to masculinity that will shape experiences of sex. Another Ugandan man living in London gave an account of how sex with his wife had changed now that she was the one with more power than him:

> First of all you don't have money in the family, you have nothing to eat in the house or a glass of wine for your wife. So you go in the bed and you're fearing to touch her. You can't say can you turn this way? (LAUGHTER) No definitely you can't. (Doyal et al. 2009 p.1904)

With these physical and psychological problems in the background, the following sections will explore the changing experiences of sex with HIV. The focus will not be on the frequency or safety of 'intercourse' that dominates so much of the literature. Rather it will explore the subjectivity of sexual experiences as positive individuals themselves have begun to report them.

Loss of Sexual Feelings after Diagnosis?

It is significant that whatever their circumstances, most people report a cessation in sexual activity in the early stages after diagnosis, and for some this will continue for the rest of their lives. Many are not well enough for sex and others are worried about doing themselves further damage. A widow in Mombasa said: 'You know, if you do that (sex) the drugs won't work properly ... the more you do sex, the medicine doesn't work. So if you want it to work you have to reduce (sex) and you know I value my body' (Sarna et al. 2009 p.786).

Alongside this, the shock of the diagnosis itself and the anxiety that so often accompanies it are rarely conducive to sexual activity. This will be exacerbated if partners and kin are not supportive. Two women in Togo explained how this affected them: 'Since diagnosis, sexual intercourse has disgusted me. I'm much despaired and will be for the rest of my life. My husband does not care for me anymore. ... He totally abandoned me. I have no desire for sexual intercourse' (Moore and Amey 2008 p.290). The second woman said: 'During the first six months after diagnosis I was very ill and was suffering a lot. I did not have the financial means to buy medicines either. So I tried to kill myself several times. Having sex was really the last thing on my mind' (Moore and Amey 2008 p.291).

A gay man in Amsterdam linked his lack of desire for sex to a range of health factors, including the side effects of the drugs he was on to cope with depression: 'I didn't feel like having sex the first months. It had also to do with problems with potency. It stiffens somewhat more nowadays. But the fact is, I'm on anti-depressants, and those inhibit the libido also' (van Kesteren et al. 2005 p.152).

Though we still have very few accounts of the feelings of heterosexual men, they too have talked about their lack of desire. One man in Uganda described how he had not been sexually active for six months: 'As I told you that I was very much scared when I knew I had AIDS. I lost interest. Up to now I am not yet ready for sex. ... Imagine from November 2005 up to now I don't know how my wife looks like' (Wamoyi et al. 2011 p.4).

Another Ugandan man living in London explained: 'Sex just crosses my mind once in a while, it is not like I think about it in terms of ... I don't think about it positively anyway. The interest is not ... it is very minimum' (Doyal et al. 2009 p.1904).

Studies have reported a significant number of people ending their sexual lives completely after being diagnosed (Undie et al. 2009). Some were just too ill or had too little energy, but others talked of lack of privacy, following health workers' instructions or doing 'penance' for their previous 'sins'. But most commonly they reported not wanting to infect others.

Routes Back to 'Normality'?

If they are able to access drugs, most positive individuals will gradually begin to reshape their lives, seeking a more 'normal' existence (Seeley et al. 2009; Wamoyi et al. 2011). However the part that sex plays in this will be influenced by a wide variety of factors. This can be illustrated with reference to a recent longitudinal study of sexual activity after ART (Allen et al. 2011). Thirty four Ugandan women and men who were HIV positive were interviewed over a period of 30 months. The majority reported, at three months after diagnosis, that their sexual desire and activity had declined or disappeared. After six months on ART, 11 out of 14 women and nine out of 20 men still reported abstinence.

Significantly, both women and men in this sample talked about the problems they had encountered before receiving ART and the need to use what little energy they had to 'normalise ' their economic and social situation and that of any dependants. One woman said: 'So now I have to look for work to help my father with that money he has spent while I was sick. So that I also make him happy while he can still see me' (Allen et al. 2011 p.536).

A man involved in local beer production was mostly concerned about his children: 'I do not have the time. I will even see a girl shaking her bum and I admire her but no. ... I only think about my children and what they are going to have for lunch' (Allen et al. 2011 p.536).

As time passed, sexual activity was gradually resumed by most of the participants, with men usually in advance of women. At six months on ART half the men had recommenced sexual activity, most with their wives.[6] A number reported being warned by health workers against 'too much sex' but most had restarted by 18 months.[7] Nine participants (seven women and two men) abstained throughout the study.

Their main reason for restarting sexual activity might have been expected to be desire for sexual pleasure. However women in particular were more likely to emphasise companionship and economic support. The story told by one Ugandan woman exemplifies the complex situation facing many. She had been abandoned by her husband after she developed tuberculosis (TB) but when her condition improved he took her back to run the household. She went to him because he had resources that she needed, including banana and maize plantations she had cultivated and some pigs she had reared. However he sometimes forced her to have sex: 'He has money. And it is mainly what I want from him. He did so many bad things to me but my friend, you bend for someone because of money' (Allen et al. 2011 p.537).

Men did talk more than women about their renewed sexual desires, but they also stressed the need for a wife who would look after them in the domestic sphere. This became especially important to them when they had found the strength to get a job or had finished a new house. A woman was necessary to complete the picture.

Searching for a New Partner?

Many people remain with existing partners (if they have one) after diagnosis, especially when they are connected by love, marriage, economic dependence,

---

6   A number pointed out that their wives expected sex and that they felt the need to oblige.

7   Obviously it is hard to know whether this was a medically or morally based comment. (See the discussion in Chapter 4 on 'therapeutic citizenship'.)

kinship and parenting ties. However others will be seeking new partners. These decisions will depend on a complex of factors, including the serostatus of any existing partner as well as their feelings about the diagnosis. But going back into the sexual arena as an HIV positive person will always pose significant challenges.

Positive Men Seeking Other Men

Most research on the quest for new partners has focussed on same-sex identified men. Of course many are searching for long-term partners with whom to establish more intimate relationships. But others report that they prefer the 'security' of casual or anonymous sex (van Kesteren et al. 2005). Many will have to overcome significant emotional barriers relating to fear of rejection and loss of confidence. A man from Amsterdam said: 'It's just being homosexual, being considered a minority and being HIV positive too. It's just like, you know, it's like a triple, it's like 3 X's bam, bam, bam, people don't want to associate with that' (Vanable et al. 2011 p.357).

Evidence from the US shows that gay men who are HIV positive will have less chance than others of being accepted as either short- or long-term partners (Raymond and McFarland 2009; Davis 2007; Courtenay-Quick et al. 2006; Smit et al. 2012). This appears to mark a move away from the collectivism and altruism of 'gay communities' in the early years of the epidemic towards what has been defined as a new form of 'radical individualism' (Davis 2007).

Positive participants in a recent study in Sydney expressed nostalgia for the era before AIDS, criticising the ways in which some gay men now ruthlessly evaluated possible partners by age, attractiveness and performance of masculinity (Holt 2011). As one man expressed it:

> The Sydney scene is all about bars, clubs etc. and if you don't really like that there are not many options. It is a very judgemental community, which means it tends to fragment into things like the young and the beautiful versus the old and the decrepit, the HIV-positive and the healthy and so on. (Holt 2011 p.863)

The process of 'serosorting' may exacerbate these problems. This is now enacted by many men as a significant part of their protective strategy. Individuals who know their status will usually prefer to choose another partner of the same status as themselves in order to optimise the safety and quality of their sexual lives. While this will help protect those who are negative, it may also have the effect of limiting the options for those who are already positive.[8]

---

8   Moreover it is not always effective. One individual may not be honest in revealing their status and/or the other may misread the signals. This can make unprotected anal intercourse (UAI) hazardous for one or both partners. The negative partner may be infected with HIV, while either partner may be infected with other sexually transmitted diseases (Butler and Smith 2007).

Positive Men Searching for Female Partners

For both women and men in high-prevalence communities, the search for a new heterosexual partner is usually focussed not just on sex itself but also on the need for support in what may be extremely challenging circumstances. As one African migrant in the UK said:

> The only thing that can make one happy is a good marriage with kids, if you are married and you don't have kids there is no happiness. If I don't have kids my future is hopeless. If I am working very hard I am working only for the cat and the dog. (Doyal et al. 2009 p.1905)

Very few researchers have explored the situation of HIV positive men seeking new partners in low-prevalence settings. However a recent Australian study showed that many felt anxious that their status would be a major obstacle to developing a new relationship. As one man said: 'I'm at the opinion that, what have I got to offer, would you gamble your feelings and emotions on a bloke who might be dead in six months?' (Persson and Richards 2008 p.802).

Surprisingly perhaps, the same study also showed that some positive men went against the general trend in preferring a negative partner. The authors write that for these men such a woman represented 'the holy grail: idealised and unattainable, an impossible desire, tangled in their own sense of undesirability as a man' (Persson and Richards 2008 p.803). Under these circumstances a negative woman would make it possible to assume a kind of 'proxy negativity' – a desired state of 'redeemed masculinity'. This highlights the important but unexplored theme of the relative influence of gender relations and serostatus in the negotiation of sexual reality within discordant partnerships.

Positive Women Searching for Male Partners

Positive women seeking male partners in high-prevalence settings may face very different challenges.[9] Many are widowed at an early age because male partners are usually the first to die. For some this will mean not only emotional distress but also significant loss of financial support. As a result, sexual desire will often be less important in seeking a partner compared with meeting the material needs of themselves and their children. But achieving these ends may be difficult with life becoming very insecure, as one positive Kenyan women described: 'The one before, my second husband he died. Actually the first boyfriend was a high school friend and he is OK (alive and well). I was with my present husband (third partner) for one year then he died ... since then I am with this one' (Sarna et al. 2009 p.787).

---

9   For excellent studies of positive women and sexuality in high-prevalence settings see Long (2009b) and for low-prevalence settings see Gurevich et al. (2007).

Women in some high-prevalence settings have described moving to another location so that potential partners will not know that they are positive (Wamoyi et al. 2011). However others report that they have attained a 'preferred' partner status, especially if they are young. Once ART has improved their looks, they may find it easy to get positive men, especially if they are without dependants.

We know much less about women seeking new partners in low-prevalence settings. However the opportunities open to them are likely to be limited, as one woman in a Toronto study described:

> [I]f you are an HIV positive woman in the straight community like I think we are still an anomaly, whereas HIV positive men in the gay community aren't. I think the gay community is a lot more knowledgeable and a lot more accepting. … But the heterosexual community, that's a community that doesn't feel any particular need to be informed and your likelihood of running across someone who's HIV positive is so much lower … and a lot of women don't have a lot of sex. (Gurevich et al. 2007 p.29)

Disclosure within Sexual Relationships

For those positive women and men who do find a new partner or retain an old one, many problems will still have to be resolved. As we have seen, the disclosure of HIV status is a crucial issue at all life stages and in all settings. But in the context of sexual partnerships there is an added edge: failure to disclose may lead directly or indirectly to the infection of others.[10] Moreover this painful process may have to be repeated several times, with each disclosure being context-and partner-specific.

An overview of what is sometimes a confusing literature indicates very marked variations in disclosure to partners in different settings.[11] In one study in the UK 68 per cent of women indicated that they had told 'important others' of their HIV status (Petrak et al. 2001). However rates of disclosure in many of the most severely infected countries seem to be lower. One study of women living with HIV in Tanzania reported only about 40 per cent disclosure to partners after four years (Antelman et al. 2001), while a South African study reported that 58 per cent of a mixed sample of women and men had disclosed their status to recent partners (Simbayi et al. 2006).

There have been few attempts to explain these differences. However it seems likely that they result from particular combinations of potential stigma, fear of violence and of losing both emotional and material support (especially in the case of women). While any kind of negative response can be hurtful, sexual rejection can be especially hard (Relf et al. 2009). A Brazilian MSM reported distressing

---

10   Although of course it is possible to negotiate safe sex without disclosure.

11   This section will only examine disclosure to sexual partners. For an excellent review of the wider literature on disclosure see Mayfield Arnold et al. (2008).

experiences which led him to give up sex altogether: 'It happened to me twice, when I told, the person didn't want to go out with me anymore. Some people think you are promiscuous just because you are HIV positive. That's prejudice and I don't even go out anymore to avoid getting hurt' (Paiva et al. 2011 p.1705).

Not surprisingly, one common finding across most settings and sexual identities is the greater likelihood of individuals disclosing to permanent rather than casual partners (Mayfield Arnold et al. 2008). An African American MSM described this in the following way:

> Maybe it's like a one night stand and you might never see this person again. ... And then again it could be a relationship that you are building up that you're trying to have. So you might have to disclose. But 9 out of 10 nobody cares if they're not going to see the person again, tomorrow or whenever. And, they just go and do what they got to do and keep on moving. (Harawa et al. 2006 p.689)

Similar points were made by a gay man in a pan-European study who highlighted the importance of being able to feel 'normal':

> If you are going out to have sex you are not actually looking for a relationship. You go out because you want to feel good about yourself and have some fun and then you get hot, and you end up having casual sex. In such a situation I would not tell that I am positive. But I would play it safe. This is much better than telling about your HIV-status. In such moments I feel like a 'normal person'. (Nostlinger 2008 p.523)

Even disclosure to long-term partners can be very difficult and is rarely done immediately. One African American gay man said:

> It was something that took me four months. Because when I met him I was in a discussion with my doctor about starting meds. In a sense, so I had to kind of tell him. I had to let him know what these ... all these pills and stuff were for and why I am taking them. But he's been cool with it ... he's been supportive and cool with it. (Relf et al. 2009 p.291)

In heterosexual relationships in particular, fear of rejection may be coupled with fear of violence. The extreme complexity many face in disclosing their status is well illustrated by the account of a young black woman from South Africa:

> I must try to make a quick plan because when he found out later he'll say maybe I got it somewhere, not maybe before the baby. Cos he'll find out that the baby is negative. I think it's a good idea ... Ja, I think it's easy to talk but it's not easy to tell him. ... I think it's crossed his mind cos you know sometimes I said to him you know, what if you find out that you are HIV? He said maybe I'll kill myself or maybe I'll go and spread it. (Long 2009b p.709)

If she 'confesses' to her boyfriend of 13 years she may put herself at risk, and others too if he seeks revenge. If she does not tell, then he may still spread it to others in ignorance so that she continues to carry anxiety and guilt. One Brazilian woman described how she had continued to hide her status as she moved between partners:

> I have to keep on hiding because maybe he could even try to hurt me. If he knew he would definitely leave me. I use condoms sometimes. … Could he hit me? Could he kill me? I just can't tell him … this HIV has been the end of three marriages of mine. (Kerrigan et al. 2006 p.2389)

The possibility of disclosure may have a profound effect on an already shifting identity. Indeed for some, the potential pleasures of sex may not be worth the pain. As one Canadian woman summarised it: 'I just didn't think I could cope with being rejected because of the HIV because, is that ultimately a rejection of me? Because that's who I am you know; I'm not a walking talking virus. But I am a woman living with HIV' (Gurevich et al. 2007 p.20).

Sex as Risk Taking

Recent 'positive' prevention strategies have focussed on spreading the message of safer sex through condom use. This has clearly had some effect, with evidence from both the USA and Africa showing an overall reduction in unprotected sex. But significant numbers of positive and negative people still report risk-taking behaviour (O'Leary and Wolitski 2009). The reasons for this have been extensively explored in recent years but the results are not always clear or consistent.

One explanation involves what has been called 'treatment optimism'. This assumes that in some settings risky behaviour reflects a growing belief that highly active antiretroviral therapy (HAART) reduces infectivity to a point where an individual is no longer able to transmit the virus. On the other hand it reflects a gradual change in attitudes towards the disease itself. If pills can reduce the symptoms so dramatically, then some people may have come to believe that HIV itself is not so serious a problem as previously thought.

A number of studies have explored the implications of these beliefs for sexual behaviour (Crepaz and Marks 2002; Crepaz et al. 2004; Kerrigan et al. 2006; Elford and Hart 2005). Again the results have been varied, but the general conclusion is that they do play a part in explaining the promotion and/or rationalising of unprotected sex in some settings. However it is clear that other psychological and social factors will also play a major part (Simoni and Pantalone 2004).

Problems of Condom Use among MSM

We know that many men will report problems with or dislike of condoms whether they are having sex with women or men or both. Indeed the reluctance of heterosexual men to use condoms is frequently cited as a major cause of HIV infection among women. However decisions relating to condom use are more complex in a heterosexual relationship when conception is a possible outcome. Hence we will begin with a brief review of condom use among MSM and return later to the heterosexual context.

The greatest risks are probably taken in casual encounters between men who are not regular partners. Most say they 'normally' use a condom in these circumstances, but there is a growing literature exploring the 'safe sex fatigue' reported by others. There is some evidence, for example, that the depression associated with HIV may lead to men not caring about their own (and sometimes others') safety. This may be enhanced by drugs and alcohol, especially during periods of anxiety and bereavement. As one positive gay man in the UK described it: 'It (depression) really influenced my sexual behaviour. You go out, you want to be used almost … you might as well let anybody do what they want to do to you' (Elam et al. 2008 p.475).

Practical problems with the use of condoms have been widely reported by both negative and positive men (Adams and Neville 2009). For some these are predominantly to do with loss of feeling. But others talk of difficulties in maintaining an erection, which may be exacerbated in the case of positive men by drug side effects or by the illness itself. The most serious challenges will often be faced by male sex workers whose economic and cultural circumstances will make it especially difficult for them to use condoms. This was illustrated in a recent study of sex workers in Chennai, India (Chakrapani et al. 2008).[12] All were positive and most were anxious not to infect others or do further damage to themselves. But structural factors prevented them from changing their sexual behaviour.

Most had little choice but to continue to try to support themselves in the sex trade. Since same-sex activities were both highly stigmatised and illegal, condoms were not always easy to access and were often expensive. As one man described it:

> How can I always carry condoms? Once I went to the market, I met with a panthi[13] … we had sex but without condoms. I did not go there to have sex … it happened. Even if I keep condoms in my pocket the old lady (mother) who washes my clothes will ask me why I have them. (Chakrapani et al. 2008 p.318)

Being caught with condoms in their possession was especially feared as they could be arrested and often faced police harassment (including sexual abuse). This presented many practical obstacles: 'I used to keep condoms in a bush in

---

12   For similar discussion of male sex workers in Dominica see Padilla et al. (2008).
13   The term used to describe a client or 'real man'.

[cruising site]. Sometimes there will be policemen standing near the bush and hence I could not go and get the condoms from there. ... The customers will not wait' (Chakrapani et al. 2008 p.319).

Others reported the difficulties they faced in trying to persuade clients to use condoms, especially when they had not done so before. They were afraid to reveal their status for fear of losing the client (and their income) and possibly of being beaten.

While these problems are especially serious for sex workers, who need to be out in the open, similar problems may present themselves for other same-sex identified men in settings where their preferred practices are illegal or highly stigmatised. In 2011 same-sex conduct remained illegal in around one-third of all countries, with the death penalty still prevailing in at least five (UN 2011).

Gay Men, Risk and Intimacy

Many men in long-term relationships will gradually be able to negotiate 'safe sex' without the use of condoms. For those in a sero-concordant relationship this will be relatively safe, provided both avoid unprotected sex with other men. But for discordant partners this will be more difficult to achieve and may well involve the risk of unprotected anal sex (UAI). Until recently, the feelings involved in such behaviour were not well understood. Indeed it was widely assumed that it was based on the denial of danger in order to achieve heightened sexual gratification. However there is now a much greater recognition of love and intimacy in same-sex relationships and the implications of this for risk taking (Rhodes and Cusick 2000; Flowers et al. 1997).

A qualitative study of the sexual lives of men in sero-discordant relationships has described them as 'fraught with contradiction and anxiety' (Rhodes and Cusick 2000).[14] In most cases the men used condoms in the early stages of their relationship. But as trust developed, they reported the desire to stop, since the condom was experienced as a symbol of emotional as well as physical separation. Negotiation towards UAI was described as a highly delicate process, characterised by caution, ambiguity and the testing of relationship boundaries.

Using Anthony Giddens' notion of the 'risk society' the authors point out the centrality of intimate relationships for the creation of secure identities in a world dominated by change and uncertainty (Rhodes and Cusick 2000). This is likely to be of particular significance for same-sex identified men in what will often be marginalised settings. For some, the protection of the relationship may then come to be seen as more important than protection against the virus. A man from London said: 'We just agreed we would do it ... and it might sound crazy to an awful lot of people out there but we really believed absolutely because of how

---

14   This study involved HIV positive gay men, drug users and heterosexual women in stable relationships. However this discussion will focus only on the gay men in the sample.

we felt about each other, and that's what made it so special' (Rhodes and Cusick 2000 pp.10–11).

Of course trust and intimacy in themselves will not protect against virus transmission. But, as Rhodes and Cusick argue, unprotected sex in such contexts can be seen not as irrational but rather as a display of faith and trust in the intimate relationship. It can be viewed as a risk worth taking and as safe *enough*. Indeed it may be less a denial of viral danger than *an acceptance of danger as part of love and life* (Rhodes and Cusick 2000).[15]

Men and Women in Long-Term Relationships: Safety, Fertility and Risk Taking

Not surprisingly, contradictions between condoms and intimacy can also be found in long-term heterosexual relationships. But there are additional challenges in the intimate relationships between women and men, especially when they are sero-discordant (Persson 2011). These can best be understood in terms of the complex dynamics relating to gender relations on the one hand and reproductive potential on the other.

It is widely recognised that men tend to be the dominant decision makers in most heterosexual relationships: at its most basic, it is they who can wear the (male) condoms. This adds considerably to the complexity of achieving safer sex. But negotiations will also depend on which partner is HIV positive. A number of studies have shown that many positive men are anxious to protect their partners through taking the appropriate action.[16] A Kenyan man from Mombasa said:

> I have changed. I am not like before. I have actually been using protection so that I do not infect my negative wife. I also avoid having extra marital affairs. ... I am able to control myself, this is the initiative I have taken to control myself and have one partner. (Sarna et al. 2009 p.786)

This is congruent with findings from a number of studies in the United States which indicate that knowledge of HIV positive status increases the likelihood that heterosexual men in general will practise safer sex (Denison et al. 2008). Similarly, heterosexual African men in the UK who are positive have been found to be significantly less likely than gay men to have unprotected sex with partners who are either HIV negative or of unknown HIV status (Elford et al. 2007).

However there are also many accounts of heterosexual men who will not change their behaviour. A recent US study explored the sex lives of 55 HIV positive women and their negative partners (Stevens and Galvao 2007). Ten of

---

15   For an interesting critique of this thesis see Davis and Flowers (2011), who argue against the 'simple opposition of love and rationality' – with each being weighed against the other in decisions about condom use.

16   However we can assume that some will face the same challenges as MSM in maintaining erections, although the lack of research makes this difficult to document.

the women reported that they had unsafe sex with their long-term partners, but all claimed that this was the man's choice.

Significantly, some women have also expressed negative feelings towards condoms, though the reasons for this will vary. For some they will be to do with pleasure. One American woman said: 'So, we tried to have sex once and that was disastrous cause, uh, he had like two condoms on and I still felt uncomfortable and couldn't do it. And I just – so it was just, uh, it just didn't work (Siegel et al. 2006 p.442).

Feelings about closeness may also come to the fore. As one British woman put it: 'Although you are about as intimate as you can be, there is still a bit of latex between you and I know that sounds really pathetic but you know, it's a consideration' (Rhodes and Cusick 2000 p.9).

Most importantly, however, there is clearly a contradiction between safer sex and conception. To women in particular, a child may be worth risking infection for (Seeley et al. 2009; Moore and Oppong 2007; Sri Krishnan et al. 2007). A positive man in Kenya described the dilemma this placed him in:

> She kept asking me how we would get a child if we keep on using condoms. Initially we agreed to use it but later on she turned and says that I am mistreating her ... this puts me in a tricky situation. Sometimes I think I should let her go out with other men ... My wife sees no use of using a condom because she wants to have a baby. (Sarna et al. 2009 p.791)

Many of the Chennai sex workers discussed above were married but had disclosed neither their status nor their sex work to their female partner (Chakrapani et al. 2008). Most were clear that they should not engage in unprotected sex, and one described the problems this could generate: 'How can I use that condom? I was just married six months ago. She would ask why we should use condoms when everyone is asking for good news (pregnancy)' (Chakrapani et al. 2008 p.319).

When it is the woman who is positive things may be even more complicated. Again there has been very little documentation of the nature of these sexual negotiations and little is known about who has the greatest influence (Persson and Richards 2008). However condoms are clearly symbolic in the context of social perceptions of masculinity and gender relations, as this graphic account from a Kenyan woman shows:

> When I told my husband [about my status] he argued that I cannot be having the HIV-virus within me, that the doctor was lying. ... We were advised to be using a condom but when I told my husband he refused and I gave up. He never wants to use it and insists that I am a prostitute – that is why I want him to use a condom. There was a time when I had it hidden in my panties. He took it and threw it away. (Undie et al. 2009 p.776)

Because of these complex pressures there are many accounts of women not disclosing their status. This could make sex itself and wider discussions about their life project very challenging. A woman from Togo says:

> My boyfriend and I used condoms at the beginning of the relationship but now we don't use them. We don't use them because my boyfriend wants to have a baby. He doesn't know of my status. I'm afraid if I tell him about it he will abandon me. He wants to marry me and have children with me. (Moore and Amey 2008 p.293)

Health and the Ethics of Sex

This overview has highlighted the ways in which HIV infection has transformed the sex lives of positive people and their partners. An activity that was largely pleasurable has become, for many, imbued with negative emotions such as fear, guilt and depression. Hence it can place major obstacles in their development of intimate primary relationships.

We have seen the many challenges facing HIV positive people in the context of their sexual lives. Behind all of these are ever-present moral pressures about infecting others which lead many to limit their sexual activities or to avoid sex altogether (King et al. 2008).[17] This can be summarised by the accounts of three African men from different settings:

> [My sex life] has kind of slowed down ... [Sexual desire] it is back now but there is that fear of infecting my partner, it does not come out of my mind. (Sarna et al. 2009 p.791)

> I don't have sex a lot. A long time ago before I was HIV positive I would just go anywhere and if I fancy a woman ... I will go to bed with her. But not now, with this on my conscience. I can tell you I am still as black as I am and you know, it's very, very difficult to stick to one partner, but not anymore. (Doyal et al. 2009 p.1904)

> I don't have sex anymore because I'm afraid I will infect my wife. If I have to die I'd rather die alone and leave my wife and child healthy. That way, my wife would take care of my child instead of both of us being killed by the virus and leaving the child an orphan. (Moore and Amey 2008 p.291)

---

17   There are of course exceptions to this, including those who actively prefer unprotected anal sex in the form of 'barebacking' or 'bug chasing ' between serodiscordant partners. This practice has received considerable publicity in recent years but appears to be relatively rare (Carballo-Dieguez et al. 2009).

Among those who do carry on with sex, many talk about loss of freedom and spontaneity (Gurevich et al. 2007). An African American woman described this in the following way: 'I can't just, you know, get loose like I used to ... I got to be careful, I can't do this here I can't do that there. Can't let them do this here; can't let them do that. You know. It's like well, get the barriers. You know?' (Siegel et al. 2006 p.443).

For many, their anxiety seems to be exacerbated by a lack of clarity over who is responsible for protecting whom under what conditions (Ridge et al. 2007; Bennett et al. 2000). Do positive people have no responsibility, do both share responsibility or is it the responsibility of the negative person? And how is this affected by gendered power relationships within the couple?

The argument that positive people were responsible for disclosure and protection was strongly resisted in the early years of the pandemic on the grounds that this would amount to 'blaming the victim'.[18] People who were negative or of unknown status were therefore encouraged to behave as though everyone else was infected (Bayer 1996). This approach has now begun to shift with the introduction of what has been called 'positive prevention', involving an expectation that those who are positive will disclose their status and play an active part in negotiating safety issues with sexual partners.[19] Indeed some even argue that the positive partner should bear the greatest responsibility, including criminal culpability for any harm inflicted (Csete and Elliot 2011). Others respond by saying that such a burden is too great for those already infected (Adam et al. 2005; van Kesteren et al. 2005). Joint moral agency would clearly be the ideal strategy in such situations, but there are a number of structural obstacles to this.

It seems from the little evidence we have that agreement about protective behaviours is easier among MSM. In long-term relationships decisions seem to be more likely to be made through negotiation between both partners. In these settings both are likely to be well informed about the relevant health issues as well as the moral arguments. Of course this does not mean that there is not continuing tension, but the basic decision is more likely to be made jointly.

Those who have sex on an informal basis will usually expect to use condoms often without any disclosure.[20] On the rare occasions when this pattern is not followed, the positive partner is likely to find the encounter morally difficult. A man from London said:

> I'd already told him [a casual partner] that I was HIV positive and he shrugged his shoulders. [Sniffs] And [um] you know, the proceedings start and he said, 'Let's not worry about the protection.' And I said, 'Well, you know, you're putting yourself at risk.' ... I got angry [um] because I thought well I've done

---

18 For further discussion see Chapter 8 on human rights.

19 See also Chapter 4 on therapeutic citizenship.

20 Unless this is negotiated in advance (sometimes online).

my best to sort of, to sort of protect you, and it's almost like you're throwing it back in my face. (Ridge et al. 2007 p.759).

In the context of heterosexual relationships, however, matters may be more complex due to the intervening variable of gender inequalities. Since the man is usually assumed to be the dominant partner it would follow that he should make the decisions. The underlying assumption here was well expressed by one Ugandan man: '... it is the responsibility of the man to protect the woman ... after counselling and discussing with her she will be satisfied because she is weak in mind and soul ... it is believed that as the man you are the leader and driver of your partner' (Sarna et al. 2009 p.792).

So long as positive men use their power to protect their female partners, then at least the women's health will not be damaged, though their capacity to exercise their own autonomy will certainly be diminished. However if men choose not protect them, then women will have very little capacity to avoid infection. As we have seen, this is not uncommon – with the majority of married women in many parts of the world being infected by their husbands. One man in Togo reported: 'I don't use condoms with my two wives because I think they are both infected like me ... I told one of them about my serostatus but the second one is unaware of it because she can't keep things secret' (Moore and Amey 2008 p.292).

These problems are exacerbated by the widespread belief that women have more moral responsibility than men for the promotion of health (including the prevention of HIV). Yet men's sexuality is frequently seen as somehow 'uncontrollable' (Davis 2007). Women will then be faced with the paradox of responsibility without power, leading to high levels of anxiety and stress. A New Zealand woman described her experiences of not being able to persuade her at-risk partner to wear a condom:

I just lie there and just think, oh my God what if? But he's a grown-up and that's his choice and I say to him. Well that's your responsibility. If you get HIV it's not my fault, so don't say that it is, because it's not. I asked you to wear a condom and you don't want to wear one and you still want to have sex, so that is your responsibility. (McDonald 2011 p.1126)

Even if the woman reveals her status there is no guarantee that the man will use condoms. Ten of the participants in a recent US study described very similar experiences of their partners' refusal to use condoms and their own guilt about living with the responsibility of unprotected intercourse. One said:

I feel responsible about having unprotected sex. I don't want anyone to go through what I have been through with HIV. And that eats me up inside, more so than me having HIV myself. My husband acts like it's not an issue but it is. I don't want it on my conscience that I hurt a single solitary soul, intentional or not intentional. (Stevens and Galvao 2007 p.1019)

Conclusion

This chapter has shown the many different challenges facing HIV positive women and men in their sex lives, whatever their gender or sexual preferences. Clearly, some will meet these challenges more successfully than others, especially as regards the degree of autonomy that they are able to exercise in the process. For many, significant obstacles will arise in their attempts to meet their desire for sex and/or their need for fulfilling primary relationships. All will face complex ethical dilemmas which will vary over time and place, with few able to avoid the painful choices shaped by love, passion, fear, guilt and anxiety. For many this will be compounded by the difficulties of achieving their major life projects: to be parents. The next chapter considers this particular problem in more detail.

Chapter 7
Shaping Reproductive Futures

The last few years have seen a rapid growth in technologies to aid safe conception for HIV positive people and to prevent the transmission of the virus from mother to child. As a result many more women and men are now able to become parents without damaging their own health or that of future offspring. However the full potential of these technologies has so far been confined mainly to those living in rich countries.

Despite the growing emphasis on reproductive rights, too many women still lack basic access to fertility control and cannot be sure of giving birth safely (Cottingham et al. 2012). In sub-Saharan Africa, for example, the numbers using modern contraceptive methods is estimated to be as low as 23 per cent, while adolescent pregnancies stand at 103 per 1,000 15–19-year-olds compared to only 17 per 1,000 in Europe (UNFPA 2010). This lack of provision affects all women of childbearing age but creates additional problems for those who are HIV positive (de Bruyn and Paxton 2005; Kendall 2009; Delvaux and Nostlinger 2007; Gruskin et al. 2007, 2008; London et al. 2008). This chapter will explore what is known about the ways in which positive status influences reproductive deliberations and experiences of childbearing within the broader framework of global inequalities in reproductive health care.

Reproduction: Paths to Pregnancy

Around 80 per cent of those living with HIV worldwide are at an age when unprotected heterosexual activity can lead to pregnancy and where parenthood is seen as the social norm. The introduction of antiretroviral therapy (ART) has left many positive people feeling healthier, more hopeful and hence more desirous of parenting (Loutfy et al. 2009).

These developments have been of particular significance to women, since it is they who must undergo the demanding biological processes of pregnancy and childbirth. New methods of assisted conception can limit the risk to a negative partner. Similarly the transmission of the virus from mother to child can be minimised through the administration of ART during pregnancy and the use of appropriate obstetric methods. These technologies are now widely available in the global north and the stigma surrounding positive parenting has somewhat diminished.[1] As result

---

1   However a number of studies have shown that even in the US high-quality services are still limited, with many marginalised groups missing out (Sauer 2006).

the total number of planned births among HIV positive women in North America and in parts of Europe has gone up significantly (Kirshenbaum et al. 2004; Blair et al. 2004; Heard et al. 2007; Sharma et al. 2007; Fiore et al. 2008).

However such developments have not occurred in the same way or at the same pace in different parts of the world (Mantell et al. 2009). Research in South Africa (Peltzer et al. 2009; Cooper et al. 2009) and Kenya (Baek and Rutenberg 2010) has shown that HIV positive status is still a major deterrent to childbearing. This reflects the fact that reproductive deliberations are affected not only by the lack of health care but also by the heightened fear of infection, illness and death found in the wider context of poverty and social deprivation (Nduna and Farlane 2009). In a recent study in Soweto only around 30 per cent of positive women using highly active antiretroviral therapy (HAART) wanted to become pregnant compared to 69 per cent of those who were negative (Kaida et al. 2010). Similarly, HIV negative women interviewed in a Rwandan study were 16 times more likely to express a desire for (more) children than their positive compatriots (Elul et al. 2009).

Under these circumstances the first priority for many positive women and men will not be to promote conception but to prevent it. Yet this reality has so far received very little attention. As a result many find themselves producing unintended children in situations that may be hazardous to their own health and that of their families (Leach-Lemens 2010; Myer et al. 2007).

It is estimated that in 2011 some 1.5 million HIV positive women became pregnant in middle and low income countries (UNAIDS 2012a). However they will have arrived at this point by very different routes. Among those who know they are positive some will have made a conscious decision to attempt conception, while others will not have. Many will have conceived intentionally or unintentionally without knowing that they (or their partner) are HIV positive at all.[2] Some of these will discover their own status (and/or that of their partner) during the pregnancy, while others will give birth without ever discovering that they are positive.

Once women become pregnant the narratives of their conception appear to be of little interest either to clinicians or to researchers. As a result, many important questions remain unexplored. What were the original reproductive desires and intentions of individual women? Were they negotiated with a partner (or others) and if so how? Did the women have access to appropriate and effective contraception? Did they use it? Did they seek a termination and if so under what conditions? A similar veil of ignorance lies over the experiences of those who go on to negotiate the later stages of pregnancy and early motherhood. The extensive biomedical literature on HIV and pregnancy focuses mainly on the reduction of mother to child transmission, while the well-being of the women themselves has received much less attention (Giles et al. 2009).

2	Around 40 per cent of all pregnancies worldwide are estimated to be unintended (UNAIDS 2012a).

Making Reproductive 'Choices'

There is now a growing body of research exploring the reproductive 'choices' or 'intentions' of people living with HIV (Nattabi et al. 2009).[3] These findings do provide insights into the ways in which couples who know one or both of them are positive may debate their options. But the analysis of 'decision making' in this area of human life (as in so many others) is often oversimplified. As a result we still know very little about how 'HIV consciousness is transformed into reproductive strategies' in specific settings (du Plessis 2003).

It is clear that there is rarely a direct relationship between desires, intentions, actions and outcomes. Many people who are HIV positive will express a desire to have a child but economic, social, health or medical factors may prevent them from bringing this to fruition. These obstacles will be especially hard to overcome for those who have few resources to turn their hopes into realities (Segurado and Paiva 2007). Even where circumstances are more propitious, couples do not necessarily embark on parenting on the basis of an unambiguous and joint decision. In some instances the conception is not actively intended by either partner but results from the absence or failure of effective contraception. In other cases the desires and/or needs of the two partners may be divergent. Particular challenges may arise in the case of serodiscordant couples who may or may not be aware of each other's status (Beyeza-Kashesya et al. 2009, 2010; Kelly et al. 2011).

Reproductive choices are therefore complex, difficult to read and often highly contested. Moreover, pregnancy and childbearing are believed in many societies to be the business not just of the woman or the couple but also of their extended families. In these circumstances those who are positive will face additional challenges: if a woman has not disclosed her status to those around her she may fear violence or rejection if she is forced to 'go public' (Feldman and Maposhere 2003). Under these circumstances women may face serious obstacles in promoting their own needs and desires and will need to find creative ways to overcome both biological constraints and gendered realities (van Hollen 2007, 2011).

Desiring Parenthood

Studies in different parts of the world have highlighted the strength of the social and cultural factors promoting parenthood. In some settings these pressures have waned, with individuals having greater freedom to make 'child-free' choices. However for many, procreation remains a 'natural' part of life rather than an option needing to be actively chosen. Parenthood remains a central life goal for

---

3   Thus far the majority of these studies have focussed on HIV positive women in the US but studies in the African region are now increasing rapidly. However we still know very little about men. A recent systematic review found 20 studies of reproductive intentions among women only, seven of women and men and only two of men exclusively (Sherr 2010).

most people in most societies and, not surprisingly, this applies to those who are positive as well as those who are not (Dyer et al. 2004).

Internalised desires and external pressures towards parenting are generally felt by both women and men, though they are experienced in gendered ways. Indeed, for many women, motherhood is viewed as a prerequisite without which it will be difficult to complete the transition to the status of adult and wife. A positive woman in a recent study in Cape Town put it very simply: 'I am going to get married and I will have a child. It is a must' (Cooper et al. 2007 p.278).

For many women, motherhood is something to be sought regardless of the risks involved. Indeed pregnancy itself may be seen as life-affirming in the wider context of poverty, deprivation and violence. A Kenyan woman explained why she wanted to conceive despite the fact that both she and her husband were HIV positive:

> I cannot live without kids. I am always alone and I am not barren. If I have a child I will take care of my child and I will be active. I can work because I know I have somebody to take care of. I will have a responsibility. (Kuoh and Best 2001 p.2)

Of course the emotional and economic implications of fatherhood will not be the same as those of motherhood. However most heterosexual men in long-term relationships also express some desire to have children.[4] Indeed there is evidence that men may sometimes express a desire for more children than their female partners. They too will experience pressure from their community, as this positive Ugandan man pointed out:

> Well as a man, you know, you want to have a family if you can, it is a positive thing. If you don't have them, the elders in that clan or in that extended family begin to say something like 'you're useless, you're worthless, up to this age you haven't got family, you haven't got children', that kind of thing. (Doyal et al. 2009 p.1904)

Among a group of bisexual and heterosexual men interviewed in Brazil, 43 per cent expressed the desire to become a father in the future (Paiva et al. 2003). A very similar percentage of positive heterosexual men in a UK study reported that they had actively considered having children (Sherr and Barry 2004).[5] Many explained their feelings as part of a desire to ensure the continuation of future generations. This has been found to be of particular cultural significance in many

---

4   Significantly, however, recent studies in South Africa have raised the issue of whether some men are anxious to have the status of father but are not necessarily desirous of being active in this role (Morrell 2001; Richter and Morrell 2006).

5   There is also evidence of a desire for children among the few studies that have explored the reproductive desires of HIV positive gay men (Sherr 2010).

African settings, especially where rapid social change appears to be undermining traditional beliefs and practices (Smith and Mbakwem 2010).

For many men, the desire for children also appears to be tied to 'proving' their fertility and hence their masculinity. Hau, a 30-year-old woman in Vietnam, explained that her husband's desire for fatherhood was so great that he threatened to take another woman if she did not 'give' him a child:

> My husband likes children very much. He always wants me to bear a child for him. When talking with his friends he often affirms that we are going to have three children in all. His friends mock him and say that 'you are infertile you just brag to save face'. They do not know we are HIV positive. (Chi et al. 2010 p 46)

A recent study has suggested that for many HIV positive people in Nigeria, having children may also play an important part in the process of 'normalisation' and the mitigation of stigma. Indeed so powerful are the institutions of marriage and parenthood that failure to achieve them will be seen as a major tragedy possibly akin to HIV infection itself. As the authors describe it:

> For people who are on ART successful marriage and childbearing are inextricably tied to protecting their social reputation, hiding their HIV-positive status and avoiding stigma. Marrying and having children offer a path to normalcy but also a way of countering the popular perception that people contract HIV because they behave in ways that flout widely accepted moral notions that connect sex and social reproduction. (Smith and Mbakwem 2010 p.346)

Most women and men who know they are positive will therefore have attitudes and emotions similar to those who are negative: all else being equal they will desire children. But, as we have seen, their deliberations and their actions will be constrained to a greater or lesser extent by the biological and social realities of their situation.

HIV, Pregnancy and Parenting: What Are the Constraints?

For women, fear for their own health is likely to be a major barrier when they consider pregnancy (Baek and Rutenberg 2010; Cooper et al. 2007, 2009; Nduna and Farlane 2009; Oosterhoff et al 2008b). The nature of such risks is not well understood and the prospect may be daunting. One Zimbabwean woman explained: 'I feel afraid of getting pregnant since some say if an HIV positive person becomes pregnant that will be the end of them' (Ndlovu 2009 p.63).

The most recent evidence indicates that pregnancy does not accelerate the progression of HIV itself (MacCarthy et al. 2009). However in some parts of the world seropositive status is becoming increasingly important as a cause of maternal morbidity and mortality (Black et al. 2009; Berer 1999). Since 1998 HIV has been the leading indirect cause of maternal deaths in South Africa, reversing a previous decline in mortality rates. It is associated with increased blood loss, urinary tract infections and bacterial pneumonia. Co-morbidity with tuberculosis (TB) and malaria is especially hazardous. A recent study showed that HIV positive women in Johannesburg were around six times more likely to die from maternal causes than their negative counterparts (Black et al. 2009).

As well as fearing for their own health, many women (and their partners) are afraid of having an HIV positive child. The moral risk of creating such a child is felt very powerfully and prevents many from going ahead. Not surprisingly, this fear is most common among those lacking easy access to care. Others may not trust the medicine being offered to protect the unborn child, and hence prefer not to take a chance. One Zimbabwean woman expressed these concerns very clearly:

> I desire to have a child but not now ... maybe when I have seen how those tablets [ARVs] work, how much they protect. Some are saying you can have a child – there is nevirapine but others are saying it is not 100% effective, some [children] can be positive, some negative. I am afraid of having a positive child. If a drug that guarantees that my child will be negative is found then I will throw aside the condoms and rush to have one. (Ndlovu 2009 p.62)

These pressures are heightened by the fact that the child of an HIV positive parent may well be orphaned before adulthood. For many this loss of maternal love seems intolerable. An African American woman in the USA described her feelings in very powerful terms:

> I'm afraid of dying and my baby has to suffer without me. Not just the fact that my baby might be sick but I loved my mother with all my heart, the one that raised me ... she's the best thing that ever happened in my life. And I'm wondering how my baby will feel if they had to lose me. (Kirshenbaum et al. 2004 p.108)

Many women are also affected by the fact that their own early death would impose a heavy burden on other family members who might eventually be required to take care of their child. A Vietnamese woman summed up the feelings of many: 'I am HIV positive. If I bear a child, it will be infected with HIV. Also, I am getting weaker and weaker. I cannot take care of a child and I don't want my child to be a burden for my family because we're poor' (Chi et al. 2010 p.S49).

For the majority of HIV positive women and men, these deliberations are of course taking place in the context of actual or impending poverty. Hence many also express their fear of being unable to afford to bring up a child. As a woman from Tamil Nadu put it:

> We will definitely not have a child. We have HIV and we do not have enough resources to take care of ourselves. It is difficult to take care of our health and the

child at the same time. We are suffering: why should we have a child and make
it suffer as well? (Kanniappan et al. 2008 p.627)

These fears of harming their own child highlight the 'double bind' that so many
positive women face (Ingram and Hutchinson 2000). On the one hand motherhood
is seen as an essential element of womanhood. But at the same time women who
are HIV positive are widely viewed as unsuitable mothers. Many are therefore
stranded between two equally unthinkable life choices. The remainder of the
chapter will explore the many ways in which gender relations and wider social
determinants interact with HIV in shaping different stages of both intended and
unintended pregnancies among those who know (or discover) they are positive.

To Conceive or Not to Conceive?

Central to the notion of human rights in general and reproductive rights in particular
is the capacity of individuals to control their fertility. As we have seen, for some
this will mean optimising the possibility of producing HIV negative children and
raising them in a healthy environment. However for others it will mean ensuring
that they avoid any risk of conception. In either case the HIV status of one or both
parents may pose specific challenges.

Trying to Conceive

Figures from sub-Saharan Africa suggest that fertility rates are 25–40 per cent
lower among people who know they are HIV positive than among those whose
status is unknown or negative. Some of this will reflect changes in sexual behaviour
that have little to do with reproductive choices. However there is also evidence
that both biological and social factors may reduce the fertility of those who do
want to have children (Kaida et al. 2006).

HIV infection in men may lead to reduced sperm production, making fertilisation
more difficult. For women, conception may be inhibited by co-morbidity with
other sexually transmitted infections and also by amenorrhoea related to weight
loss. Under these circumstances there will often be a need for supportive health
care services, but these are rarely available in those parts of the world where HIV
prevalence is highest (van der Spuy 2009). Even in countries such as Argentina,
where services are relatively well developed, positive women have reported on
the very low priority which many doctors give to parenting desires: 'I asked the
gynaecologist "what happens if I want to have a child?" She said "well first get
pregnant". That's completely ridiculous! I need help' (Gogna 2009 p.817).

Health workers will have varied and often ambivalent views about HIV positive
women attempting to conceive, and may impose these on service users (Harries
et al. 2007; Orner et al. 2011a, b). One woman in a recent study in Gauteng and
the Eastern Cape region in South Africa reported that she was encouraged to come

and discuss pregnancy plans: 'at the clinic they are always saying that if you are on HIV treatment you can take the pills for a while ... if you want to have a child, they invite you to go and talk to them and they will see how they can help you' (Nduna and Farlane 2009 p.S64). However another woman in the same study reported receiving a very different response: 'Why are you making babies ... what is going to happen if you die? They are making sure that there should be no orphans' (Nduna and Farlane 2009 p.S64).

Even though assisted reproduction was available, a recent study of 17 positive Australian women in serodiscordant relationships found that most wanted to conceive what they called the 'natural way'. Four had achieved this through unprotected intercourse, but all talked about the potential stigma involved. Even though these had been joint decisions by the couple, the women reported fearing that they would be accused of 'putting their partners at risk' – and all had constructed alternative narratives to tell family and friends. As one woman described it:

> When we got pregnant, it wasn't so bad with Jon because Jon was positive, but with Allan people would say, 'How could you risk Allan's life like that?' And I'm like, Oh, you know it was just the once, lie, lie, lie. Because people can't deal with it and it's not like how can *he* risk his life? And I think well, it's not a secret from him that I've got HIV; he knew as soon as he met me. I've always been upfront and I know that if he did get HIV his family would say it was my fault. (McDonald 2011 p.1123)

Both women and men who are HIV positive may also face difficulties in creating a family because they have no suitable partner. This can be especially distressing for women, as Violeta from Bolivia describes:

> I want very much to have a baby but I want to be confident he or she will be okay in every sense. ... I want to make sure I am with the baby and the baby's father ... I have many fears around having a child and at the moment I don't have a partner to support me in this choice. It's difficult because most men don't want to be with a woman who might become sick. (Bell et al. 2007 p.116)[6]

Trying Not To Conceive

But what about those who do not want to conceive? It is estimated that at least 215 million women currently wish to avoid pregnancy but are not using contraception (UNFPA 2010). Thus there is a significant unmet need for birth control around the world. It is not known how many of these women are HIV positive, but they clearly make up a significant subset of an already disadvantaged population (Leach-Lemens 2010). Estimates of how many

---

6   For further discussion of constraints on choice of sexual partners see Chapter 6.

pregnancies among HIV positive women are unintended vary between 51 per cent and 91 per cent depending on the settings (Wilcher and Cates 2009). A review of recent studies estimated that around 160,000 unintended births to HIV positive women in sub-Saharan Africa could be avoided each year through appropriate birth control (Wilcher and Cates 2009).

Most forms of contraception are medically suitable for HIV positive women (Leach-Lemens 2010; WHO 2008a).[7] However they are rarely offered a real choice. Male (or female) condoms are the most effective method because of their capacity for dual protection against both infection and pregnancy. But, as we have seen, they are often unavailable or resisted by male partners (or occasionally women themselves) on the grounds of reduced sensitivity (Pool et al. 2000).[8] The desire to use condoms may also be seen by men as an indication of a woman's 'promiscuity'. One young woman from Johannesburg said:

> At first I didn't use a condom but I got to a point where I realized that I should use a condom because I now know about the HIV/AIDS virus. And when you're supposed to tell your partner, it gets hard because he will ask why we should use a condom now and that maybe you are cheating on him and there is no more trust in the relationship. (MacPhail et al. 2009 p.489)

Many positive women express a preference for continuing to use hormone-related methods to prevent conception. But recent studies have shown that they may be inhibited by changes in menstrual patterns. Women whose periods cease have reported heightened anxiety that they are not expelling 'bad blood'. Conversely, where the drugs cause 'withdrawal bleeding' this is seen as a constant reminder of their own condition and also as a possible risk to male partners (Laher et al. 2009, 2010).

In many parts of the world sterilisation is promoted as an option to contraception, but we know very little about how this is used in the context of HIV. Recent studies have found evidence of coercive sterilisation in a number of countries, including Chile, Namibia, Mexico, the Dominican Republic, Venezuela and South Africa (Essack and Strode 2012). However the power of doctors may also work in the opposite direction. A recent Brazilian study found many refusing to sterilise positive women who saw this as the most practical way of exercising their autonomy at this critical point in their lives (Hopkins et al. 2005).

These examples highlight the complex problems many HIV positive women face in attempting to control their fertility while at the same time preventing their own re-infection and/or the infection of a partner within what are too often male-dominated sexual relationships and authoritarian medical settings. There is

---

7   Though the reliability of some hormonal contraceptives can be affected by antiretroviral drugs. For detailed discussion see WHO (2012).

8   See discussion in Chapter 6.

now growing interest in the development of women-initiated/women-controlled methods such as female condoms and microbicides (Long 2009b; MacPhail et al. 2009).[9] But in the meantime too many positive women continue to become pregnant each year in situations that will pose significant challenges to their health and well-being.

Where is the M in PMTCT?

In the absence of any medical intervention, around 40 per cent of children born to HIV positive mothers will themselves be infected. The recognition of this reality and its social implications has led to the creation of a wide range of programmes under the general heading of prevention of mother to child transmission (PMTCT) (WHO 2010a,b). These policies were ostensibly designed with several aims: to reduce HIV transmission to potential mothers; to prevent unintended pregnancies among positive women; and to stop mother to child transmission of HIV. They were also intended to provide care, treatment and support for mothers, their infants, partners and families. But in practice it is the prevention of mother to child transmission which has received by far the greatest attention.

These programmes have led to a significant reduction in the numbers of paediatric infections, with about 60 per cent of positive pregnant women in low and middle income countries now receiving antiretroviral treatment to protect their children (UNAIDS 2012a). However this represents only a partial success. The rate of mother to child transmission still remains high in many low income communities, varying between 20 per cent and 45 per cent of newborns (Moland et al. 2010).[10]

Even more importantly, few pregnant women are receiving the treatment they need either before or after delivery to treat their own HIV (Coovadia 2009; International Treatment Preparedness Coalition 2009; McIntyre 2010; Mnyani and McIntyre 2009). Around 1.5 million women in low and middle income countries were pregnant in 2011 of whom 75 per cent lived in the African region (UNAIDS 2012a). A recent UNAIDS estimate suggested that only about 30 per cent of those women who were eligible were receiving ART with the figure for the Democratic Republic of Congo as low as 13 per cent (van Rompaey et al. 2010).

Findings of this kind led Stephen Lewis, former UNAIDS Rapporteur on HIV and AIDS, to describe many of these programmes as a 'shameful example of double standards' (International Treatment Preparedness Coalition 2009 p.iv). In 2011 UNAIDS initiated the rather oddly titled Global Plan Towards the Elimination of New Infections among Children by 2015 and Keeping their Mothers Alive.

---

9   For a detailed account of positive women's own views on these issues, including the covert use of barrier methods, see MacPhail et al. (2009).

10   The comparable rate is as low as 2 per cent in developed countries.

However, little progress was reported on the latter target in the first progress report in 2012 (UNAIDS 2012a).

It is clear that many challenges will have to be faced if maternal deaths associated with HIV are to be prevented (and of course if mothers are to be guaranteed ART throughout their lives). The next section will examine some of the problems that will need to be faced through an exploration of the ways in which HIV positive women experience pregnancy and childbirth both inside and outside the context of PMTCT services. It will highlight the complex social, economic and cultural constraints on the lives of these women as they negotiate decisions about fertility control as well as the twin challenges of pregnancy and HIV, often with very few resources at their disposal (Abdool-Karim et al. 2010; Turan et al. 2008).

Dealing with the Diagnosis

Central to the strategy of PMTCT programmes is that all pregnant women should be offered voluntary counselling and testing (VCT) at their first antenatal visit. However it is estimated that in 2010 only about a third of those in low and middle income countries were actually tested (WHO, UNICEF and UNAIDS 2011). Moreover there is now a growing body of evidence to suggest that they may not always be treated with sensitivity during this process. The ethical principles of informed consent and confidentiality appear to be treated less seriously in the context of obstetric care. Instead the emphasis is often on getting the test done, with little or no counselling, and many women report that they were not aware of what was actually being done to them. One South African woman explained:

> When I was pregnant and went for antenatal care I was told to have a blood test. They did not tell me what the test was for. Every woman who came to the clinic had to have their blood tested. They did not explain at all what kind of test they were doing. I realized it was the AIDS test when I received the results. (Bell et al. 2007 p.119)

It seems that many counsellors are not adequately trained and are often extremely busy. Some may see their job as persuading women to be tested, with the boundaries between counselling and coercion being unclear. Gloria, a counsellor in Tanzania said: 'You give the woman a choice, but you tell her that the best she can do is be tested. When you do pre-test counselling and she disagrees I encourage her to be tested until she agrees' (de Paoli et al. 2002 p.147).

Issues relating to confidentiality appear to be frequently ignored. Out of 52 women who delivered their babies in a hospital in Hanoi, 14 reported that their test results were not kept confidential. Ten of these were sent results through the commune health station, while the others were told through relatives (Nguyen et al. 2008).

Studies have shown that post-test counselling is often especially problematic and rarely adapted to the specific needs of antenatal care. Many women have reported that they were shown little respect once their diagnosis was known. One group of Vietnamese patients reported that, after testing positive, they were not allowed to sit down during counselling sessions without covering the chair with newspaper (Nguyen et al. 2008). Yet this is a time at which many women have to cope with a combination of two potentially devastating pieces of information. They are pregnant and they are also HIV positive. When a group of 504 positive women in Angola were asked how they felt, 42 per cent described themselves as 'unable to cope with the HIV diagnosis', while 32 per cent wished they had not been tested at all (Bernatsky et al. 2007).

One of the declared aims of testing during pregnancy is to prevent transmission not just to the child but also to sexual partners, and this will require disclosure. However the context of their diagnosis means that positive women are often given little help in thinking through their options. A number of studies have found that those tested in antenatal settings are less likely to disclose their status to sexual partners than those tested in specialist HIV clinics. Rates of disclosure have been shown to vary markedly, ranging from as low as 16.7 per cent in some settings to as high as 86 per cent in others (Medley et al. 2004). The majority of those who did not disclose cited fear of violence, emotional abuse, accusations of infidelity, rejection and loss of economic support (Visser et al. 2008).

The challenges faced by many women after their diagnosis will be heightened by the failure of their partners to test (Kizito et al. 2008). In a recent study in an Entebbe hospital, 62.8 per cent of women accepted HIV testing but, despite encouragement, only 1.8 per cent of their male partners did the same! Hence the onus usually lies with the women to pass on any bad news and to cope with the consequences. (Kizito et al. 2008).

Termination or Not?

For many women, the discovery of their pregnancy alongside their HIV status will raise the question of whether or not to seek a termination. However few attempts have been made to explore the numbers of HIV positive women obtaining or being denied access to abortion. We know that around 20 million women have unsafe abortions each year – most of them in low and middle income countries. It is not known how many of these are related to an HIV diagnosis, but studies carried out in the USA before the HAART era indicate that rates were high among those who were HIV positive. There is evidence to suggest that termination may be more dangerous for positive women, especially if it is not carried out in a medical setting. This reflects their immune-compromised status and their greater likelihood of developing bacterial vaginosis, chlamydial cervicitis and anaemia.

Studies indicate that some positive women are pressurised to have a termination against their wishes (de Bruyn 2005) while in other settings they may be counselled against termination or even denied it (Cooper 2007; Oosterhoff et al. 2008b; van Hollen 2007; Orner et al. 2011a,b). Where choice is available, many women report receiving little help making what will often be very difficult decisions. A Vietnamese woman had hoped to get advice but left disappointed:

> One doctor was terrible … So when I left I wondered if I should keep my baby or should I have an abortion? I wished at that time that the doctor could have given me advice and that we could have discussed the disease, the transmission rate from mother to infant, my financial situation, whether or not I could feed the child formula, or what I would do if I died, who would take care of my child. But the doctor did not say anything. (Nguyen et al. 2008 p.7)

A recent study explored the experiences of 12 positive women from Tamil Nadu who were faced with making such a choice (van Hollen 2007). All were of low socio-economic status and lower-caste backgrounds, with six being Hindu and six having converted to Christianity. All found their situation very difficult, with an obvious tension between the cultural mandate for motherhood and the fear of transmitting HIV to a child. Though termination was available in principle, all the women decided to continue with the pregnancy.

Maliga was encouraged by her husband and family to abort the child at eight months but made her own decision not to do so. She reported that: 'Some said there was a 10% chance the baby would be HIV positive. So they felt it would be better to abort. For me … I am a woman. There is not reason to live if I do that. For a complete family you need a baby' (van Hollen 2007 p.28). In practice the major constraint on Maliga's decision making was her very late diagnosis. However she drew positively on her Christianity as well as the symbolic significance of motherhood as justifications for making her choice.

Vijay had a daughter with her first husband, who then died of AIDS. When she was pregnant with the child of her second husband she felt no need to produce another child for herself. However she decided to continue for the sake of her husband, who would otherwise not have his own biological child to care for him in old age. Moreover the grandparents were anxious to have a male heir and Vijay felt she should continue the pregnancy in the hope of meeting these needs. Punitha too was motivated to keep her baby for the sake of her in-laws and because of her Christian faith, but her membership of the Positive Women's Network was also a key factor:

> When the doctors first explained to me that even with the medicine to prevent transmission of HIV, there was a chance that the baby could be HIV positive, I told the doctor that I could live a happy life myself even with the HIV virus and I told him that I knew how to raise a baby whether the baby was HIV positive or HIV negative. (van Hollen 2007 pp.37–8)

A comparable study of decision making in Vietnam explored the experiences of 13 women, all of whom eventually opted for a termination (Chi et al. 2010). As was the case in Tamil Nadu, abortions were easily accessible in Vietnam – but again the choices were complex, with many different factors influencing the eventual outcome. The 'double bind' of motherhood and HIV was the key theme to emerge: most wanted to continue the pregnancy but felt that it was not in the child's own best interests. To be a 'good mother' was therefore to abort the foetus, but for many this meant losing important aspects of their own identity as women.

Nga was a hairdresser married to a miner and living on very little. She became pregnant after a miscarriage and was expecting twins. She was very happy, imagining the perfect family life: 'I so much wanted to have a child. Having children would make my husband come back home early. He would look after them while I prepared the dinner. After dinner we would go out together. I made a sketch of dreams but real life was not like that' (Chi et al. 2010 p.S45).

After a slight discharge of blood at three months she was diagnosed as HIV positive. It was a turning point in their lives, with her husband then admitting that he had probably been infected through sharing needles. One month later they decided on a termination and Nga was in great torment: 'I feel my husband does not love me anymore because as a woman I cannot have a child and we have no ties. ... Sometimes I think I am in this situation because my ancestors led immoral lives' (Chi et al. 2010 p.S46).

Most of the women in the study reported going through traumatic experiences of this kind. Most had conceived the child while in ignorance of their status. Hence many were aborting much-wanted children because they could see no way of sustaining them in their current circumstances.

Continuing with a Positive Pregnancy

As we have seen, about 1.4 million HIV positive women do continue with a pregnancy each year (WHO, UNICEF and UNAIDS 2011). The vast majority live in poor countries, and again we know almost nothing about their experiences. However a study in Angola found that two-thirds of HIV positive pregnant women reported what the authors call 'significant emotional distress'. This was a much higher proportion than that found in a comparable control group (Bernatsky et al. 2007).

All mothers in all settings worry about whether or not they will have a healthy baby. But for those who know they are HIV positive these anxieties are likely to be greatly heightened. One South African woman described her feelings to Carol Long: 'Ja you know, you just dream of your child being positive – not healthy. That hair loss, whatever. So you always think about these things. You know, ja, that makes you very sad. ... You just imagine a monster, you know (laughs) coming out from you' (Long 2009a p.111).[11]

---

11   This is one of the few studies to focus on HIV positive pregnant women in a developing country (South Africa). The author interviewed 50 women, some of them more than once, adding an important longitudinal aspect to the research design.

Many know that they are themselves at risk of significant morbidity and possibly early death while carrying a new life for which they will have the major responsibility. And all too often they have to carry these fears alone.

Hlengiwe was another of Long's participants. She was eight months pregnant with her first child and was diagnosed two months previously. She was working, was not married and lived with some cousins. Her boyfriend of three years was drinking excessively and she was afraid he would leave her:

> Mm, in terms of HIV I think he has done better compared to other men because if you tell them that you are HIV they run away, but he didn't. But I said to him 'But the way you acting, eh, for me, I do understand that it's difficult but you make me suspicious: I cannot rest.' But I have to be prepared; I know I am stronger. (Long 2009a p.35)

She had not seen her mother since she became pregnant and felt isolated from her family and financially and emotionally dependent on her boyfriend. She had kept her status secret from most people for fear of being badly treated.

Pumla was three months pregnant when she discovered she was HIV positive. At the time she was living with her boyfriend of 10 years. When she disclosed her status he 'chased her away', claiming that she was infected through 'sleeping around'. Although she sought help from her mother, this was refused because she was no longer earning money to contribute to the household. This was devastating and Pumla felt rejected and stigmatised (Long 2009a p.39).

Many HIV positive women who are also pregnant will therefore face major challenges to both physical and emotional well-being. In too many cases the support they might reasonably have expected from health workers will not be available (Turan et al. 2008).[12] Some reported abuse even at the highly stressful time of delivery itself. Two Vietnamese women described such experiences:

> The doctors treated me well when they didn't know my status. But right after my delivery, they found that I was infected and they became rude. They did not tie the umbilical cord immediately. I was in so much pain.

> When they knew my HIV status, they shouted at me and did not allow me to sit, even when I was bleeding and was weak. ... They asked other patients to keep far away from me. Then they transferred me to a special room. When I gave birth, there was no staff. I gave normal birth, no operation. (Nguyen et al. 2008 p.8)

---

12 This is not something associated only with HIV. A number of studies have highlighted the discriminatory experiences many poor women have with health workers (especially nurses) in obstetric settings. For an important discussion of these issues in South Africa see Jewkes et al. (1998).

Another woman in the same study talked about the insensitivity she experienced during and after labour:

> I was in an isolated room when I woke up. Crying, my relatives stood far from me. I was not dressed and was left with only a thin sheet. Later on, I found out that the health staff informed all my relatives, neighbours, and friends who came to visit me of my status. I didn't understand why. Health care workers examined me carefully but said nothing. I couldn't see my beloved baby either. Some days later, my husband told me everything; that I was infected with HIV. (Nguyen et al. 2008 p.8)

Contradictions of Positive Parenting

Just as we know little about the experiences of HIV positive women during pregnancy, so the early phases of motherhood also take place largely behind closed doors (Ingram and Hutchinson 2000). The main focus of interest is usually the baby, yet HIV positive women have major challenges to deal with on top of those experienced by many negative mothers in the postpartum period: dealing with the uncertainty of not knowing their child's HIV status for example (Shannon and Lee 2008). As Long has described it in her study of South African mothers: 'there was a sense of women having to hold their breaths through this uncertainty, not quite being able to say one way of another and hence not being able to speak' (Long 2009a p.108).

The HIV status of babies cannot be ascertained at birth since they will still have their mother's antibodies. Hence most positive mothers undergo a period of severe anxiety. In the early phases of the pandemic tests usually required a wait of 18 months until the mother's antibodies had disappeared from the child's blood. A nurse counsellor from Tanzania described the terror and anxiety of the mothers when the child is tested:

> The mothers will not sleep until they have had the results. When I tell them they are shaking. When the child is negative they kiss me, kneel down and praise the Lord. They will not worry about themselves. It is very painful to reveal positive results. One mother fainted. They will cry and complain to God. 'What did I do my Lord, the sin is mine. The child is clean.' (Blystad and Moland 2009 p.113)

The development of a new polymerase chain reaction (PCR) test means that a diagnosis can now be made at six weeks while in some cases results can be obtained even earlier. This is now standard practice in most rich countries, but it is expensive and requires sophisticated equipment. Hence there are many countries where a long wait is still inevitable. This is clearly problematic for the baby's health since it means a delay in treatment for those who are positive.[13] And the stress on the mothers will be intense, as Long found in a study in Johannesburg:

> Not knowing is very terrible, it's very terrible. … Because whenever he is sick I feel that it has something to do with it even when he has got a cold. The last time he was very sick, he had this terrible cold and I thought maybe he is too sick, and then I took him to the hospital and they told me it was just bronchitis … flu or something like that – but it was horrible. (Long 2009a p.114)

The reality of the mothers' own illness as well as uncertainty about their child will usually have a significant impact on the bonding process itself. Most reported a continuous process of monitoring and observation in which they sought to know the unknowable through minute inspection of the child's appearance and behaviour. Most are hypervigilant, as Ayanda described:

> The baby, you check the baby, you look everywhere, and it's very hard. These are hard times you know, you look, even if you see this … like now I told the doctor that this rash, he says to me 'haii, this rash is normal' … I said please give me something. He just gave me aqueous cream … (laughs). (Long 2000a p.116)

Another study carried out in Johannesburg after the introduction of PCR testing confirmed that a shorter wait caused less suffering, but it was still an extremely difficult period (Lazarus et al. 2009). Moreover, for some mothers the anxiety remained even when the child tested negative since they felt unable to trust the result. In both studies most of the mothers whose children were found to be positive expressed guilt and shame. As one put it: 'when I think of what my baby has contracted from me I wish there was a way of eradicating it from my baby's system and rather doubling it in mine' (Lazarus et al. 2009 p.332).

Inevitably, they also worried about the children's future health. How long would they live, would they ever be well and who would look after them if one or both of their parents died: 'my baby is suffering – they often have to take blood from her … she is not like other children because she comes to the clinic often and she will have to start treatment soon' (Lazarus et al. 2009 p.332).

Fears about Feeding

In the early years of the pandemic it was recognised that HIV could be transmitted through breastfeeding, and positive women were therefore advised to use substitute methods.[14] However this has posed problems in settings where infection is hard to

---

13   About one-quarter of positive babies will be dead by the end of the first year and about one-third by the end of two years if they are not treated.

14   This followed a pre-HIV period during which breastfeeding was seen as by far the most desirable method and this was widely publicised by WHO and other organisations.

avoid and the cost of formula often very high. The current advice is to use either breast or bottle feeding alone until weaning since 'mixed methods' seem to have the worst outcome of all (WHO 2010c). The preferred option is formula feeding, but only if the woman can afford to buy enough milk or if it is available free and if she has access to clean water (Moland et al. 2010).

For many mothers this advice may be very difficult to follow. The authors of a recent study carried out in Ethiopia and Tanzania highlighted the problems involved in negotiating local beliefs about infant feeding on the one hand and guidelines based on (changing) biomedical knowledge on the other: 'For the large majority of the HIV positive mothers in the study, life was a daily battle to avoid sickness and disclosure, to maintain respectability and to secure their daily food and shelter' (Blystad and Moland 2009 p.113).

Conflicting messages are presented to mothers. Some are told they should not breastfeed because there is virus in their milk, but others are recommended to do so because they are too poor to do anything else (Leshbari et al. 2007). Thus scientifically based recommendations may be altered by social circumstances. As a result both mothers and health workers may feel under-informed and uncertain. These problems are often exacerbated by an authoritarian relationship between the two, leaving many mothers feeling disempowered in making what may be a life or death decision for their child.

These constraints on women's autonomy are reinforced by the fact that infant feeding practices are socially and culturally embedded in wider communities – with mother, partner, kin and even neighbours all having their own expectations. This will be especially challenging if the mother does not wish to reveal her status. A number of studies have explored these difficulties and women's strategies for managing them (Desclaux and Alfieri 2009; Doherty et al. 2006; Leshbari et al. 2007).

In most settings breastfeeding remains the culturally preferred option and for many women this will be central to their sense of themselves as mothers. Not to breastfeed will usually be seen as failing to do the best for your child. But over the years the symbolism attached to mother's milk has gradually begun to change from a substance essential to the sustaining of life to a source of infection and even death. The experience of these contradictions may cause both emotional and physical problems for those women who are too poor to bottle feed. One reported: 'Every time the baby was sucking my breasts I felt like throwing up' (Koricho 2008 quoted in Blystad and Moland 2009 p.111).

This anxiety and the self-loathing that often accompanies it may even limit the milk supply itself. Under normal circumstances the baby would be given supplementary food, but this 'mixed feeding' is against the medical guidelines. The experiences of one Tanzanian mother offer an illustration of the complex

---

For a detailed account of the scientific debates about HIV and breastfeeding and a history of guidelines see Moland et al. (2010) and Coutsoudis et al. (2008).

challenges faced by so many as they struggle to follow these recommendations. Since she could not afford formula, Eli was advised that she must only breastfeed:

> She was upset and frightened but felt she had no choice … After two months she felt extremely tired. She did not have enough food to eat and worried that her milk was not sufficient for the baby … Her mother who visited said Eli had to introduce complementary food – otherwise the child would not grow. Eli recalled the argument with her mother; 'She said I would kill her grandchild.' (Blystad and Moland 2009 p.110)

For those who opt for substitute milk, similar problems are likely to arise. First, and most importantly, in a heavily affected area the fact that a child is not being breastfed is frequently read by others as an indicator of HIV in the mother (and possibly the child). As a result women may try to conceal their feeding practices, though this is difficult in what are often close-knit communities. One South African woman described her attempts to avoid disclosure: 'when they see me coming with the tins they laugh at me, they say I have HIV, and I tell them I do not have AIDS it is because I have TB and a lot of people know I have TB and I hide the tins' (Doherty et al. 2006 p.94).

A number of studies in African settings have shown that those women who are living with the father of their baby will usually expect him to pay for the milk (Tijou Traore et al. 2009). However if they are still keeping their status secret it will be difficult to get the money without declaring that they are HIV positive. Some women may be offered substitute milk from the PMTCT programme but supplies are often irregular, causing great anxiety. Health workers may not treat the mothers well and they are forced to go away with nothing to feed the baby. Mulu, who was homeless and lived on the streets in Tanzania, revealed how she tried to keep her baby from becoming malnourished: 'Every day I go to the big traffic lights in town where the cars stop and I beg. I carry my daughter on my back and when people see her they give me a few coins so that I can buy cow's milk to feed her' (Blystad and Moland 2009 p.112).

Thus far research on these difficulties has focussed mainly on the experiences of African mothers. However we can glimpse similar problems in another setting from a study carried out in the Indian state of Tamil Nadu (van Hollen 2011). Here poor women face comparable dilemmas, but they are exacerbated by the importance of breasts and breast milk in the context of Tamil culture. Both Tamil language and identity are seen to be transmitted through breast milk, while formula feeding is negatively associated with the British colonisers (van Hollen 2011 p.508). Hence the failure to breastfeed will weigh even more heavily against women. Importantly however, the study also describes how some women are beginning to make an active choice for formula feeding not only for the sake of their children but also as a form of resistance against discrimination: '… some HIV positive women are actively negotiating and refashioning the discourse of global health agendas and international rights movements in local idioms to serve their own interests' (van Hollen 2011 p.515).

Moving through Motherhood

Pregnancy and childbirth can therefore be very challenging for positive women, especially those with few resources. These challenges are likely to intensify since, as we have seen, only a minority currently receive ART to sustain their own health. Hence both the current patterns of service delivery and the circumstances of many women's lives will severely limit the benefits they can achieve from PMTCT programmes. Many will have to battle with serious health problems of their own while raising their children who may also be positive. In 2010 only about 23 per cent of those under 15 were covered by provision of ART, and an estimated 250,000 children under 15 died from AIDS-related causes (WHO, UNICEF and UNAIDS 2011).

A recent study in South Africa was one of the first to explore women's experiences of the loss of a young child to AIDS. The women were living in very deprived circumstances and most talked of the immense hardships they faced in coping with their own illness while trying to care for a dying child, often as single parents. Many described their situation as very lonely and the distress (and often guilt) at the child's eventual death could be overwhelming:

> When my daughter was sick, I was the breadwinner. Even though she was sick, I had to leave her alone and go and sell vegetables so that we can have food on the table. I did not have anyone to help her. I used to think that if there someone at home working and bringing in income, I was going to provide better care to my daughter. I was going to stay at home and look after her. That is what makes me feel guilty and have lots of regrets. I did not provide better care. (Demmer 2010 p.4)

There is evidence that for many women, concern about their own and their children's health is further exacerbated by hostile attitudes from those around them. A study from Vietnam indicated that women are often marginalised within the family once their HIV status has been revealed. Indeed some are not even allowed to care for their babies, with this role being taken over by mothers-in-law. One woman explained: 'She is afraid that if I take care of the baby, there will be more risk of him contracting the disease. She has been with the baby since he was born. I just help wash up or do the vegetables' (Brickley et al. 2009 p.1201).

Positive mothers in Malawi have also reported being abused because of their status: 'They say look at the nevirapine baby referring to your baby because they know that HIV positive mothers are given nevirapine during labour … They give us all sorts of names like "HIV person" (Wakachirombo) surviving on top-ups' (ARVs) (Østergaard and Bula 2010 p.219).

In a recent study in the very different setting of Scotland, most women with older children reported that the cultural identity of 'good mother' had been the central focus of their lives (Wilson 2007). This had meant protecting the children as much as possible from the reality of their mother's illness, and for many it also involved the denial of intimate relationships for themselves: 'The women's narratives were suffused by motherhood. It seemed that their identities as mothers were hugely significant to their perception and experience of their illness ... the respondents' narratives further pointed to the complexity of their identities as mothers, incorporating elements of both fragility and strength' (Wilson 2007 p.611).

If their children were also HIV positive then ensuring their survival had obviously been a key goal. But where (as in most cases) the children were negative the mothers' main aim was to ensure their own survival so long as they were needed. For most this meant living until the child reached the age of 16. As one woman described: '[Sixteen is] when they're responsible for themselves [...] they dinnae need anyone else to be their guardian or anything [...] It's like cutting the umbilical cord' (Wilson 2007 p.618).

For some of the women in the study this became such a powerful influence on their lives that they became concerned about themselves when their children were approaching adulthood: 'When they turned 16 I got a bit paranoid, you know, cos I thought "have I lived to this age for that reason and now am I gonnae die?" you know because my *quest* is over' (Wilson 2007 p.619).

Thus what has been called 'empty nest syndrome' will have a particular poignancy for most of these HIV positive mothers (Murphy et al. 2012). On the one hand it may involve loss of physical care as well as emotional support. But, most importantly, it may diminish the centrality of motherhood in the woman's sense of herself making space for illness and fear of death to become more dominant. As one American woman expressed it:

> Being a mother is one of the things that ... gives me a sense of normality. You know what I mean? Like ... I'm able to do the normal things that other people do, being a parent, doing the everyday, day to day things a mother does. And in a way, staying busy all the time it does allow me not so much time on HIV. I think when she's gone I'll have a whole lot more time to think about it. (Murphy et al. 2012 p.395)

Conclusion

This chapter has shown how the combination of HIV and motherhood will often pose dramatic challenges, especially in situations of scarcity. Most (but not all) potential parents in the global north can now benefit from a range of material, medical and social support. This will help to optimise their own well-being and that of their children. However, for the majority of those in the global south, HIV infection will still create severe constraints on what many regard as their most important life project: becoming parents. This will be denied entirely for some. Others may succeed in the physical acts of conception, pregnancy and childbirth but may be severely disadvantaged in their later capacity for caring for themselves and their children. Clearly, the more difficulty they have in satisfying their own basic needs the greater the harm generated by these inequalities is likely to be.

Chapter 8
Human Rights: Paths to Cosmopolitanism

Throughout this book we have illustrated the ways in which structured patterns of inequality and disadvantage worsen the lot of so many HIV positive people. They are all equal in the sense that they require the satisfaction of the same basic needs to pursue their critical interests. Hence if we accept Aristotle's famous dictum that justice requires equals to be treated equally, then the pandemic represents a particularly invidious example of global injustice. It is with this in mind that activists have turned to the discourse of human rights in demanding greater equality and justice in the provision of treatment along with the basic need satisfaction required to optimise its effectiveness. As we shall see, the language of human rights is by its very nature a language of universal entitlement. Nelson Mandela made this point with great simplicity when he spoke out about the death of his son: 'AIDS is no longer a disease, it is a human rights issue'.[1]

Human Rights: An Overview

It was the recognition of injustice in so many aspects of society, along with the terrible destruction of the Second World War, that led many nations to collaborate in developing a moral framework of 'universal human rights' and creating a legal framework to ensure its implementation.[2] The 1948 Universal Declaration of Human Rights (UDHR) provided the foundational statement on the inherent dignity and worth of the individual, something that no group should abuse. All were said to be of equal value and entitled to equal treatment on the basis of their common humanity. Article 25 specifically stated that: 'Everyone has the right to a standard of living adequate for the health and well-being of himself and his family, including food, clothing, housing and medical care and necessary social services.'[3]

This initial formulation was ratified in 1976 with Article 12 of the International Covenant on Economic Social and Cultural Rights (ICESCR), which enunciated 'the right of everyone to the enjoyment of the highest attainable standard of physical

---

1   http://www.southafrica.info/mandela/mandela-son.html.

2   For an excellent account of these developments and other issues discussed in this chapter see Wolff (2012 Chapters 1–3).

3   Note the close overlap between this list and the 'intermediate needs' described in Chapter 1, the appropriate satisfaction of which will be necessary to optimise the satisfaction of the basic needs for survival/physical health and autonomy.

and mental health'.[4] Thus it was not just health care but (attainable) health itself that was formally placed on the human rights agenda. In the same year the International Covenant on Civil and Political Rights (ICCPR) was put in place to protect individuals from various forms of discrimination and persecution.

To the degree that many nations have formally endorsed these Covenants, they both form a part of international law. What this means in principle is that nations have an obligation to *respect* the rights of their citizens, avoiding prejudicial and unfair discriminatory practice. Further, citizens must be *protected* from human rights abuses, however inflicted. Finally, there is a requirement on nations to *fulfil* these obligations to the best of their abilities.[5] What these duties entail as regards the highest attainable standard of health was further articulated by General Comment 14 in 2000 from the Committee charged with monitoring and providing guidance to the ICESCR.[6]

It was recognised that certain 'minimum core obligations' should be the primary focus of discharging these duties, obligations closely linked to the satisfaction of intermediate needs described in Chapter 1. Equally, it was recognised that at any given time all nations could not attain the same standards of health for all of their citizens. Poverty and lack of resources may be key factors here (along sometimes with corruption and inefficiency). For this reason, General Comment 14 also embraced the notion of 'progressive realisation' along similar lines to our earlier discussion of the 'adequacy' of intermediate need satisfaction, also in Chapter 1.

Thus the notion of human rights has been tied from a very early stage not only to the basic need for autonomy (including critical autonomy) but also to the satisfaction of the basic need for survival/physical health. If such rights are taken seriously, the entitlements and claims associated with them trump the preferences of others even when these others are in a majority (Dworkin 1984 pp.153–67; Dworkin 1977 p.xi). This is why the moral focus of human rights entitlement is on the individual and the responsibilities for human rights delivery are on the nation state rather than the other way around. It is hardly surprising, therefore, that throughout the world the concept of human rights has been at the forefront of struggles against poverty associated with various forms of international, national and cultural injustice as well as shaping much of the advocacy relating to HIV and AIDS.

This was reflected in the 2001 UN Declaration of Commitment on HIV and AIDS and the Political Declaration on HIV and AIDS (2006) and consolidated in the *Handbook on HIV and Human Rights for National Human Rights Institutions* (UNAIDS 2007).[7] While there is no legally binding international treaty or covenant that specifically addresses HIV, there are a number of human rights treaties and declarations that have major significance for the effectiveness and morality of the

---

4   We will normally refer to these as 'economic and social rights' unless circumstances require otherwise.

5   http://www.ohchr.org/en/professionalinterest/Pages/InternationalLaw.aspx.

6   http://www.unhchr.ch/tbs/doc.nsf/(symbol)/E.C.12.2000.4.En.

7   http://data.unaids.org/pub/Report/2007/jc1367-handbookhiv_en.pdf.

response to the pandemic. These include the Convention on the Elimination of all Forms of Discrimination Against Women (CEDAW) as well as the Convention on the Rights of the Child (CRC).[8] The latter has been particularly influential in national attempts to minimise mother to child transmission.

Much has been achieved through the use of these various institutional mechanisms of human rights as well the aspirational power of their associated rhetoric. The moral significance of the pandemic was formally recognised in 1996 with the creation of UNAIDS and the issuing of the *International Guidelines on HIV/AIDS and Human Rights* in the same year.[9] The importance of non-discrimination and equal treatment in the delivery of services was emphasised as well as the active participation of relevant populations in planning and evaluating care. These developments reflected the continuing demands of activists who were taking up the idea of human rights in a number of different ways, and it is no accident that this period began to witness increasing funding for HIV and AIDS research and treatment.

It was clear from the early stages of the US epidemic that many positive gay men were receiving immoral, insensitive and hostile treatment at the end of their lives. Jonathan Mann (Director of the Global Programme for AIDS at WHO) played a key role along with colleagues in placing this on the international agenda (Fee and Parry 2008). As a result the reality of 'stigma' was increasingly accepted as a moral harm from which positive individuals should have the right to be legally protected (Bayer and Edington 2009).

At the same time there was extensive debate about whether or not positive individuals should be entitled to what could be seen as specially tailored rights within the clinical context. While they clearly had the same rights to informed consent and confidentiality as anyone else, it was argued that the nature of their illness meant that these should be taken a stage further. Thus the notion of 'voluntary counselling and testing' and the associated right to remain ignorant of infection emerged.

Lively discussion also took place about whether or not the partners of those diagnosed positive had the moral and/or legal right to be informed of the potential threat posed to them. In the early years it was generally thought that their rights were trumped by what was perceived to be the absolute right to confidentiality of those who were positive.[10] However recent years have seen the emergence of a much more nuanced position on this debate highlighting the challenges that may arise when an individual's right to privacy has to be balanced with the right of a partner to make an informed choice about whether or not to risk exposure to the virus.[11]

---

8   http://www.un.org/womenwatch/daw/cedaw; http://www.unicef.org.uk/UNICEFs-Work/Our-mission/UN-Convention.

9   http://data.unaids.org/Publications/IRC-pub07/jc1252-internguidelines_en.pdf.

10   It was widely argued that disclosure would open them up to hostility and hence dissuade them from seeking care.

11   For a more detailed discussion of this point see Chapter 6.

As more effective treatment began to emerge, there was a marked shift in the focus of advocacy towards the right of all individuals to access whatever therapy was available. Indeed many called for those who were positive to have the right to participate in the potentially hazardous clinical trials taking place in the US in the early years. Campaigns for the right to treatment spread rapidly as widening access in rich countries highlighted the exclusion of millions in poorer settings from these potential benefits. Activists, international organisations and charities all stressed the moral imperative of guaranteeing access for all in need.[12] Indeed, as with legal claims with respect to discrimination against those who are positive, it was also argued that treatment for HIV and AIDS should be accepted as the legal right of all infected individuals (Novogrodsky 2009).

Viewed from another perspective, activists have also identified specific abuses of human rights as leading to HIV infection itself. Here the main focus has been on what we could broadly define as the right to physical security, including the failure to protect women from gender violence[13] or to provide men in prison with condoms.[14] Similar abuses have been identified in the case of injecting drug users denied the right to clean needles.[15] While standards may still be internationally variable, there can be little doubt that there has been considerable improvement on these issues in some parts of the world in recent years.

It is clear then that human rights discourse and practice have been (and continue to be) of enormous value in shaping a coherent ethical response to the pandemic because of their identification with reasoned argument about defined moral and legal claims. But, as we shall see, there are still many challenges to be faced if their full potential is to be realised (Gruskin and Tarantola 2008; London 2002; Stemple 2008). The most important of these relate to the inherent contradictions between the goals of equality and equity that are central to human rights-based institutions and the very different values that shape the unequal and unfair worlds of national and global capitalism in which they are embedded.

Constraints on the Human Rights Approach in Practice

Most of the responsibility for the upholding of human rights currently falls to individual nation states in respect of their own citizens. Yet there is huge diversity between countries in their access to resources as well as their levels of political commitment to the underlying principles of equality and social justice. This in turn raises complex legal and philosophical issues concerning the universality of

---

12   http://www.thebody.com/content/66751/tag-at-20-early-campaigns.html;   http://www.thebody.com/content/69487/on-a-darkling-plain-the-years-of-despair.html. Also see Wolff (2012 pp.53–9).

13   http://www.paho.org/english/ad/ge/Viol-HIV_FS0705.pdf.

14   http://www.avert.org/prisons-hiv-aids.htm.

15   http://www.avert.org/needle-exchange.htm.

human rights in practice. With this in mind, the bright sunlight of those early UN declarations and covenants has run into some dark clouds.

Within the UN system it is individual nations that have responsibility as collective duty-bearers. Yet not all countries have signed up to all the relevant conventions.[16] And even when they have, the mechanisms for enforcement are limited. Countries are expected to report regularly to monitoring bodies and the resulting 'constructive dialogues' are intended to highlight deficiencies in practice. In recent years this process has been enhanced by the introduction of 'shadow reports', usually produced by non-governmental organisations (NGOs) as a critical commentary on the official picture. However there is a woeful lack of information about actual or potential abuses, especially in relation to economic and social rights, and there may be little opportunity for effective legal redress if countries are not compliant.[17]

Individuals can also raise their own human rights claims, which can be potentially adjudicated legally or reviewed in other ways in a range of national, regional and international settings (Gruskin et al. 2007b). These have increased in recent years and, as we have seen, have had some impact on national policy and law (Mason Meier 2012; Novogrodsky 2009). However the ease with which they can be mounted is highly variable. Moreover, even when individual claims can and have been legally adjudicated, there may be a lack of congruence between them and wider population needs. Wolff notes as follows: 'it is claimed in Brazil there is now an "epidemic of litigation" under the heading of the right to life and health, for access to therapies for not only HIV/AIDS but also for diabetes, Alzheimer's, and multiple sclerosis, among other conditions' (Wolff 2012 p.38).

To make things even more complex, HIV and AIDS care in many of the poorest and most affected nations is funded through aid from other countries, international organisations or philanthropic institutions. The terms of this aid often include conditionalities that may reflect the strategic interests or moral values of the donors themselves as much as or more than the needs of recipients. This has been especially evident in the highly contested arena of sexual and reproductive rights (Gruskin et al. 2007b). The anti-prostitution stance of the US President's Emergency Plan for AIDS Relief (PEPFAR), for example, has meant a denial of rights to both positive and negative sex workers. Similarly the required focus on abstinence and faithfulness in many aid programmes has led to significant limitations on individual choice and hence on overall effectiveness.

In many settings, the special needs of women and children have (correctly) been highlighted. But the rights of other potentially vulnerable groups have been largely ignored (Stemple 2008). Heterosexual men, for example, are usually treated instrumentally in most rights-based HIV strategies (Peacock et al. 2009).

---

16   For example, among some others the United States itself did not sign up to the ICESCR.

17   Backman et al. (2008). Also see discussion in Wolff (2012 pp.32–5).

That is to say they are mentioned only in relation to their significance for the rights of women with little or no attention being paid to their own rights or needs.[18]

The rights of men who have sex with men (MSM) have received especially low priority in many settings. This reflects in part the homophobic values in many of their own domestic environments, but it is also a consequence of ambivalent attitudes towards same-sex desires among some aid donors (Jurgens et al. 2010; Persson et al. 2011). Thus many policies supposedly based on a human rights model have ended up being less than fully universal in their approach.[19]

These problems are exacerbated by the limited financial and organisational capacity of many nation states to respond to wider human rights claims even if they have the political will to do so (which many do not). They may be unable to marshal the necessary resources, while at the same time their sovereign powers are declining by contrast with the growing strength of non-governmental entities whose cooperation may be necessary if human rights claims are to be met.[20] Located at the heart of the global economy, multinational corporations in particular are able to exercise significant control over the rights-related policies of individual countries (Koivusalo 2011).

The realities of an increasingly globalised world have highlighted important questions about the relationship between individual rights and nationality. Put simply, should everyone everywhere have the same human rights or should they be dependent on an individual's citizenship status? This issue has been extensively debated in recent years, with some wishing to limit the scope of human rights to specific national jurisdictions while others take what has been called a 'cosmopolitan' position. The latter argue that human rights must be treated as universal so that each individual will have an equal chance of having their basic need for survival/physical health and autonomy met (Brock 2009 Part 1).

Thus there are many practical (and ultimately political) challenges that need to be faced if the human rights approach to HIV and AIDS is to reach its full potential, and these will be discussed further in Chapter 9. However it will be important to start by exploring in more detail the conceptual foundations of the discourse of human rights itself. Too often advocates (and others) have simply taken their existence for granted without any formal attempt at moral justification. This can lead to confusion, especially when the same 'rights talk' is invoked by stakeholders as diverse as the World Bank, transnational corporations and anti-globalisation movements. As one commentator has put it: 'the concept of human rights has become a vessel for moral frustrations and idealism: the dominant moral

---

18   Obviously any attempt to remedy this situation would pose challenges to the promotion of gender equality, but these potential paradoxes need to be faced rather than ignored (Doyal and Payne 2011).

19   This issue is discussed in more detail in Chapter 9.

20   This again is the pragmatic background to the 'progressive realisation' clause concerning the highest attainable right to health referred to in General Comment 14. http://www.unhchr.ch/tbs/doc.nsf/(symbol)/E.C.12.2000.4.En.

discourse of our time. That said, its influence remains profoundly uneven both geographically and socially (Gready 2008 p.735).

If human rights supporters are to move forward in their campaigns for greater equality and justice, it will be essential that they are armed with the most effective arguments. We have seen that the ICCPR and the ICESCR respectively stipulate two different categories of rights. The civil and political rights of the former concern the range of *freedoms that individuals have to do things* they choose: for example, to pursue their critical and other interests provided that in the process no one else is harmed in ways deemed to be socially unacceptable. Conversely, the economic and social rights of the latter relate to cognitive, emotional and social deprivations that *restrict individual freedoms to pursue such interests.* There is considerable debate about the implications of distinguishing between human rights in this way, debate that can have important consequences for activism and policy concerning HIV and AIDS. The remainder of this chapter will explore these issues in a little more depth through outlining some of the arguments from which the concept of universal human rights continues to draw its moral strength.[21]

First Principles: What Are 'Human Rights'?

Human rights are (moral or legal) 'claims' possessed by 'right-bearers' that corresponding 'duty-bearers' must take seriously.[22] If, for example, freedom of speech is accepted as a 'strict' *moral right,* then individuals have a moral claim that others must not stop them from speaking, provided that recognised boundaries are observed for not harming others in the process. In this sense a strict right corresponds to a 'perfect' duty. Rights and duties always correspond in this manner. If the right has *legal* status within a relevant jurisdiction then any attempt by the duty-bearer to impede the right-bearer could lead to litigation or even criminal prosecution. Strict legal rights of this kind are said to be judicially 'enforceable'.[23]

We have already outlined the difference in international law between civil and political rights on the one hand and economic and social rights on the other. In philosophical attempts to clarify this difference an important distinction has been made between 'negative' and 'positive' rights (Fried 1978 p.110). The 'negative right' of freedom of speech entails only the 'negative duty' of non-interference, so that on the face of it duty-bearers will be required to do nothing except allow right-

---

21   Readers who find these more philosophical sections especially interesting can use the references to explore related issues in more depth.

22   For an excellent general introduction to the concepts and literature concerning human rights, see Human Rights, *Stanford Encyclopedia of Philosophy*, http://plato. stanford.edu. Two further classic and readable analyses are Nickle (2007) and Shue (1996).

23   Obviously, people can disagree about who has a right to what. Using the language of rights and duties does not settle moral arguments, but it puts them into a particular context.

bearers to go about their business; again, so long as no one else is unacceptably harmed in the process. Specific examples would be the right to freedom of movement, to buy and sell property and to not be discriminated against on the grounds of arbitrary prejudice. Thus 'negative rights' are identical to 'civil and political rights' since they form the bedrock for sustainable and coherent social cooperation. They were the rights most stressed in the evolution of the concept of human rights and most commonly incorporated into national law and institutionally enforced.[24] In this context they are often referred to as first-generation rights.[25]

By contrast, positive rights entail 'positive duties'. They are claims for direct assistance from duty-bearers rather than just their negative forbearance. Such claims usually involve the right to goods and services of various kinds that individuals cannot provide for themselves. This may be because they are too poor or too ill to acquire them or because the 'public good' is perceived to demand their universal provision. Adequate health care and education are good examples. Hence positive rights are identical to 'economic and social rights'. They are referred to as second-generation rights because they primarily gained international traction through the UDHR and the ICESCR.[26]

Like negative rights, all claims to positive rights potentially entail strict or 'perfect' duties on the part of others, either directly or through institutions supported by taxation. This is very different from the 'imperfect' duty of giving charity, which will not be obligatory in the same sense though may still command strong moral force. We will return to the distinction between perfect and imperfect duties shortly. For now, its potential relevance to arguments about the strength of individual entitlement to basic need satisfaction should be clear.

So if positive economic and social rights are taken seriously by nation states, they will be incorporated into law and potentially enforced in the same way as negative civil and political rights. For example, if a woman has a positive right to appropriate antenatal care then she should be able to obtain this from a designated institution on the basis of need rather than her ability to pay. The resources for providing such care will come from legal and enforceable taxation on other citizens as duty-bearers. This is why positive rights are at the heart of all 'welfare states'. If the relevant institutions do not adequately fulfil their duties through meeting welfare claims embodied in law, legitimate right-bearers can in principle seek enforcement through the courts. The same applies to the 'right to health' institutionalised within the UDHR and the ICESCR, although claims and adjudication can only be made through mechanisms established by nations that have endorsed the relevant treaties.

---

24   Except of course in countries governed by authoritarian regimes where, for example, freedom of speech or freedom from torture (another negative right) may be very low on the list of national priorities.

25   http://www.globalization101.org/three-generations-of-rights.

26   See previous footnote.

As we have seen throughout this book, meeting the needs of people with HIV or AIDS can raise issues related to what can be called both negative and positive rights. To take a simple example, the failure to protect a female sex worker known to be HIV positive from angry neighbours would be a violation of her negative (or civil and political) right to protection from physical harm. However the failure to treat the same woman with a CD4 count of 200 when antiretroviral therapy (ART) was available would be a violation of her positive (or economic and social) right to appropriate health care. Where such laws do not exist, the claim may 'only' be moral but it may well provide the basis for campaigns to make it legal.

This distinction between negative and positive rights is widely used in much of the relevant philosophical literature and does offer a neat framework into which we can fit different types of claims and the moral or legal responses associated with them. But no matter how convenient it happens to be, this typology of rights is by no means as simple as it may seem. For example, as we shall see, the ability of a duty-bearer to execute their negative civil and political duties may be dependent on the degree to which their own positive economic and social rights are respected by others.

As a result many of the most recent UN documents appear to elide the distinction between positive and negative rights through summarising state responsibilities together in the one phrase 'respect, protect and fulfil human rights'. The obligation to 'respect' means that states must refrain from interfering with or curtailing the enjoyment of human rights. The duty to 'protect' requires states to protect individuals and groups against human rights abuses, while the responsibility to 'fulfil' means that states must take positive action to ensure that the basic human rights of their citizens are ensured. Yet note that when the phrase 'respect, protect and fulfil' is applied to specific circumstances it will concern *either* negative civil and political rights *or* positive economic and social rights or both.[27]

We will return to further discussion of these distinctions later in this chapter and in Chapter 9. But in the meantime we need to address the more basic question of how to justify the existence of any rights at all. Are human rights 'real' or are they just rhetorical devices? Do they apply to everyone or just to a favoured few? And how do we coherently answer the question: who has a right to what? Who is obligated to give what to whom and how much? A number of different arguments have been put forward to defend the existence of universal rights. As we shall see, these are not simply abstract philosophical debates but are central to discussion about the implementation of rights-based policies of all kinds, including those concerning HIV and AIDS.

Good Reasons to Believe in the Universality of Human Rights

There can be no doubt that the existence of universal rights is endorsed by almost all nations. But why? The most immediate historical reason for the formulation of

---

27   As an example see http://www.humnrightsimpact.org/hria-guide/glossary-of-terms/resources/view/7/user hria terms.

such rights might be seen to be the Second World War. But moral outrage alone is not enough. Nor does the existence of the Universal Declaration itself provide the ultimate justification. The fact that the existence of a right is stated in an impressive document does not make it true. Hence we need to look more closely at various moral justifications lying behind the discourse of human rights. We will examine three major arguments used to achieve this.

The first group of commentators base their commitment to the notion of universal human rights on the fact that the conditions for basic need satisfaction are the same for everyone, whatever their circumstances. As we saw in Chapter 1, it is in the critical interests of all of us to actively engage in the social interaction that enables us to discover who we are and what we can be. Through the exercise of our autonomy or 'agency' we can attempt to live what we believe to be a good life. But our success in this endeavour will be proportional to the adequacy or 'sufficiency' to which our basic needs are satisfied.

This has led many to the conclusion that all individuals must be accorded the same level of entitlement to the satisfaction of these basic needs as a matter of universal right. Such arguments assume that the satisfaction of shared 'interests', 'capabilities' or 'dimensions of well-being' go to the heart of what it means to be human and what is necessary for every individual human to try to realise their potential to act and interact in the world (Nussbaum 2000 Chapters 2, 4 ,5 ; Powers and Faden 2006 pp.15–49; Sen 2009 pp.231–47, 355–90). Thus if we claim that as individuals we require our basic needs for survival/physical health and autonomy to be satisfied to optimise our own capabilities and well-being, why should this not apply to everyone else who is human in the same sense that we are? Depending on cultural variations and different perceptions of critical interests, the details of such rights claims may differ. However, they will all focus on some conception of universal and adequate basic need satisfaction.

However a second group of supporters of universal human rights base their arguments on a very different approach. They suggest that in practice there is less commonality of belief between individuals than the former argument implies. On the contrary, there are frequent disputes both between and within nations about the validity of particular moral claims, especially when they are defined as 'rights'. This can lead to a situation where justice is denied because of a failure to agree either about moral goals themselves or about those who should be treated as moral 'equals'.

This is powerfully illustrated by continuing disagreement about sexual and reproductive rights, where sex and gender differences continue to be used by some to justify radically different entitlements to a range of resources for women and for men (Doyal and Payne 2011). The same situation occurs when individuals are denied medical or other resources because they are HIV positive.

In light of such problems, this second group of commentators argue for the development of a more overarching approach to human rights through the creation of some form of 'social contract'. Their basis for such claims takes the form of a 'thought experiment'. Hypothetical representatives of a wide range of communities are assumed to meet in what John Rawls called an 'original position'. They would be armed only with what he perceived to be knowledge about the critical interests common to all human beings and the basic needs that would have to be met if these were to be acted upon (Rawls 1972 pp.118–66). Their task would then be to create a constitution which would protect those interests for everyone.

More importantly they would meet under a 'veil of ignorance' and would not know what would happen to them when the deliberations ended – for example, neither the country/culture to which they would belong nor their socio-economic status, age, health or sex/gender. Most importantly in the context of our current concerns, they would not know whether they themselves would be infected with HIV.

Since these representatives would be unable to see into the future, reason (as well as self-interest) would dictate that they design a constitution to include both negative and positive rights for all, including those with life-threatening diseases. This would protect the satisfaction of the basic needs necessary for the potential well-being of all individuals whatever their circumstances (Rawls 1972 pp.118–92; Brock 2009 pp.45–63; Caney 2005 pp.107–16). It is unlikely therefore that they would design a constitution that would allow widespread poverty for example, or poor health care, discrimination against women, older people or those with stigmatised social conditions. Proponents of this view argue that institutional arrangements designed on this basis are a moral requirement for a just society.[28]

The third argument put forward for justifying the existence of human rights is based on their importance in facilitating what has been called 'moral reasoning'. The successful practice of such reasoning is important for everyone since it provides the moral glue which holds social life together. Citizens with what may be ostensibly very divergent interests are enabled to negotiate their way through the resulting dilemmas while causing as little harm as possible to others. But the capability of individuals to successfully exercise such reason will be linked to the extent to which their own basic needs are met. As Jeremy Waldron correctly observes:

> Only a few heroes are capable of thinking and acting morally under conditions of oppression and terror. For most of us, such conditions – and others like the panic of starvation or exposure – overwhelm our faculties and crowd out moral deliberation. If something like this is true, then freedom and the satisfaction of basic needs may be cited as the necessary perquisites for morality. And they may be claimed as rights for everyone from whom moral action and social responsibility are reasonably expected. (Waldron 1988 p.731)

---

28   Interestingly, however, although there is a consensus about what it means to argue for a social contract using the methodology of the original position, different conclusions can be reached about the universality and importance of economic and social rights vs. civil and political rights. For an excellent summary of these debates see Brock 2009 Part 1. The existence of such disagreement underlines the importance of exploring the philosophical questions to be raised in the next section of this chapter.

This link between need satisfaction and the capability for moral reasoning and subsequent action should not be taken to imply that those who are disadvantaged will never be able to act morally. Many certainly do so. But 'ought implies can' and they may be unable to do this with any degree of consistency. It follows that if individuals are to be expected to fulfil their duties and to treat others in morally acceptable ways, they must be physically, emotionally, intellectually and socially in a position to do so. And this will only be possible if their own basic needs are met to an adequate level. Not surprisingly, poverty breeds not only disease but also prejudice, misunderstanding, distress, desperation and anger. The most effective way of combating this will be through the creation of a universal framework of human rights that will protect the satisfaction of those needs for every individual (Doyal and Gough 1991 pp.91–115). Thomas Pogge makes the same point:

> A commitment to human rights involves one in recognizing that human persons with a past or potential future ability to engage in moral conversation and practice have certain basic needs, and that these needs give rise to weighty moral demands. The object of each of these basic human needs is the object of a human right. (Pogge 2008 p.64)

This will apply across all areas of social activity and has particular resonance in the context of daily life with HIV and AIDS. We have seen, for example, that women who believe it is their moral duty to disclose their status to sexual partners may feel unable to do so out of fear when their need for physical security is not met. Similarly, parents who wish to adhere to an ART protocol in order to provide appropriate care for their children may be prevented from doing so by the failure to meet their need for food security.[29] Thus the recognition of the universal right to basic need satisfaction should be endorsed not only for the good of the individuals concerned but also in order to optimise their capacity to carry out their responsibilities as duty-bearers in their moral interaction with others.

Debates continue about the value of such arguments in defence of universal human rights, and indeed there are still further arguments on offer.[30] All of these can be seen to reinforce each other in providing a strong foundation for rights-based practice and advocacy, whether in the context of HIV and AIDS or more

---

29 For a variety of similar examples of the problematic imposition of duties on those who are practically unable to fulfil them see the discussion of 'therapeutic citizenship' in Chapter 4 and also the last section of Chapter 6 on ethical dilemmas in sexual activity.

30 For example, Jürgen Habermas bases his justification for the existence of universal rights on what he calls an 'ideal speech situation' designed to optimise rational decision making about moral and other issues. The central idea is that if the impediments for such collective decision making are removed, it will be clear to decision makers that negative and positive rights should be respected and institutionalised. For these and similar arguments see Caney (2005 pp.28–9, 68–70). This idea will be further discussed in the next chapter when we evaluate the morality and rationality of distributive justice in health care.

generally. However the validity of these arguments is not accepted by all. Hence it will also be important that we explore some of the most common opposing views. This will provide a valuable preparation for future advocacy surrounding universal access to HIV care and, perhaps most important of all, for the wider social change that will necessarily accompany it.

Challenges to the Universality of Human Rights

As we have seen, the wording of the ICESCR includes what has been called a 'progressive realisation clause', meaning that national compliance with the covenant is required only as resources permit. As Hein and Kohlmorgen comment:

> The 'right to health' is codified in slightly different formulations in a number of other international agreements. As such it constitutes binding international law but it is widely seen as an example of 'soft law' which corresponds to the principles of basic human rights but is certainly also far from being an obligation enforceable by any institutionalized process. (Hein and Kohlmorgen 2008 p.84)

There is little chance of these social and economic rights being respected without significant redistribution of resources and power both within and between countries. Yet the current circumstances make that hard to achieve, especially since many do not take seriously the implication in General Comment 14 that more wealthy nations have a strict duty to provide aid to those who are poorer.[31] Here we will outline and critically review three major arguments that are commonly used to resist global redistribution through the universal implementation of human rights (Hunter and Dawson 2011 pp.77–88). This will involve a defence of the 'cosmopolitan' approach to human rights and its importance in tackling the HIV and AIDS pandemic.

1. Libertarianism: Non-Existence of Positive Social and Economic Rights

The first challenge to universal human rights is based on the notion of libertarianism and is linked to neo-liberal or neo-conservative economic and social policy. 'Libertarians' do accept the duty of the state to protect negative or civil and political rights: indeed they see these as universal. This is not surprising since, as we have noted, such freedoms are part of the necessary foundation for the functioning of all societies, particularly in protecting life and property. Moreover they are assumed to require relatively little from individual citizens except non-interference with the legal and non-harmful actions of others.

Positive economic and social rights on the other hand will place an obligatory and sizeable burden on taxpayers, which libertarians see as an unjust intrusion on

---

31   See footnote 6.

their freedom of choice. They claim that it is only through their own initiative and efforts that 'better-off' individuals have been able to build up wealth. Why then should they be forced through taxation to pay for the health, education and welfare of those who did not try as hard? According to libertarians, such provision should not be required of them even in relation to the most minimal 'safety nets' such as the provision of basic health care (Nozick 1974; Narveson 2000).

Since libertarians do not believe that taxpayers should be forced to pay for the minimal need satisfaction of the poor in their own countries, they will certainly find it unacceptable that they should be required to do so for those to whom they have little emotional attachment. This is not to suggest that libertarians would never be convinced by the moral argument that they should be charitable towards the vulnerable wherever they may live. No doubt some do give generously. But this does not count as support for positive economic and social rights and vulnerable recipients can only hope that those who are better off will be generous in their hour of need (Narveson 2003, 2004). So how can we respond to these arguments?

Counterargument: The Myth of Self-Sufficiency

The libertarian rejection of positive rights rests on two main assumptions. The first is that individuals should have total control over their income and wealth on the grounds that it is they (or their families) who have earned it. However this assumes that the race of life is run on a level playing field when it clearly is not. Many different forms of arbitrary disadvantage (including bad luck) will limit what individuals will be able to achieve. The only way to limit such unfairness is to create a society where negative civil and political rights are protected and a range of organisations are given the strict duty and adequate resources to ensure sufficient basic need satisfaction necessary for dignity, fairness and acceptable levels of opportunity for all (Gilabert 2006; Kymlicka 2002 Chapter 4).

The second problem with the libertarian argument is that their assumption that civil and political rights can be provided to all citizens at little cost is incorrect. Even these so-called negative rights will require expensive agencies such as police, fire services and highway departments. Moreover even these will not function effectively unless citizens are educated enough to understand the moral importance of their civil and political duties and healthy enough to act on them. They will also require access to sufficient resources to ensure that they will not be tempted to break the law in order to survive (Shue 1996 pp.13–87; Waldron 1993 pp.24–5).

Thus respect for negative rights generates what Waldron calls 'waves of duties' towards individual citizens, highlighting again the practical impossibility of separating negative (civil and political) and positive (social and economic) rights (Waldron 1993 pp.211–13). Charity alone will not be adequate to meet these needs. Yet a failure to do so will mean that the poor and vulnerable are unlikely to identify with the moral values of personal freedom and security so valued by libertarians.

And in a globalising world this will run the risk of increasing civil unrest both nationally and internationally. The resulting insecurity and social instability may not just pose a threat of physical violence but may also generate health hazards that do not respect national borders.

In short, if libertarians wish to continue to enjoy the civil and political freedoms that they hold so dear (and as a result of which many are able to lead a high-quality life) they will need to recognise the universal economic and social rights of all those on whom their security (and their wealth) depends. And these rights will need to be taken seriously.

2. Liberal Nationalism: Bordering Human Rights

A second group of commentators base their argument for restrictions on the universality of human rights, on what they see as respect for individual autonomy within the context of particular 'nationhood'. Each nation has a common language, a history, a set of dominant cultural beliefs about what makes a good citizen and a set of political institutions within which social and economic policies are developed and legitimated. As we saw in Chapter 1, women and men discover who they are and what they are capable of within these national and cultural settings in which they are born and grow up. Hence they provide the backdrop against which most individuals make choices about their critical interests.

Yael Tamir argues that if these nations incorporate democratic political institutions and respect for human rights, then the communal bonds that they create are of great value and significance (Tamir 1995 Chapters 1–5). Similarly, the group of commentators also referred to as 'liberal nationalists' believe that conceived in these terms the notion of 'nationalism' itself can avoid the negative associations that it has so often elicited in both the past and the present.[32] Indeed they argue that the common heritage of national liberal institutions expands rather than restricts the scope of personal choice. Will Kymlicka and David Miller, for example, both argue that the webs of belief associated with dominant national cultures constitute shared visions of the good that are central to reciprocal trust between individuals. Going further, they argue that democratic governance and the collective provision of welfare is impossible without a strong commitment to such ideals. Kymlicka says on democracy:

> ..., democracy requires us to trust, and to make sacrifices for, those who do not share our interests and goals ... Democracy requires the adjudication of conflicting interests, and so works best when there is some sort of common identity that transcends these conflicting interests. Within nation states, a common national identity ideally transcends (such) differences. (Kymlicka 2001 p.239)

---

32   This section draws heavily on Brock (2009), Caney (2005) and Jones (1999, Chapter 6), all of whom provide excellent commentaries on 'liberal nationalism'.

Miller makes similar comments about welfare states:

> ... the redistributive policies of the kind favoured by socialists are likely to
> demand a considerable degree of social solidarity if they are to win popular
> consent, and for that reason socialists should be more strongly committed than
> classical liberals to the nation-state as an institution that can make such solidarity
> politically effective. (Miller 1995 p.92)[33]

Miller argues that, viewed in this way, national cultures are somewhat analogous
to families. He sees them as constituting bounded communities of 'special
relationships' where: 'The duties we owe to our fellow-nationals are different
from, and more extensive than, the duties we owe to humans as such' (Miller
2000 p.27). He continues this theme, though concluding that there is no point in
striving for a universal strategy for meeting human needs based on conceptions of
universal rights. Instead such initiatives must be planned and carried out within
nation states themselves:

> We do not yet have a global community in the sense that is relevant to justice as
> distribution according to need. ... It is ... unrealistic to suppose that the choice
> lies between distributive justice world-wide and distributive justice within
> national societies; the realistic choice is between distributive justice of the latter
> sort, and distributive justice within much smaller units – families, religious
> communities, and so forth. (Miller 1988 p.648 quoted in Jones 1999 p.167)

With these ideas in mind, liberal nationalists argue that the imposition of the idea
of human rights on nations of different moral persuasions can be construed as a
threat to their sovereignty: to their right to self-determination and to the autonomy
of their citizens. Instead Miller argues that each nation must assume responsibility
(or not) for the basic need satisfaction of its own members (Miller 1995 pp.108,
191–2; Miller 1999 pp.193–7). With the exception of genocide, famine or other
forms of natural disaster, liberal nations are said to have no strict obligation to those
beyond their borders. Of course they may (and often will) choose to be generous
in offers of assistance to others but, as we saw in the case of the libertarians, this
may be based more on forms of 'national altruism' rather than strict respect for
universal economic and social rights incorporated within international law. Or, to
put it another way, such nations would claim that how they ultimately choose to
help (or not) those countries in need should remain a matter for them.

---

33   This same solidarity reinforces respect for the autonomy of minority cultures
which adhere to the core values of liberal national cultures in which they are located.
Kymlicka (1996) argues that multiculturalism would be unable to thrive within nations that
did not promote respect for indigenous cultures even when they rejected some central tenets
of the dominant national culture.

Thus for liberal nationalists the acceptance of human rights commitments can only be mediated through national cultures and associated political institutions: they cannot be regarded as universal because whatever international law or other international agreements may say in principle, choices about their own practice begin and end at home. So are the liberal nationalists right?

Counterargument: Perplexities of Moral Pluralism

It is certainly true that the cultural context within which individuals are raised will have an important impact on their perception of the good life and the strategies they will choose to achieve this. Hence these values will always need to be acknowledged and taken seriously. However there are major problems with any argument that moral principles should be inextricably linked to the dominant (or minority) culture(s) within particular nations.

First, the concept of a dominant national culture lacks clarity. While individuals living within the same nation may all accept a variety of common principles, they may not accept them all and may differ in how they interpret them. As Waldron puts it:

> [He] may live in San Francisco and be of Irish ancestry, he does not take his identity to be compromised when he learns Spanish, eats Chinese, wears clothes made in Korea, listens to arias by Verdi sung by a Maori princess on Japanese equipment, follows Ukrainian politics, and practices Buddhist meditation techniques. He is a creature of modernity, conscious of living in a mixed-up world and having a mixed-up self. (Waldron 1995 p.95)

Such existential mingling can lead to wide disagreement between citizens about who has a right to what and why. And when this occurs, notions of human rights are frequently drawn in from outside the national culture to be used as a central theme in campaigns for change.

The United States, for instance, would surely be defined as an example of a liberal nation. Yet debate continues to rage about whether or not women should be able to make their own choices about abortion. If the clock is turned back (as many are arguing for) and most terminations become illegal, the struggle that would undoubtedly ensue would be based on what were defined as the universal human rights of women irrespective of domestic cultural, political and judicial processes. The same argument will be applied to citizens without health insurance who are seriously ill and cannot get appropriate care.

Within national boundaries, the same arguments will be used by minority groups that are at odds for whatever reason with the dominant culture (Patten 1999). Liberal nationalism entails respect for such groups, ensuring their right to follow their own traditions and beliefs provided that those of the dominant national culture are also respected. But again, things become problematic in the face of cultural disagreement. Forced marriages for example; the wearing of the veil in public; female genital mutilation or the freedom to express a range of views that may offend others are all currently the subjects of debate in a number of national settings. In such circumstances, members of minority groups will frequently appeal to universal human rights – particularly to rights assumed to protect their autonomy – in order to defend their case. Ironically however this may involve them in calling upon the very discourse of rights to defend beliefs and practices which would themselves be seen as unacceptable from a human rights perspective.[34]

Second, there are also significant problems with the ambivalence of the liberal nationalist position on support for foreigners. Those writing within this tradition do acknowledge that all countries have some responsibility toward non-nationals. However there is a lack of clarity about precisely what this should involve. We have seen that Miller argues that only in extreme situations can nations be said to have strict obligations to protect the human rights of foreigners. Indeed, he argues that sometimes these countries may have only themselves to blame for what happens to them and their citizens.

This might make some sense were nations islands unto themselves, but history shows that the poverty of many nations is at least in part a result of the actions of others that are now wealthy (Caney 2005 pp.129–36; Pogge 1992). Hence it makes little moral sense to allow those social and economic entities currently configured as nations to avoid taking responsibility for identifiable breaches of the human rights of those in other nations on the grounds of some myopic (and ahistorical) version of moral national sovereignty.[35]

To understand the final problem with the liberal nationalist position we need to go back to our earlier discussion of 'moral reasoning'. Here we argued that without the requisite basic need satisfaction, individuals cannot be expected to carry out the moral duties entailed by citizenship in a sustained and consistent way. It is implicit in the notion of a national culture of reciprocal obligations that all members should be able to do as well as they can in striving for the nationally accepted vision of the 'good'. Yet this will not be possible unless the nation(s) in question ensure the satisfaction of the basic needs required for citizens to have the opportunity to do their best (Doyal and Gough 1991 pp.91–115).

It follows that the advocates of liberal nationalism cannot consistently support the right of nations to place arbitrary limitations on the basic need satisfaction of their citizens. To do this would be to deny them the chance to develop the very individual autonomy and moral reciprocity that liberal nationalists themselves argue are so central to national identity. Hence there can be no real 'nation' worth its salt unless its citizens can optimise their freedom to participate socially

---

34   For an interesting analysis of related points as regards minority religions see Nussbaum (2012).

35   For an interesting through problematic discussion of this point in relation to the United States see Koh (2003). More generally, a useful analysis of some of the complexities of the concept of sovereignty is in Shebaya (2009).

within it. Discretion in this regard cannot be justified on the grounds of national sovereignty. Without serious respect for economic and social rights, 'nationality' is transformed into little more than ideology which at its worst promulgates the pretence of intellectual and emotional unity in the face of suffering of the kind we encountered in Chapter 1 with Sumalee, Lena and Simon.

To conclude, liberal nationalism begins with understandable premises: an emphasis on the autonomy of national cultures and the way in which they shape the choices of their citizens. However, the further premise – that the scope and content of human rights should be allowed to vary between national boundaries – is problematic. If citizens within some settings are entitled to the rights enabling them to pursue their own critical interests, then why should this not apply to all citizens everywhere (Brock 2009 pp.261–70; Caney 2005 pp.85–96)? To deny the universality of such entitlement opens the door to forms of relativism that are both inconsistent with liberalism and often associated with ideological justifications of nationalism at its worst. Indeed there can be no better recent example of this than the opportunistic nationalist support of Thabo Mbeki's disastrous policies concerning HIV and AIDS in South Africa (Caney 2005 pp.89–90; McGreal 2002).

3. *No Claimability, No Rights*

The third challenge to a universalist position on human rights can be illustrated through the work of Onora O'Neill. Like the libertarians, she accepts the status of negative civil and political rights as an essential part of a universal moral order. However she argues that the same cannot be said for positive economic and social rights such as education or health care. This is not because she rejects the moral goal of improving basic need satisfaction implied in this concept. Far from it. Rather she argues that positive rights are quite different from negative rights in their 'claimability'. In the case of negative rights, individual duty-bearers who do not comply (who attack someone for example) can potentially be identified and claims made against them through the appropriate authorities (whether civil or legal). However this is not the case with complex goods and services (such as health care). She therefore challenges the notion that any individual can be said to be responsible for providing ART for compatriots in need in the same way that they clearly can be held responsible for stealing from a neighbour.

Under these circumstances O'Neill argues that it is only specially created institutions and not individuals who can be designated as relevant duty-bearers. If positive rights can be said to exist, it must be possible for claims to be made against these institutions by those who believe that they have not received their entitlement. Such claims should be potentially enforceable, under appropriately formalised arrangements. O'Neill develops this position as follows:

> [T]he correspondence of universal liberty rights [negative rights] to universal obligations is relatively well defined even when institutions are missing or weak. For example, a violation of a right not to be raped or of a right not to

be tortured may be clear enough, and the perpetrator may be identifiable, even when institutions for enforcement are lamentably weak. But the correspondence of universal rights to goods and services to obligations to provide or deliver remains entirely amorphous when institutions are missing or weak. Somebody who receives no maternity care may no doubt assert that her rights have been violated, but unless obligations to deliver that care have been established and distributed, she will not know where to press or claim, and it will be systematically obscure whether there is any perpetrator, or who has neglected or violated her right. (O'Neill 2000 p.105)

O'Neill's basic argument is that without such mechanisms of claimability, rights of the type encoded in the ICESCR are no more than 'aspirational'. They imply imperfect duties which she powerfully argues on other grounds should be met but which in the end remain a form of charity despite their strong moral force (O'Neill 2005). Thus she would presumably agree with the libertarians that the work of the Bill and Melinda Gates Foundation in fighting HIV and AIDS constitutes altruism rather than respect for the positive right of individuals to ART (although she strongly disagrees with other aspects of the libertarian position) (O'Neill 1996 pp.141–6).

O'Neill does not deny the existence (or the potential value) of positive rights in contexts where they are formally embedded in the legal system. However she points out that many nation states do not have the institutions necessary to ensure the 'claimability' of the positive rights their citizens might otherwise be deemed to possess. Even those international institutions whose mission is defined in the language of universal rights (UNAIDS or WHO for example) do not have the legal clout or the material resources to realistically enforce rights claims. It is for these reasons that O'Neill argues that we need to be very careful about claiming positive rights in the many situations where there is clearly little or no chance of them being met. Indeed she suggests that it may be dishonest or harmful to do so: 'Proclamations of universal "right" to goods and services without attention to the need to justify and establish institutions that identify corresponding obligations-bearers may seem a bitter mockery to the poor and needy, for which these rights matter most' (O'Neill 1996 p.133).

These are important arguments, some of which will be revisited in Chapter 9. But do they amount to a refutation of the concept of positive economic and social rights?

Counterargument: Complexities of Claimability

O'Neill's argument that rights do not exist unless there are corresponding institutions through which to claim them is clearly true in one sense. But it runs the risk of confusing legal and moral rights. Unless we decide to resolve the issue by definition, the fact that particular rights and duties are not currently enshrined in law does not mean that they do not have a moral status that should be taken just as seriously. As Elizabeth Ashford has aptly put it:

Human rights claims are claims of basic justice. Each person is entitled to the objects of their human rights and can justifiably insist on them as their due. These claims ought to be institutionally guaranteed, but since human rights are grounded in fundamental moral principles they are independent of established institutional standards. For this reason, a central function of human rights is to evaluate existing social institutions: a test of whether any institution is minimally just is whether it acknowledges human rights. For example, societies that legalized slavery clearly failed that test and were fundamentally unjust. (Ashford 2007 p.185)

The same criticism could obviously be made of a society that has not legally and practically guaranteed universal access to health care in general and to HIV and AIDS services in particular.[36]

A related criticism is that O'Neill does not sufficiently acknowledge the range of international institutions through which universal positive rights can already be morally claimed and these claims recognised and recorded. As we have seen, the UDHR, the ICCPR and the ICESCR all constitute international law, at least as regards those nations that have endorsed them. While it is true that individual claims of the sort that O'Neill has in mind have more traditionally been made to the ICCPR, the situation is changing.[37] As Noah Novogrodsky has convincingly argued in relation to access to ART:

The impact of the juridical, advocacy, and enforcement revolution surrounding treatment is apparent in at least three ways. First, the successful demand for ARVs has had a synthesizing effect on the corpus of human rights law as a whole. Enforcing right-to-health claims serves to collapse the distinction, if any exists, between civil and political and economic, social and cultural rights. With ever greater frequency, courts, government officials, and advocates are defining the interest in treatment as a core human rights concern rather than as a policy priority. Second, the treatment cases have generally been decided in domestic courts and have been announced within national laws and processes, not at a supranational level. We might refer to this as the grounding effect of socio-economic rights adjudication. Third, the global treatment cases have catalyzed treatment claims, investing them with a sense of urgency and priority, a process that has elevated public health and development claims while simultaneously devaluing private intellectual property rights. (Novogrodsky 2009 p.17)

---

36   For excellent expositions of this point and many others concerning O'Neill's arguments, see Ashford (2007), Tasioulas (2007) and Jones (1999 Chapter 4).

37   Of course there are a range of practical problems concerning enforceability, which again will be discussed in more detail in Chapter 9. For a comprehensive discussion of the range of these institutions and other related issues concerning HIV and AIDS, see Wolff (2012 Chapters 2–3).

Even when potential claimability (and enforceability) is much more tenuous, it is essential to recognise the existence of other mechanisms for exposing the immoral violation of economic and social rights to health. As we have seen, these include the UN organisations whose work is based on the monitoring of human rights implementation in different parts of the world. NGOs of many kinds will plough their critical furrows by means of reports of rights violations and suggested guidelines for improvements in relation to the operation of the ICESCR. True, much of this might be characterised as 'soft law'. But soft law can (and has) become hard law and the move from one to the other needs to be at the heart of political struggle for human rights. Hence the absence of strict claimability in O'Neill's sense cannot and should not be seen as a refutation of universal economic and social rights in themselves.

O'Neill is certainly right in implying that international claimability should be the goal for the 'progressive implementation' of economic and social rights. However it can be argued that she is not correct in stating that legitimate moral claims can never be made against individuals as duty-bearers. Corporate institutions can and should be held morally accountable when they are identified as responsible for the harms that they have caused to citizens of poor nations. And those in control of these organisations should come under particular scrutiny.

Similar arguments could also be applied to citizens of those countries who have benefitted from harm done through lack of respect for the rights of those living elsewhere. Though they will not usually be individually identifiable, it can be argued that they have a strict duty to support changes in national policy in their own countries that will address such harm and respect such rights in the future (Ashford 2007 pp.215–18). Responding to O'Neill's denial that there is a positive right to food because there are not identifiable duty-bearers to provide it, Charles Jones disagrees: 'Who has the responsibility to supply food to all those who need it? ... All of us' (Jones 1999 p.94).

Finally, it is important to highlight the fact that legal claimability alone will not be enough to ensure that even negative civil and political rights can be claimed and enforced in law. Many potential claimants for such rights do not have the necessary physical health and autonomy to make their claims effectively. In the absence of positive social and economic rights, they may lack sufficient food, education, housing and health care to do so: 'If a man is subject to chronic unemployment in a depressed area, he will not thank you for the information that he has the basic rights of liberty' (Raphael 1967 p.87). In such circumstances, the claimability of negative rights can become no more than a moral abstraction, despite the existence of institutions that might sustain such claims. And ironically in her excellent writing in moral philosophy, it is precisely such abstraction that O'Neill rightly castigates.

To conclude, O'Neill maintains that universal economic and social rights are no more than aspirations. But the poor record of respect even for the many rights that are already institutionalised is testimony to the importance of maintaining such aspirations, as many HIV and AIDS activists will confirm. Indeed it underlines the urgent need both to improve existing institutions and to create new ones in precisely the ways that O'Neill herself outlines.[38] In short, if we are to take negative civil and political rights seriously, we must do the same for positive economic and social rights and recognise that aspirationally *and* institutionally they reinforce each other. As Waldron suggests, they are: 'two sides of the same (moral) coin' (Waldron 1981 pp.1–34). O'Neill has not demonstrated that it will be impossible to achieve these goals: only that it will be hard work.

Cosmopolitanism and Human Rights: The Way Forward

It would seem then that there are many weaknesses in the arguments of those who wish to deny the universality of human rights. It cannot be that individuals are the sole authors of any material success they achieve and thus have the prerogative to deny to those who are suffering the goods and services that they need. Nor can it be that nations have a similar prerogative to deny their own citizens or those outside their boundaries the right to the basic need satisfaction they require to live decent lives. Finally, it cannot be that the sole foundation for human rights is their incorporation into existing institutions or laws, either nationally or internationally.

Rather we must base our understanding of why such rights exist on the kinds of justifications outlined in this chapter. First, we argued that an overlapping international consensus exists about the importance of basic human needs in the successful achievement of critical interests. For this reason, if one individual has the right to have these needs met then the same applies to all. Second, it is clear that for the same reason, constitutional negotiators in ignorance of their own economic, social and cultural futures would agree on a rational social contract endorsing the equal right of all individuals to basic need satisfaction. Third, we saw that the civil, economic and political interaction necessary to further human interests must be based on sustained and coherent moral reasoning. This in turn will be impossible to maintain unless the right to the basic need satisfaction of those involved is recognised in principle and respected in practice. We can conclude that moral rights based on these arguments are just as 'real' as legal rights and should be applied universally. They are identifiable and justifiable entitlements that should enable all individuals everywhere to pursue their critical interests with a realistic potential for success.

Where national and international institutions do not exist to make such rights claimable and enforceable then this should be the object of sustained activism, whether it is focussed specifically on HIV and AIDS or not. Such universal

---

38   O'Neill accepts that such institutionalisation is possible: 'Systems of universal institutionalized rights to goods, income, or services with distributed counterpart obligations, are both conceivable and coherent. Moreover, such rights have been at least partly achieved both in the welfare states of Western Europe and in the countries of formerly existing socialism' (O'Neill 1996 p.132).

entitlements would minimise the harmful patterns of inequality and corrosive disadvantage that we discussed in Chapter 1 in relation to Sumalee, Lena and Simon. Indeed for Simon such a move toward levelling the playing field could mean life itself.

This emphasis on the right of each individual to the preconditions for well-being – where 'every human being has a global stature as the ultimate unit of moral concern' – lies at the heart of 'cosmopolitan' theories of justice (Pogge 1992 p.49). It is this perception of a universal morality that establishes our commonality as humans and provides us with a yardstick for deciding when we are respecting and caring for others to a standard that they and we deserve. As Gillian Brock states:

> global justice requires that all are adequately positioned to enjoy the prospects for a decent life, such that they are enabled to meet their basic needs, their basic liberties are protected, and that there are fair terms of cooperation in collective endeavours. This calls upon us to ensure that there are social and political arrangements that can underwrite these important goods. (Brock 2009 p.322)

Navanethem Pillay, the United Nations High Commissioner for Human Rights, expresses this same commitment even more succinctly: 'The principle of universality admits no exception. Human rights truly are the birth right of all human beings' (Pillay 2008).

The next chapter will examine what it means to put this cosmopolitan theory of justice into practice as regards HIV and AIDS and human rights. But before doing we need to discuss the potential contradiction between a commitment to universal human rights on the one hand and what has been called 'HIV exceptionalism' on the other. This ambiguity is often evident in debates about the pandemic, with little recognition of the logical confusion involved. It is therefore important that we confront these issues in light of the urgency of developing alliances and shaping future advocacy.

What about 'Exceptionalism' in the Context of Human Rights?

We have seen that HIV is unique in terms of its natural history in affected individuals, its particular configuration of symptoms and its history of rapid development in what are often marginalised groups. The (mainly) sexual mode of transmission and the mutability of the retrovirus make primary prevention difficult, while the 'long waves' of infection challenge mitigation strategies. But what are the policy implications of these differences? They have frequently been used as the justification for what could be seen as 'special moral treatment' but in recent years such claims have been increasingly challenged. We need to ask how this sits in the context of a commitment to equality and universal human rights.

A number of commentators have argued that 'too much' is being spent on HIV and AIDS in comparison with other health problems. It has been pointed out, for example, that the number of people who die from AIDS each year is roughly equivalent to the annual number of deaths of children under five in India: while AIDS causes fewer than 4 per cent of deaths every year it receives 25 per cent of international health aid (England 2008). Critics have argued that these claims for extra resources have been made not on scientific grounds but in the interests of those individuals and groups within the 'HIV/AIDS establishment' itself (Pisani 2008; Chin 2007). This high level of spending is said to have weakened health care systems through diverting resources and staff away from other problems (Shiffman 2008). HIV advocates on the other hand have responded by pointing out the large sums of additional funding that have been brought into health care systems and the infrastructure and good practice initiatives that have often followed (Piot et al. 2009; Yu et al. 2008).

These conflicting empirical claims are difficult to evaluate. However a recent study comparing expenditure on HIV and AIDS across a range of countries found overspending relative to need in some but far too little spent in others (MacDevette 2011). Most importantly, the total 'surplus' in overspending countries was dwarfed by the size of the 'underspend' in others. This indicates that global HIV and AIDS resources are currently inadequate to bring all countries into line with their levels of need based on the relevant disease burdens. Hence the answer would not seem to lie in robbing Peter to pay Paul by moving funds away from HIV and AIDS to other health problems. Rather it should be to increase the levels of funding for global health overall and then to allocate it on the basis of need.

Social justice would then require that decisions about the allocation of health resources should be made with reference to the specific needs of populations in particular settings. Thus the needs of those with HIV should be considered alongside those of people in need of sexual and reproductive services, for example, or those infected with TB.[39] Where prevalence is high HIV and AIDS services may well receive the greatest priority. However there will be other situations where it will be 'normalised' as part of the wider public health agenda (Whiteside and Smith 2009; Smith et al. 2011). Thus the struggle to protect the rights of those with HIV and AIDS cannot be divorced from the more general struggle for health in the context of the complex political and economic conditions that place arbitrary limits on its achievement.

This same point has been argued from a different perspective by Paul Farmer, who draws on the practical work of Partners for Health with deprived communities around the world. He stresses the fact that whatever the state of their health or the nature of their circumstances most people can identify what is required for their own basic need satisfaction. The central objective must therefore be to ensure that the right of all to the highest attainable health is met using the most practicable means possible. Much more will be required than just 'rights talk'. As Farmer

---

39   Of course in many instances these will be the same people.

himself recently put it, the next phase of HIV campaigning will need to focus much more on 'human rights in the doing':

> ... if we believe that health care is a right, we need to address problems such as AIDS and maternal mortality with the highest standard of care possible. If we believe that the treatment for hunger is food, we need to address food insecurity with both short-term and long-term strategies, even if this means that we must learn about improving seed quality and procuring fertilizer and promoting fair trade, which means taking on rich-world agribusiness subsidies ... If we put even a shred of stock in the notion of solidarity, then we must press for basic social and economic rights for the poor. (Farmer 2008 p.13)

Conclusion

This chapter has highlighted the value of the human rights approach in tackling the HIV pandemic. We have seen how the discourse and practice of universal rights have been at the centre of attempts to improve the well-being of those who are HIV positive. We have also outlined both the political and the intellectual challenges that have to be tackled if the human rights approach is to be used even more effectively. Given the obvious strength of the 'cosmopolitan' approach for HIV and AIDS activists, this was highlighted as central to the continuing campaign against the HIV epidemics. However it was also argued that in the context of universalism there is nothing privileged about HIV and AIDS as regards the right to attainable health and the fight for health care. Hence Chapter 9 will explore the challenges facing the promotion of the human rights agenda not just for those who are HIV positive but for all those harmed by the current crisis in global health.

Chapter 9
Back to the Future

Throughout this book we have highlighted the importance of a commitment to universal human rights in meeting the needs of those who are disadvantaged. The main focus has been on those who are HIV positive, but parallels have been drawn between their lives and those of people damaged by other health problems and by poverty itself.

This final chapter identifies the challenges that will need to be met if as many people as possible are to be saved from sickness and early death. It will begin by examining changes in the pattern of HIV funding over recent years and assess the implications for the future. Given the likelihood that the scarcity of health-related resources will remain (or even intensify) strategies will be needed to ensure that they are used more fairly and also more effectively in order to tackle not only HIV and AIDS but also other sources of socially generated harm.

Several interrelated strategies will be proposed for achieving this. First, a broader evidence base will be needed, with greater collaboration between biomedical researchers and those from a range of social sciences.[1] Second, fairer mechanisms for resource allocation will be required both within HIV and AIDS care and between HIV and AIDS and other health problems. This will be an essential component in a strategy that enforces existing rights and duties more effectively but also generates new entitlements and more accountability at both national and international levels. Means will have to be found to maximise the resources available for the realisation of these universalist or cosmopolitan goals for promoting global health. And this in turn will require a clear commitment to the placing of health needs at the centre of post 2015 development strategies (Kim et al 2011; Fox and Mason Meier 2009).

The Challenges of Funding: Past, Present and Future

As the HIV and AIDS pandemic spread, it initially attracted an unprecedented level of resources for a single health problem. Funding rose six fold over the period 2002 to 2008 but began to level out in 2009. It then dropped off markedly in 2010 despite evidence of increasing levels of need (Kates et al. 2011). As early as 2008 there were reports of cutbacks in clinic services in many settings, with existing patients turned away and new ones denied access (Médecins Sans Frontières

---

1   This will of course need to include what we could regard as the 'bridging' discipline of social epidemiology (WHO 2008b).

2009). This posed a major challenge at the very moment when more interventions were needed to improve the well-being of those infected and also to limit onward transmission of the virus (WHO 2012a).

Early History of HIV and AIDS Funding: Protection and Pragmatism

The 1990s saw demands from a growing number of civil society organisations for greater priority to be given to issues of poverty and social justice in the face of economic globalisation. This led to the emergence of a large number of what have been called 'normatively driven institutions of public health' with an initial emphasis on the very broad goal of *Health for All by the Year 2000* (Mason Meier 2012; Fidler 2008–2009). At the same time the world's richest countries (then the G8) began to recognise global health as a legitimate item on their agendas.

The first large-scale funding targeted specifically at HIV and AIDS was spent on medical research in the US and other countries of the global north. This was in part a response to advocacy on the part of gay men. However it was also a protectionist strategy as it became clear that HIV transmission might not be confined to specific groups.

As the pandemic spread into poorer parts of the world, concern increased in the centres of power about its global implications. On the one hand it was feared that what was then termed 'HIV/AIDS' constituted a serious 'security issue'. On the other it was seen as a potential obstacle to economic growth. This led the 2000 meeting of the UN Security Council on HIV/AIDS to pass Resolution 1308 warning that 'unchecked the pandemic will pose a risk to stability and to security'. Following a similar line, US Vice President Al Gore claimed that: 'it (HIV) threatens not just individual citizens but the very institutions that define and defend the character of a society'.[2] As a result HIV/AIDS took its place alongside emergent terrorism as a perceived threat to the global order (McInnes and Rushton 2010).

Thus two strands – one based on wider social justice principles and the other on more pragmatic or libertarian concerns – converged to produce dramatic increases in funding directly targeted on HIV (Forman 2011). However the last few years have seen a growing recognition among many of those holding the purse strings that the neo-liberal arguments for this expenditure are not as strong as had first been assumed.

The pandemic was initially seen as a potential cause of everything from the fall of national governments to roving bands of orphans with no commitment to social order. However recent research has concluded that its impact on security has been much less dramatic than expected (Becker et al. 2008; McInnes and Rushton 2010). In the case of South Africa, for example, although political activism was behind the push for universal treatment it never directly threatened the government itself. Alex de Waal (2006) attributes this to pervasive denialism

---

2   http://clinton5.nara.gov/WH/EOP/OVP/speeches/unaid_health.html.

as well as to the fact that HIV and AIDS have not been a priority for the majority of voters, and hence not for their leaders either. He argues that, at least for the moment, African political systems have proved to be resilient in the face of the pandemic. Indeed some elites have learned to co-opt international AIDS efforts to their own political ends.[3]

Similar problems emerged in identifying the direct impact of the pandemic on economic growth in high-prevalence countries (WHO 2009). It is now clear, for example, that the loss of individuals of working age may not be as serious for employers as had been feared since, at least in the case of unskilled jobs, there will usually be a large reservoir of unemployed labourers. In some settings there has also been considerable restructuring of labour forces, with women picking up some of the slack as men weaken and die (Johnston 2008).[4] Thus the interests of the rich and powerful have not been seriously threatened by the pandemic. Indeed the economic growth rate of around 6 per cent for the African region as a whole in 2011 is striking by comparison with that of the Organisation for Economic Co-operation and Development (OECD) countries (UNAIDS 2012b).

Of course this does not mean that their circumstances are not causing harm to affected individuals. In the first place much of this economic development has offered little to the populations involved. And, as we have seen, HIV and AIDS have seriously harmed or killed many of the poorest people in the world. As the number of people living with HIV continues to increase it is these effects on human rather than economic development that are likely to intensify (Boutayeb 2009). Yet those funders who were motivated mainly by a desire to stabilise the existing economic and social order now appear to be cutting back on their commitments as the financial crisis deepens (Horton 2009; Gill and Bakker 2011).

Current Funding Cuts and Future Crises?

The last two decades saw the creation of a wide range of funding organisations, including the Global Fund to Fight HIV/AIDS, Tuberculosis and Malaria in 2002; the US President's Emergency Plan for AIDS Relief (PEPFAR) in 2004; and the Bill and Melinda Gates Foundation in 2000. Together with other multilateral, bilateral and philanthropic programmes they have so far contributed about 60 per cent of all external HIV and AIDS funding to sub-Saharan Africa (Ravishankar et al. 2009) as well as providing support for a range of other health problems (Garrett 2007).

The Global Fund has been especially important in providing about two-thirds of all international funding for TB and malaria services and one-fifth for HIV. Hence it came as a major shock in 2011 when the Fund announced the cancellation of its

---

3   For an interesting commentary on de Waal's work go to the website of the South African Social Science Research Council at http://www.ssrc.org/programs/pages/hiv-aids-program/aids-and-power-why-there-is-no-political-crisis-yet.

4   See Chapter 5 on HIV and work.

next funding round. While existing projects were to be financed in the interim, no new applications would be considered until 2014.[5] A recent review of the expected impact of these cuts concluded that Bangladesh, Bolivia, Zimbabwe, Zambia and the new Republic of South Sudan would be among the hardest hit. In the case of South Sudan, 80 per cent of the national AIDS plan was left unfunded – including services designed to help those returning from neighbouring countries with high HIV prevalence (Podmore et al. 2012).

The current situation of economic austerity and insecurity, as well as other challenges such as climate change and rising oil prices, has led many donor governments to reduce, delay or cancel their contributions to these initiatives. This reluctance was reinforced when fraud was identified among some of the Fund's recipients, leading to significant changes in procedures to avoid such problems in the future (Lopez Gonzales 2012; Podmore et al. 2012). Yet the funding needed to sustain services not just for HIV and AIDS but also for other diseases, including TB and malaria, will increase significantly in the coming years.

It is difficult to estimate precisely how much will be required for HIV and AIDS because of the biological, social and economic uncertainties involved (Friedman et al. 2006). However the AIDS 2031 Initiative estimated that in the absence of a 'game-changer' such as a vaccine the cost of providing universal prevention and treatment in low and middle income countries will have risen to as much as $35 billion per year by 2031. This can be compared with the $15.6 billion spent in those countries in 2008 (Hecht et al. 2009 p.1597).

Paradoxically, the main reason for this dramatic increase is that so many of those who would have died without antiretroviral therapy (ART) will have survived but will continue to need treatment. At the same time it is assumed that there will be at least a million new infections each year, all of whom will need drugs and associated health care throughout their lives. Moreover, an unknown number will require the much more expensive second- or third-line drugs. Financially then the picture is grim. And the burden is likely to become increasingly unequal as recent rises in the cost of food and fuel push more people back into poverty, making the circumstances of those who are positive even more difficult to sustain (Gill and Bakker 2011).

Not surprisingly considerable pressure is now being exerted for as many countries as possible to 'take ownership' of their own HIV epidemics (Haytmanek et al. 2010). A recent report from UNAIDS pointed out that if individual countries

---

5   This was later revised when the US Senate Appropriations Sub-Committee voted to fund the Global Fund to fight AIDS, Tuberculosis and Malaria at the president's budget request of $1.65 billion – which would fulfil the US four-year, $4 billion pledge to the Fund. However, it appears that the Senate had allocated approximately the same amount of funding to the Global Fund plus the US President's Emergency Plan for AIDS Relief (PEPFAR) as it did the previous year, but apportioned the money differently to fulfil the US pledge to the Global Fund. This translated into a reduction in PEPFAR funding by approximately $350 million.

in Africa increased their HIV spending at the same rate as their economic growth an increase could be expected from \$2.5 billion in 2010 to \$3.2 billion in 2015 (UNAIDS 2012b). Over the next few years the growth rate of a number of the middle income or BRIC countries (Brazil, Russia, China and India) should put them in a position to meet the needs of their own positive citizens and also to work collaboratively to help some of those in other countries.

But the fact remains that for the millions in the poorest settings domestic funds will simply not be available. High levels of indebtedness, international trade policies and structural adjustment have limited the volume of national expenditures on health care (AIDS2031 2010; Rudin and Sanders 2011).[6] While many African countries are increasing the resources spent on their positive populations, 80 per cent of all ART consumed in the region is currently paid for by outside sources. This reflects the very limited domestic expenditure on health overall. More than half of African countries still spend less than the WHO minimum recommendation of \$34 per capita per annum and by 2011 only three were on track to meet the health-related Millennium Development Goals (MDGs) (MSF 2009; UNAIDS 2012c).

Thus the future appears to be one of increasing need and declining resources. This applies not just to HIV but to a range of other health problems. Under these circumstances, rights-based activism needs to be expanded. An important part of this will involve an extension of the existing evidence base, with a particular emphasis on the economic, social and cultural contexts within which the health and well-being of individuals are shaped.

Reshaping the Research Agenda: Bringing the Social and the Biomedical Together

Throughout the history of the pandemic, the biomedical paradigm has been dominant in research. It has been vital in developing a range of therapeutic interventions, and adequate funding will continue be needed in the search for a vaccine as well as a cure. However the last decade in particular has begun to highlight the limitations of the biomedical model used in isolation (Auerbach et al. 2011; de Wit et al. 2011; Adam 2011). Hence a broader and more interdisciplinary approach will be needed.

The foundational belief of biomedical science is that it is possible to make a decontextualised measurement of aspects of physical reality through the gold standard of the randomised controlled trial (RCT). This use of the 'scientific method' has obvious advantages in clinical settings but it obscures the complexity of 'the intermingling of ecosystems, economics and politics, history and specific

---

6   For an excellent review of the financial background to this situation, especially the role of the International Monetary Fund (IMF), see Baker (2010).

exposures and processes at every level, macro to micro from societal to inside the body' (Krieger 2008 p.227).

Biomedical methodologies are central to the development of new treatments and to their testing for safety and efficacy. However all medical interventions, whether preventive or treatment oriented, are also social events.[7] In order to maximise their effectiveness they will therefore need to be based not just on medical science but on an understanding of community and individual life, with testing done in different settings on a range of people (Kippax et al. 2011; Padian et al. 2008).

The WHO Commission on the Social Determinants of Health (2008) has reworked traditional arguments for the centrality of the social sciences in explaining and mitigating inequalities in global health (WHO 2008b; Blas et al. 2008). This provides an essential baseline for further investigation of these issues. However more detailed examination will be required of the ways in which a range of societal influences interact in the context of specific diseases. This will be particularly important in the case of HIV and AIDS where the success of practical strategies based on structural approaches has so far been relatively limited:

> ... the arsenal of structural interventions – or more generally, evidence-based and evidence-informed strategies that can be demonstrated to actually achieve social change – is quite small; and developments in this arena have been hampered by significant methodological and evidentiary obstacles that have yet to be fully explored and addressed. (Auerbach et al. 2011 p.2)

In order to remove these methodological obstacles we need to begin by reminding ourselves of the differences between HIV and AIDS and most other diseases associated with social disadvantage. As we have seen, the link between HIV and poverty is not straightforward. This is because the immediate 'cause' of HIV is not differential exposure to harmful aspects of the external environment or to lack of basic need satisfaction. While these will obviously increase vulnerability, the virus itself is transmitted by particular practices carried out by individuals and groups in specific social contexts (Kippax 2008; Auerbach et al. 2011).

Hence it will be essential not to lose sight of the personal narrative of individuals while exploring the wider social context of their lives (Krieger 2001, 2008; Forde and Raine 2008). To put this another way, it will be essential that researchers pay proper attention to the individual experiences of the people whose lives they are investigating. Rather than treating them as 'opaque entities' they need to see them as active agents with beliefs, habits, routines and unconscious cognitive processes

---

7   A number of recent studies have provided important illustrations of how this works in the context of preventive interventions currently in development. These include vaccines (Newman 2009), pre-exposure prophylaxis (PrEP) (Golub et al. 2010) and microbicides (Montgomery and Pool 2011).

who are living within a broader network of human relationships (Hedsrom and Ylikoski 2010).

HIV also differs from most other 'diseases of inequality' in that the absence of a cure leads to a requirement for continuing health care. Thus what have been called the 'social drivers' of the pandemic are relevant not only to the process of infection itself but also to experiences of the illness over a lifetime. As we have seen, a complex mix of economic and social factors determines access to therapy and influences its long-term use (or discontinuation). These range from fear of stigma or of violence to lack of money for drugs or clinic visits, the maternal desire for a child or the urge to maintain a 'real masculine identity'. An understanding of these cognitive and emotional factors, as well as the structural determinants of human behaviour, will become even more important as the strategy of 'treatment as prevention' (TASP) becomes a central mode of intervention (Montaner et al. 2006; Montaner et al. 2011; Nguyen et al. 2011).

In the context of sexual behaviour, for example, what had previously been treated as a simple 'biological event' has now been recognised as a complex expression of cultural beliefs and practices. Indeed even the definition of a 'sex act' may raise complex methodological challenges that need to be tackled before such acts can begin to be counted or categorised.

These challenges are linked to a longstanding debate within the social sciences: how far is apparently personal behaviour shaped by outside forces (or social structures) and how far is it the result of individual 'agency'? To put this more simply, how far do people behave 'as they please' and how far are their actions shaped by wider societal factors even in the most intimate of circumstances? The answer of course is that social factors will influence the beliefs and behaviour of individuals whose actions will in turn (re)shape attitudes and practices in the communities of which they are members. This continuous interaction has been defined as 'structuration' (Giddens 1984).

It can be illustrated here through a case study of young women and transactional sex carried out by researchers from HEARD[8] in Mbekweni Township in South Africa (Brown and Labonte 2011). The researchers found that the motives of young women who engaged in sex for money were very different from what might commonly be assumed. While some were simply trying to meet their basic needs, many had a very different approach, seeing this work as a gateway to modernity through the purchase of material goods – especially fashionable clothes. In some cases they described themselves as 'hunters' seeking out those men who would give the best deal in terms of money. For many this led to increased fatalism with regard to HIV.

The authors relate this to the spread of consumerism in the wider context of global capitalism and the radical changes it has engendered in the sexual attitudes and activities of this particular group of women. This in turn is seen to have led to

---

8   Health Economics and HIV/AIDS Research Division at the University of KwaZulu-Natal in Durban.

changes in sexual values and practices in other members of the local population of which the women are a part.

Thus the effectiveness of any HIV or AIDS intervention (whether biomedical, behavioural or social) will require a clear understanding of this interweaving of the external and internal realities that shape individual lives. The nature of the interaction will vary according to personal characteristics and physical embodiment as well as social circumstances. If these complex processes are to be accurately reflected in policy making, a range of methodological approaches and disciplinary perspectives will be required.

Any call for greater collaboration between medical and social sciences must of course begin by acknowledging that this will be no simple task (Mykhalovskiy and Rosengarten 2009a and 2009b; Hirsch et al. 2007). There can be no doubt that medicine still has higher status as a discipline, playing a dominant role in policy making and with greater access to funding. However there are signs that this divide is beginning to break down, with the exigencies of the pandemic itself playing a significant part in this process (Blank et al. 2008). This will need to be further developed through more open and informed debate about the appropriate balance of research between different disciplines as well as an increase in 'mixed methods' projects in the wider context of research into global inequalities in health.

But however much the efficiency and effectiveness of health care can be increased through an improved evidence base it is clear that funding will continue to be scarce. If available resources are to be allocated fairly then much more attention will need to be paid to the processes involved in making the relevant decisions. Without more clarity on these issues it will not be possible to ensure that the human rights of all those in need have an equal chance of being met.

Putting Fairness into Resource Allocation: Substantive versus Procedural Justice

There is a broad consensus on the basic moral principles to be adopted in rationing the public provision of health care. Those who face life-threatening illness should be given priority over those whose condition is less serious. When there is not enough health care to go around, individuals or groups should have an equal chance of accessing whatever is available. They should not, for example, be discriminated against (either implicitly or explicitly) because of the country they live in or because of what is perceived to be moral status of their illness. There is nothing exceptional about these moral guidelines. Indeed they are at the heart of the triage practised in any well-managed emergency clinic (Doyal 1997b).

But these guidelines are rarely followed in the context of national or international health planning. This reflects in part the very fragmented and highly contested principles on which such decisions are usually made. But it is also a consequence of the global inequalities in allocation of resources. Based on the life-threatening character of their illness, everyone diagnosed with HIV should – in principle –

receive treatment as necessary, along with those infected with malaria, TB and any other serious health problem for which therapy is theoretically available. But of course there will rarely be enough resources to treat all those in equal need especially in settings of poverty where need is greatest. Hence 'tragic choices' will often have to be made (Nussbaum 2011 pp.36–9).

Unfortunately, substantive moral principles in themselves can offer little guidance in these circumstances. This is because they have to be interpreted in practice and sometimes there can be disagreement about how to choose between the many people who can be shown to be equally deserving. In light of these limitations there have been growing calls for greater fairness to ensure that those in equal need have an equal chance to receive the care that they require (Doyal 1995). This can best be assured through the adoption of clear procedural principles designed to optimise such equality and negotiated in practice on the basis of what has been called 'public reason' (Gruskin and Daniels 2008; Rawls 1997 pp.93–141).

Until now, decisions about health policy and funding have been made mainly by officials and medical experts. They may be made at international, national or local levels and may involve wider public health issues or focus only on one disease. But whatever their scope, the grounds on which they are made are rarely open to scrutiny and the decision makers themselves are not held accountable for their choices. If 'public reason' is to be applied effectively and equitably, these deliberations will need to be done in ways that optimise their 'communicative competence' and ultimately their rationality and fairness (Gruskin and Daniels 2008; Doyal and Gough 1991 p.124).

This will require that decisions are made by a representative group of stakeholders, with any vested interests openly declared. The group should include some of those in need of the resources under discussion and the process should not be dominated by experts. Conclusions should be based on sound evidence rather than professional or other prejudice. Moreover the evidence under review should go beyond traditional measures of morbidity and mortality into the wider social and economic impact of particular choices

Deliberations and the reasoning behind them should be made public and there should be a revision and appeals system along with clear lines of accountability. Very importantly, there must be coherent links between the evidence used, the reasons given for particular decisions and the rationale for whatever principles are used in making them (Daniels and Sabin 1997; Daniels 2008; Powers and Faden 2006 Chapter 7; Samia et al. 2011 pp.173–83). Under these circumstances the use of a simple 'democratic' vote will not suffice (Doyal 1998).

The use of these needs – and rights – based principles will produce a more morally nuanced and broader evidence-based approach to decision making in the context of what are often very complex policy issues. We can illustrate this through looking at ongoing debates about prevention versus treatment in tackling HIV and AIDS.

Saving Life and Preventing Death

Much of the debate about the morality and effectiveness of the allocation or 'rationing' of scarce medical resources has focussed on the use of methodologies – including quality-adjusted life years (QALYs) and disability-adjusted life years (DALYs) – which purport to maximise the greatest good for the greatest number. However, these have been much criticised in clinical medicine because of their inevitable bias in favour of those healthier or younger people rather than those for whom treatment may be more expensive and who may benefit for a shorter period. When individual lives are at risk and the moral emphasis is on immediate access to treatment on the basis of need, the tensions posed by such maximising strategies are clear (Bastian 2000, Doyal 1995, Powers and Faden 2006 pp.150–70).

However, when we move from clinical medicine to public health, these utilitarian strategies can seem much more appealing. For here, the moral emphasis is inevitably focussed on the well-being of populations rather than individuals. On these grounds, it is not difficult to see why spending more money on prevention than treatment may be seen to offer greater rewards (in terms of lives saved).[9] This is an argument frequently used either explicitly or implicitly in the context of debates about HIV. One recent example of this is the argument by Brock and Winkler (2009) that many people already infected will have to be allowed to die in order to prevent the disease in others: 'If stressing treatment will not augment resources sufficiently to overcome the greater number of lives that could be saved by favouring prevention over treatment, then we find no convincing moral argument for giving priority to treatment when a lack of resources forces us to choose' (Brock and Wikler 2009 p.1675). There are (at least) two problems with this position. The first is empirical, while the second is moral.

Most of these debates make what can only be heroic assumptions about both the cost and the potential effectiveness of behavioural prevention in particular (de Wit et al. 2011). While some initiatives have been shown to be relatively cost effective, others are very labour intensive – especially those involving individual or couple counselling. Moreover very few have had their impact on rates of HIV infection measured over time. Hence neither the effectiveness nor the cost of particular interventions can be easily predicted: 'No one thought 25 years ago that HIV prevention would prove as difficult as it has proven to be ... We need to remain humble as we approach the issue of how to keep the virus from moving from one person to another' (Coates et al. 2008 p.669).

The moral objection to a major shift of this kind away from treatment towards prevention rests in the potential fate of the millions of positive people (most in the poorest parts of the world) who are clinically in need of ART but are not currently receiving it. Unless the amount of funding rises dramatically they will pay for such

---

9   For a range of interesting discussions about this moral tension, see: Dawson and Verweij (2007).

a decision with their lives. This raises serious questions about human rights and about the duty to treat equals equally.

How could we choose who would not be allowed to start treatment or, even more difficult, to have their treatment terminated? And why should their lives be seen to have less worth than those of other positive people or those who are still negative (and not even identifiable) but who *might* be prevented from becoming infected in the future? There are strong arguments that the former have a greater claim on resources not only because of the threat to their lives but also because of the implications for those with close bonds of attachment to them (Powers and Faden 2006 pp.171–7).

These questions are of course further complicated by the fact that so long as they remain alive, positive individuals can be a potential source of infection and hence their survival could be seen as a threat to prevention (though this disturbing truth is rarely stated openly in debates about resource allocation). On the other hand, it is increasingly clear that ART can have the double effect of preserving life while also making transmission to others less likely (Ambrosioni et al. 2011; Cairns 2012; Cohen et al. 2011; Granich et al. 2010; Lancet 2011). So how are the evidential grounding and the moral balance between these options to be evaluated?

This should not in any sense be taken as an argument against an increasing focus on prevention. However it does highlight the limitations of the use of simplistic and ultimately utilitarian measures of anonymous lives saved in making such vital policy decisions in conditions of scarcity. Instead principles of both substantive *and* procedural justice will need to be deployed in debates about complex dilemmas of this kind.

Of course even after procedurally appropriate deliberations, where the substantive principles of social justice are taken into account there may rarely be a single 'right' answer.[10] There will always be a number of possible outcomes, with some winners and some losers. But at least we can say that these decisions have been made as fairly as possible and (most importantly) those who are negatively affected are more likely to understand why they have lost out (Powers and Faden 2006 pp.179–90).

Reframing Human Rights in the Context of Globalisation

As we saw in Chapter 8, significant benefits have flowed from the use of the human rights approach in the context of HIV and AIDS. However existing mechanisms will need to be used more effectively alongside the development of new policies if individuals throughout the world are to be able to optimise their well-being. As Laura Stemple has put it: 'the health and human rights framework holds many promises but is not without limits at least as it is currently actualized' (Stemple

10 For an example of how this works in practice see Gruskin and Daniels' (2008) case study of maternal mortality.

2008 p.S115). Indeed a recognition of this reality led a number of NGOs to issue a recent document entitled: *Human Rights and AIDS: Now More Than Ever* (Cohen 2009). Making progress will of course also be of value in tackling a range of other deadly and disabling diseases (Hunt 2007).

Promoting Human Rights to Health at a National Level

Given the centrality of individual states in implementing the UN human rights framework there is much to be done in monitoring their actions (or lack of them) as duty bearers (Schrecker et al. 2010). Despite their limited resources some low and middle income countries are well known for having made notable progress in meeting the health care needs of their populations: Cuba, Costa Rica and Kerala State in India are good examples. In relation to HIV and AIDS, Brazil stands out as one of the most successful, having been the first of the middle income countries to implement a universal right to ART. This entitlement was outlined in the 1988 Brazilian Constitution and institutionalised in the 1990s by the creation of the Unified Health System (SUS) (Galvao 2005).

Brazil's success has been made possible in part by the rapid increases in economic growth which made it the fifth largest economy in the world by 2011 (Kleinert and Horton 2011). However the allocation of a significant proportion of these resources to health care reflects the origins of SUS in the democratisation of Brazil after the fall of the military dictatorship in 1985. This meant that policies were devised in active collaboration with a range of rights-based civil society organisations. They also involved government participation in wider global politics to win the right to undertake domestic manufacture of pharmaceuticals (Fleury 2011; Galvao 2005).

Finally and very importantly these developments in health care have been underpinned by systematic attempts to tackle poverty in what has historically been one of the most unequal societies in the world.[11] Of course Brazil still has many problems to solve but it does offer an important example of feasible ways forward. Thus the reality of moral social and economic rights as vital aspirations in the struggle for better health and health care explored in Chapter 8 is well illustrated by this Brazilian experience and achievement.

By contrast there are still a large number of countries that despite declarations of intent have not set up an effective national health care system. A recent study showed for example, that only 56 of the 160 countries that had ratified the International Convention on Economic, Social and Cultural Rights had legally recognised the right to health as specified in the Convention, and 88 were severely deficient in monitoring and accountability mechanisms (Backman et al. 2008). In the context of HIV in particular, this leaves many millions without the treatment necessary for survival.

---

11   This is enshrined in the new Programa Brazil sem Miseria (Brazil Without Extreme Poverty Programme) (Padilha 2011).

Some countries have progressed through the creation of some form of Human Rights Commission.[12] These are usually quasi-independent and strategically located between state institutions and civil society organisations. Hence they are well placed to contribute to the promotion of health and human rights. In those settings where the epidemic is widespread some have taken on a wide range of responsibilities, with the monitoring of HIV and AIDS services and the review of national plans often being a key focus (UNAIDS 2007).

In many countries their role in encouraging collaboration and networking between a range of HIV and AIDS organisations has been of particular value. This is partly because of the acknowledged importance of ensuring active participation of people living with HIV in related programming. But it also enables more focussed and collective political action for rights-based policies by community organisations.

The Canadian Human Rights Commission, for example, has been actively engaged in a wide variety of policies to prevent discrimination against HIV positive people. They have placed particular attention on workplace issues opposing both pre- and post-employment testing and encouraging the development of formal HIV policies. In Asia the example of Vietnam is widely quoted as a success story. The AIDS-related work of its Human Rights Commission has been broad in scope and represented a major turnaround from past attitudes. Working with the United States Agency for International Development (USAID) Health Policy Initiative, it has introduced a rights-based HIV strategy that includes harm reduction services for injecting drug users (IDUs) and sex workers in settings which had previously relied on mandatory rehabilitation centres.

Of course many human rights organisations are poorly resourced and have little power to push through changes that challenge traditional social values. Hence one of their most important roles may be to provide a focal point for wider political activism. In India, for example, HIV prevention was included as a priority in the country's second National AIDS Strategy. However this led to outreach workers being arrested and charged under obscenity and sodomy laws. These activities were taken over by a new civil society programme led by the India HIV/AIDS Alliance which brought together 200 community-based organisations in 17 states.

A central focus for most organisations concerned with human rights and health within their own countries has been ensuring access to ART itself. As we have seen, many health services are still placing obstacles in the way of access for vulnerable groups – whatever their formal entitlement to care. These include the major populations of 'at risk' people, including sex workers, MSM and IDUs as well as other vulnerable groups such as truckers, prisoners, soldiers, refugees and orphans (Beyrer et al. 2011; Overs and Hawkins 2011).

Human rights activists have also highlighted the fact that services need to be delivered in ways that respect the moral and legal rights of users: autonomy, confidentiality and human dignity. This will not be achieved without the active

---

12   For a list of these see http://en.wikipedia.org/wiki/Human_rights_commission.

participation of users themselves in the development and monitoring of services as well as the implementation of appropriate mechanisms of accountability. In many settings it will also necessitate specialist human rights training for health workers, many of whom will not be sensitive to the relevant rights issues.

Moving on from service delivery itself, activism related to human rights and HIV is also vital in uncovering the role of national legislative frameworks in denying civil and political rights to particular groups (Global Commission on HIV and the Law 2012). The criminalisation of HIV transmission, sex work and injecting drug use offers obvious examples (Csete and Elliot 2011). There are more than 60 countries in which it is defined as a crime to expose someone else to the HIV virus, and at least 600 people have been convicted in 24 countries (Barr et al. 2011). Such laws can cause major harm to positive people, yet they are likely to be counterproductive in terms of prevention: 'They are impossible to enforce with any semblance of fairness, they impose regimes of surveillance and punishment on sexually active people living with HIV, not only in their intimate relations and reproductive and maternal lives, but also in their attempts to earn a living' (Global Commission on HIV and the Law 2012 Chapter 2).

The extreme homophobia that lies at the heart of some of this legislation is exemplified in the widely publicised Uganda draft law of May 2010 which included not only compulsory testing for HIV but also public disclosure (Barr et al. 2011). The law also included life imprisonment for homosexuality and was poised to be passed in 2013. Though 123 countries have passed legislation to prevent discrimination against HIV positive people, these are rarely used. Again emphasising the difference between the reality of both moral and legal rights, change motivated by the former will be needed in the legal systems of many countries if the basic human rights of HIV positive people are to be upheld:

> The legal environment can play a powerful role in the well-being of people living with HIV and those vulnerable to HIV. Good laws, fully resourced and rigorously enforced, can widen access to prevention and health care services, improve the quality of treatment, enhance social support for people affected by the epidemic, protect human rights that are vital to survival and save the public money. (Global Commission on HIV and the Law 2012 p.11)

Finally, it will be important for those concerned with ensuring respect for human rights to pay particular attention to national budgetary priorities. What is public money being spent on and why? In those countries with a high level of unmet need for health care in general and HIV care in particular, local, regional and national governments will need to be held accountable for patterns of resource allocation, taxation, redistribution and the overall transparency of their financial operations. Without such systematic audit there is evidence that some may exaggerate the limitations on their resources or in the worst cases may be fraudulently accumulating funds meant for humanitarian purposes. The fact that such abuses often occur within the law highlights once again the force of moral rather than legal rights in the defence of the vulnerable.

These different elements provide a basic agenda for national advocacy on human rights and HIV. They offer a preliminary plan for action within the normal democratic processes (where they exist) as well as providing a focus for wider civil society activism. In the next section we open the lens wider to explore the political goals to be sought at a global level.

Promoting Human Rights to Health at a Global Level

As we have seen, some of the key challenges in progressing the health and human rights agenda lie in the wider context of what is an increasingly globalised world. The sovereignty of individual countries is being limited by the growing power of a range of international and global entities while the dominant discourses of neo-liberalism are frequently at odds with the aspirational discourse of economic and social rights.

In what has been called the 'post-Westphalian' world, nation states are no longer the only key players.[13] There is now a more complex system made up of a wide variety of interest groups: public and private, corporate as well as philanthropic. The sovereignty of most nations has been curtailed by the emergence of these powerful and genuinely transnational actors leading to much more diverse processes of policy making and implementation at a number of different levels (Kickbusch and Gleicher 2012).

We can look at the implications of this from two perspectives. On the one hand, much of the power concentrated in this new 'global architecture' functions to sustain the existing inequalities between the 'rich world' and the 'poor world'. On the other hand, the resulting trans-nationalism can be seen to offer glimmerings of a global 'demos' with individuals as global citizens. This will enhance the potential for further human rights developments across international borders: the very vision of cosmopolitanism outlined in Chapter 8. A review of strategies for the mitigation of the HIV pandemic and for the wider promotion of global health will need to begin with a clear understanding of the significance of these new realities and the tensions and contradictions between them.

The most powerful organisations outside nation states are multi-national corporations whose role is clearly identified with the pursuit of profit meaning that they have a huge impact on the distribution of world resources. Aligned with these institutions are the organisations set up to regulate the operations of the international economy, including the World Trade Organization (WTO), the International Monetary Fund (IMF) and the World Bank. These are effectively controlled by representatives of the wealthier and more powerful nations which

---

13   The term 'Westphalian' is used by scholars in international relations to describe a world made up of sovereign states with political self-determination, legal equality between states and the principle of non-intervention by one state in the affairs of another.

make up their membership. Whatever their officially stated objectives, they too play a key role in maintaining the current distribution of global resources.

At the same time, some of the earlier international organisations which began with a human rights mandate have gradually weakened. This is especially true of the World Health Organisation which has become increasingly dependent on its richer donors and now has a predominantly technical rather than a values-based focus (Kickbusch et al 2010). But over the same period there has been a marked increase in the number of other organisations concerned in one way or another with health issues. As the leadership of WHO began to fade a new set of actors emerged as both autonomous and partnering players with nation states and international organisations (Hein and Kickbusch 2012; Ng and Ruger 2011).

Among these are private for profit and civil society organisations as well as public institutions. By 2010 more than 200 public–private partnerships were working in the health field, while 185 health related NGOs were officially accredited with the UN. These include faith-based, community-based and patient-based organisations as well as professional associations, workers' groups and those concerned more broadly with the 'politics of health': 'In just over two decades global health has gained a political visibility and status that some authors have called a political revolution' (Kickbusch 2011 p.1)

It is in this new political space that the battles over health and human rights will be fought. Victories will not be easy to achieve because of the greater power and resources that lie with those individuals, corporations and international regulatory agencies that currently hold the reins of global capitalism. Moreover in the context of such domination, the lack of leadership among the diversity of progressive interest groups has sometimes led to what has been described as 'anarchy and chaos'. This poses a challenge of how such 'creative plurality' can be coordinated in the most effective way to tackle the HIV epidemics and to promote wider human well-being (Hein and Kickbusch 2012).

The first step will involve democratic debates to achieve the greatest possible convergence in normative values between these different groups aiming to promote the optimisation of human well-being. As we saw in Chapter 8, it is in this context that a rigorous and firmly grounded philosophy and discourse of individual human rights can play an especially important role. The second step entails more collaborative advocacy in an attempt to ensure that the current processes of social and economic restructuring are as health-centric as possible (Fidler 2008, 2008–9; Hein and Kickbusch 2012). Ilona Kickbusch has summarised this as follows: '... we need to be pushing beyond a narrow focus on health services to a 'whole of government' and 'whole of society' approach. This of course echoes what Paul Farmer said about HIV and human rights at the end of Chapter 8.

Such change will not of course be easy to achieve. Despite their collective commitment to work for health reform, it cannot be assumed that these very diverse organisations will necessarily want to work together in any formal way. Indeed it is obvious that in many cases they do not. They may well have different immediate interests and be competing for a dwindling pool of resources, as we have already demonstrated in the context of 'AIDS exceptionalism'. As David Fidler has succinctly commented: 'The Gates Foundation may no more march to the tune of WHO than the US will to the cadence of the UN' (Fidler 2008 p.8).

Despite such fragmentation, this is an opportune moment for activism since a broad range of individuals and organisations are currently collaborating in the creation of what is referred to as the Post-15 Agenda. The UN Millennium Development Strategy officially ends in 2015. While the pursuit of the eight development goals or MDGs had mixed success, the need for the formulation of a new global development strategy has been agreed by the UN and debates have begun (UN 2012). Many different stakeholders are now attempting to learn from earlier mistakes and to build on the achievements of the MDGs.

Debates have focussed on three interrelated issues that have been central to the themes of this book: health, inequalities and human rights. It therefore seems appropriate to undertake a brief review of the links between these themes and future development strategies with HIV and AIDS as a central focus.

Limited Progress on Health

The original MDGs were closely linked to health issues although only three were focussed on specific targets: reducing childhood deaths (MDG4), improving maternal health (MDG5), combating HIV and AIDS, malaria, TB and other major diseases (MDG6). Progress on meeting these targets has been variable both between regions and countries and also between specific goals. The number of childhood deaths fell from 12 million in 2000 to 7.6 million in 2010. And as we have seen, many more people are now able to access ART. However the WHO target of universal access by 2010 was missed by a wide margin. Deaths from both malaria and TB have fallen but both continue to take a severe toll in the poorest parts of the world. Attempts to reduce rates of maternal mortality have made least progress with around half a million women continuing to die each year (UN 2012).

One of the major criticisms of the Millennium Development Strategy has been the failure to make appropriate links between these different health targets, with separate and what have often been competing strategies directed towards each problem. These comments were borne out by the analysis in the preceding text. We have seen for example the obstacles posed by the failure to link interventions tackling maternal mortality and TB with HIV in particular.[14] In short, 'joined up' policy and practice will be essential.

If greater success is to be achieved post-2015, access will need to be guaranteed to integrated health services based on sustainable foundations at affordable cost. Within these services there will be an urgent need for more effective and appropriate reproductive and sexual health care both for its inherent benefits in promoting the well-being of users but also as an essential element in reducing both

---

14   See Chapters 4 and 7.

maternal mortality and HIV transmission.[15] It will be essential that these are based on the model of sexual and reproductive rights elaborated at the International Conference on Population and Development (ICPD) in Cairo in 1994.[16]

Empowering Women?

A second major criticism of the MDG strategy was its failure to make close enough operational and conceptual links between health and the very broad goal of MDG3: promoting gender equality and empowering women. During the last two decades, women in many parts of the world have made considerable gains in education, access to jobs and livelihoods.[17] More countries now guarantee equal rights in property, marriage and other domains. Gender gaps in primary schooling have begun to close while in a third of all countries girls now outnumber boys in secondary school. Women now make up about 40 per cent of the global labour force and 43 per cent of its farmers (World Bank 2012). But despite this progress, inequalities and thus disadvantages remain in many areas. Primary and secondary school enrolments for girls are still much lower than for boys in many Sub-Saharan African countries and some parts of South Asia, especially among disadvantaged populations.

Women are more likely than men to work as unpaid family labourers or in the informal sector and generally earn less than men. Indeed estimates indicate that women make up about 3/5 of the global poor. Poor women in particular still have less say over decisions and less control over household resources. And in most countries, fewer women participate in formal politics than men and are hugely underrepresented among decision makers (World Bank 2012).

We have seen throughout the book that gender inequalities play a significant part in shaping the physical health and autonomy of both women and men, operating at individual, interpersonal and structural levels. This is especially evident in the context of HIV where as we have seen, the limitations many women experience on their capacity to control their sexual lives as well as their fertility greatly increases their vulnerability to infection. Their more limited access to a wide range of resources including income, status and entitlement to informal care are also of major relevance in shaping the well-being of those who are living with HIV.

Hence gender inequalities will need to be a central element of any rights based health practice. While this will focus mostly on the greater disadvantage suffered by women, the gendered nature of men's lives will also need to be taken into account. In the context of HIV and AIDS in particular, much more thought will need to be given both to the implications of male gender for men's own health as

---

15   See Chapter 6.

16   The strengthening of sexual and reproductive rights is already a central part of the planning for the ICPD Beyond 2014 conference.

17   Although these cannot all be attributed to the Millennium Development Strategy they are usually included in related evaluations.

well as the relevance of a range of different male and female sexualities for the development of appropriate services.

The reduction of discrimination relating to gender and (where appropriate) sexuality will therefore need to be identified as explicit goals but also to be mainstreamed through all aspects of health policy. This will require much more consistent use of existing gender-related human rights legislation particularly the Convention on the Elimination of All Forms of Discrimination Against Women (CEDAW) and the Platform of Action from ICPD.

Human Rights, Health and Development: Poverty and Inequality

In the final section we need to explore the implications for HIV and AIDS of what is often represented as the most fundamental of the Millennium Targets: the reduction of poverty and hunger (MDG1). Much has been achieved with the number of people living in extreme poverty falling in all regions including sub-Saharan Africa. The proportion of people living on less than $1.25 per day fell from 47 per cent (over 2 billion) in 2000 to 24 per cent (less than 1.4 billion) in 2010. Despite recent slowdowns in the fate of improvement due to the post-2008 financial crisis, it is estimated that the MDG1 target of halving those in extreme poverty will be met by the 2015 deadline (UN 2012).

But despite this reduction estimates indicate that by 2015 at least a billion people will still be living on less than $1.25 a day, four out of every five of whom will be in sub-Saharan Africa and South Asia. This geographical overlap between those living in poverty and those living with HIV and dying with AIDS draws our attention back to the issue of basic and intermediate needs discussed in Chapter 1 and the implications of the failure to satisfy them not just for human flourishing but for survival itself.

For millions of those living with HIV, poverty is likely to mean they will be harmed by lack of access to ART, along with clean water, nutritious food, and appropriate sanitation. They are also likely to lack a range of opportunities that might have enabled them to realise more of their potential despite their biological disadvantage. As we have seen, an obvious example of this would be the opportunity to have children and raise them to adulthood. If their well-being is to be improved and their life expectancy increased, ways will have to be found to deal with the profound local, national and global inequalities that still lie behind the relative poverty and disadvantage of such a large proportion of the world's population.

Thinking about Inequality and Poverty

The last few years have seen a marked shift in development discourse from an emphasis on the elimination of poverty to the reduction of inequality. This shift has occurred during the period when inequalities in income, wealth and power have dramatically increased both within and between countries. Indeed the World Economic Forum's own Global Risk Report identified inequality as one of the top risks for the near future (World Economic Forum 2013).

To give just a few examples: in the US the share of national income going to the top 1 per cent of the population has doubled since 1980 from 10 per cent to 20 per cent. In the very different circumstances of China, the top 10 per cent now take home nearly 60 per cent of the income while South Africa is now the most unequal society on earth with greater inequality than that found during apartheid. At a global level a recent Oxfam study estimated that the top 100 billionaires added 240 billion to their wealth in 2012 alone – enough to end world poverty four times over (Oxfam 2013).

The dangers of this growing inequality have been identified from a number of different perspectives. They are economically inefficient since they limit investment as well as reducing demand. As a result, economic growth in more equal countries is more effective at reducing poverty. They are also an obstacle to democracy since those with the greatest wealth are able to use it to influence both national and international decision making in their own interests. And finally of course we can see inequality as unfair since the poverty and disadvantage that it promulgates act as major obstacles to the adequate meeting of basic human needs. Recognition of this reality will need to be central in future attempts to fulfil the human right to the highest attainable health. As a recent Oxfam report stressed 'Post-2015 *must place tackling inequality front and centre*' (Oxfam 2013). But how can this be done?

The conceptual work of Thomas Pogge is frequently used as a starting point for formulating a feasible human rights framework to achieve this. He begins with the argument that the harm caused by poverty is the most important cause of ill-health and the single most important obstacle to the realisation of human rights. He traces this poverty back to the profoundly unequal economic relationships between countries which are sustained by international corporations and organisations over which the poor countries have little or no control (Pogge 2007, 2008).

Under these circumstances Pogge argues that there is little to be gained from formulating policy focussed only on the positive economic and social rights of individuals to access particular goods and services. While in some circumstances, this may be effective – the increased provision of ART to some seropositive individuals for example – the therapeutic success of the drug may still be obviated by the effects of continuing poverty. Equally, as Onora O'Neill correctly reminded us in the last chapter, the institutionalisation of such positive economic and social rights cannot necessarily be relied upon. However important their moral force and aspirational influence may be, national, corporate and individual inertia may lead to them being ignored or not properly enforced.

In the face of such uncertainty, Pogge argues that human rights claims can most effectively be framed in terms of the negative right of individuals not to be forseeably and preventably harmed in ways that conflict with their critical interests. In making this claim, he invokes a central and widely shared moral principle:

that it is wrong to harm innocent people in pursuit of minor gains. Respect for this principle therefore imposes a strict duty on individuals and organisations to protect others from harm of this kind for which they can be deemed responsible. If this principle is to be upheld it will require a dramatic shift in economic and social values as well as the reform of those institutions currently promoting the privileges of the rich at the cost to the poor. Pogge explains his position in this way:

> An institutional order is human-rights violating when it foreseeably gives rise to greater insecurity in access to the objects of human rights (physical integrity, freedom of movement, adequate nutrition, etc.) than would be reasonably avoidable through an alternative feasible institutional design. Moral claims on social institutions are also, indirectly, moral claims against those who participate in designing and upholding these social institutions. Such agents, too, are violating human rights by imposing an institutional order under which access to the objects of human rights is foreseeably and avoidably insecure for some or all participants. (Pogge 2005 p.43)

Such criticism can be directed not only at international institutions such as the WTO but also at multinational corporations that cause harm through disadvantaging millions of people by limiting their earning power and/or controlling their access to necessary goods through lack of supply or high prices (Koivusalo 2011). This complex mix of profit-seeking economic activity and one-sided regulation is in urgent need of moral scrutiny and appropriate reform if basic human needs are to be met – and not just for those who are HIV positive. Again Pogge offers a dramatic illustration of this point:

> ... it is reasonably possible for us *not* to deplete African fish stocks, *not* to distort world markets through massive subsidies and other protectionist measures that hamper exports from poor countries, *not* to insist on pharmaceutical monopolies that deprive the poor of access to generic version of advanced medicines, *not* to recognize and arm rulers who oppress their compatriots and steal their resources. (Pogge 2011 pp.243–44)

Taking Action for Health

Working with Pogge's conceptual model (or something similar to it), research will be needed to bring the direct and indirect harms caused by different elements of the present economic order into the light of day. And adequate resources for identifying these will need to be built into further strategies for development. But even if this information can be produced it will not be easy to generate the necessary reforms in a world where different types of power are so heavily concentrated.

The most obvious strategy is likely to be one of 'naming and shaming' those national and corporate decision makers whose policies run counter to the civil and political and social and economic rights of so many of the world's poorest people

(Pogge 2008 pp.70–73; Benatar and Doyal 2009; Navarro 2011). Vicente Navarro has put it very plainly: 'It is not inequalities that kill people. It is people that produce and reproduce inequalities through their public and private interventions that kill people. In most cases we have the specific names of those responsible for those inequalities and therefore for those deaths' (Navarro 2009 p.15). Pulling the veil away from these individuals and organisations is in itself an important political act in a situation where, as Bob Dylan famously suggested: 'the executioner's face is always well hidden' (Dylan 1962). However this will not be enough.

More formal processes of institutional change and collective accountability will also be required if the satisfaction of the basic needs of the disadvantaged is to be improved. Returning to the Millennium Development Strategy, it was widely criticised for failing to specify the mechanics of change, to formulate strategies for implementation and to develop rigorous modes of accountability. Hence it will be essential to spell these out in planning the Post 2015 Agenda.

Solving what Kickbusch has called these 'wicked problems' will not be easy in such a complex scenario without obvious leadership (Kickbusch et al. 2010). The notion of a world government would be hopelessly idealistic as well as a threat to the legitimate autonomy of individual nations. However this should not be assumed to rule out a more effective and rights-based system of what is now termed 'global governance'. That is to say, this would entail the creation of concrete cooperative problem-solving arrangements, many of which would increasingly involve not only the United Nations or individual states but also 'other UNs', namely international secretariats and other non-state actors (Pang et al. 2010).

Of course, such institutions of governance would need to be designed to operate with progressive values. They would require a central focus on social justice to meet the needs of the most disadvantaged. In this way they could inject greater equality and fairness into the management of problems relating to economic interdependence and the uneven distribution and ownership of wealth and natural resources. The constituent institutions would be centrally focussed on social justice and the recognition of moral culpability for the poverty and many varieties of harm, including ill health, that they impose on individuals: 'At present the consideration of the needs of the global poor are not part of the mandate of any of the powerful parties in global interaction and this needs to change' (Johri et al 2012 p.8).

The importance of initiatives of this kind has been highlighted by Paulo Teixeira, former director of the Brazilian National AIDS Programme, on the basis of his own experience:

> The biggest challenge for the future of the Brazilian National AIDS Program is the maintenance and the sustainability of the policy of free and universal access to ARVs. This is directly linked to a change in the world economic order with regard to medicines. It will depend not only on a firm position by Brazil, in the defence of its policy of production and distribution of ARVs, but also on

the strengthening of international alliances that are beginning to form with the World Health Organization, the World Trade Organization, the United Nations Special Session on HIV/AIDS, and the Global Fund to Fight AIDS, Tuberculosis and Malaria. (cited in Galvao 2005 p.1111)[18]

Similar strategies will be needed to deal with a range of global problems, including the food insecurity that is now reaching crisis point in so many parts of the world (Hunter 2007; Murphy et al. 2005; McIntyre and Rondeau 2011; Gill and Bakker 2011). Again, adequate nutrition has been defined as a human right in Article 25 of the UN Declaration. However the mechanisms for putting this into practice have proved extremely limited, with the World Food Programme in its current form making relatively little impact as a result of the commercial imperatives shaping so many of its policies.

Increasing the number of safe, productive and fairly paid jobs and promoting secure and sustainable livelihoods will also be central to a health-promoting development strategy. According to the International Labour Organisation (ILO) 45–50 million new jobs will be needed annually over the next ten years just to keep up with the growth of the world's working age population and to reduce the unemployment caused by the economic crisis (ILO 2012) Most of these will need to be created through domestic policies designed to achieve full and productive employment. However they should be framed within a set of international regulations designed to secure 'decent' work for all. This initiative would of course need to be accompanied by progress towards universal access to a basic set of income guarantees and social protection floors to protect those whose capacity for work is limited or non-existent (ILO 2012).

These reforms in global governance will need to be done on the basis of a common set of values. They will need to be democratic in form and appropriate mechanisms of enforcement will be necessary to ensure that each organisation is held accountable for any harm it does to those it is intended to serve: 'Overall global health governance needs to resolve the current imbalances and bring a greater sense of coherence to the "big picture" of global health' (Gostin and Mok 2009 p.9). While these developments will not be easy to achieve, they lie at the heart of the campaign for the optimisation of health through the realisation of both negative civil and political rights *and* positive social and economic rights.

---

18   Following this line, Gillian Brock has argued for what she calls a TRIPS Commission. This would be a 'neutral, high level body to review and assess development proposals and recommend new intellectual property regimes for pharmaceutical products' (Brock 2009 Chapter 9). While this would need to respect justifiable rights for inventors and developers, it would also need to focus on meeting the needs of the millions who still require not just ART but other drugs for all poverty-related diseases, some of which remain entirely neglected.

What about the Money?

Thus far our discussions have assumed that resources for global health in general and HIV in particular will always be scarce. And realistically this is likely to be the case. But that does not mean that current levels of public funding should not be interrogated. The existing level of resources allocated to HIV and AIDS in particular and to 'public expenditure' more generally is not 'natural' but politically determined and could potentially be increased (Navarro 2009; Schrecker 2008; Pogge 2008).

Hence it is important to place current levels of public expenditure in some broader context. At this stage in history (2013) the most obvious sums to compare would be the many trillions of dollars mobilised over a short time to save the US and UK banks and financial services, compared with the $750 billion promised (but not yet delivered) to meet all the Millennium Development Goals over a 15-year period. Similarly we can compare this long-term MDG budget with the annual US defence budget of around $1 trillion.

We must continue to ask questions about the morality of such priorities. While the US has contributed a large volume of health aid to poor countries this has still amounted to only about 0.01 per cent of its own GDP. Other wealthy countries have contributed still less. Given the arguments made throughout this book, there seems no way that such very limited redistribution can be morally justified. If the maximum available resources are to be directed towards human rights implementation, much more money will be needed for health care, water, food, sanitation and a range of other intermediate needs. To achieve this goal, a number of different taxes have been suggested that could be levied on particular forms of global activity such as air travel, emails, share transactions and carbon emissions (Brock 2011 Chapter 5).

Schemes of this kind could play a part in meeting the gap between public needs and available resources if global mechanisms for their collection could be made to function effectively. But sufficient funding is unlikely to be achieved without redistributive policies that change the rules of the game. Most importantly, the issue of tax evasion needs to be moved to the top of the agenda. Only money identified by the relevant authorities can be taxed. As a result billions of dollars are stashed in tax havens, Swiss bank accounts and other financial boltholes every year. Indeed an authoritative recent study came to the staggering conclusion that the world's super rich were currently holding some $21 trillion in unaccountable wealth siphoned off through tax evasion and avoidance (Tax Justice Network 2012). The most striking finding of all was that when the nationality of the beneficiaries is taken into account Africa as a whole becomes a creditor rather than a debtor region (Shaxson et al. 2012; Stewart 2012). This clearly casts a very different light on the assumed 'inevitability' of the burden of poverty and HIV and AIDS currently being carried by the people of the region.

Alicia Yamin has summarised the situation succinctly:

A post-2015 development agenda must recognize that we need systems of global responsibility and global redistribution if we are to have an international order in which the rights and freedom set forth in the Universal Declaration of Human Rights can be fully realized. If the basic rules of the game are not changed simply aligning the language used to describe the post 2015 goals with international human rights norms as has been suggested by some, is beside the point. Indeed it may amount to no more than co-opting rights rhetoric to give a patina of legitimacy and universality to a deeply flawed neo-liberal paradigm in which the mantra of scarcity is invoked for the masses while the elite continue to live in luxury. (Yamin 2011 p.2)

Conclusion

In this book, we have examined the experiences of HIV positive people from diagnosis to (eventual) death via a variety of what will often be very different routes. We have outlined the needs and rights that they all have in common with others afflicted by poverty and explored some of the reasons why these so often go unmet. Recommendations have been made for the formulation and implementation of strategies at both national and international levels to begin to remedy these disadvantages. However we have also noted the major obstacles that stand in the way of such changes.

Turning back to the HIV and AIDS pandemic itself we can see this story as changing shades of darkness and light. It began with those dark years when a positive diagnosis was an inevitable death sentence. But light was shed for some with the success of new therapies as well as greater prosperity. While this light has gradually filtered out from the global north, it still shines much less brightly in many of the poorest parts of the world where the numbers living with HIV are continuing to grow. Some have had their lives revitalised by access to health care but there is a real danger that they may still be unable to sustain an adequate quality of life. Their access to drugs may be ended by reduced funding. And even if it is not, the gathering economic crisis may reduce their capacity to maintain the minimally healthy lifestyle necessary to enable optimal use of ART.

Finally of course we need to consider the millions who are still in the darkness, waiting for relief from sickness and impending death, often in circumstances where they are stigmatised and rejected rather than respected. 'Human immunodeficiency virus: its first name is "human". To defeat it, the world and its laws must embrace and promote what every living person shares: the fragile, immensely potent human rights to equality, dignity and health' (Global Commission on HIV and the Law 2012 p.89).

References

Abbott F (2005) The WTO medicines decision: world pharmaceutical trade and the protection of public health. *American Journal of International Law* 99 (2) 317–58.

Abdool-Karim Q, AbouZahr C, Dehne K, Mangiaterra V, Moodley J, Rollins N, Say L, Schaffer N, Rosen J, de Zoysa I (2010) HIV and maternal mortality: turning the tide. *Lancet* 375 (9730) 1948–9.

Abdool-Karim S, Abdool-Karim Q, Friedland G, Lallo U, El Sadr W, Wafaa M (2004) Implementing antiretroviral therapy in resource-constrained settings: opportunities and challenges in integrating HIV and tuberculosis care. *AIDS* 18 (7) 975–9.

Abrahams N, Jewkes R, Hoffman M, Laubsher R (2004) Sexual violence against intimate partners in Cape Town: prevalence and risk factors reported by men. *Bulletin of the World Health Organization* 82 (5) 330–37.

Aceijas C, Oppenheimer E, Stimson G, Ashcroft R, Matic S, Hickman M (2006) Antiretroviral treatment for injecting drug users in developing and transitional countries one year before the end of the 'Treating 3 million by 2005. Making it happen'. The WHO Strategy ('3 by 5') *Addiction* 101 1246–53.

Adam B, Husbands W, Murray J, Maxwell J (2005) AIDS optimism, condom fatigue or self-esteem? *Journal of Sex Research* 42 (3) 238–48.

Adam B (2011) Epistemic faultlines in biomedical and social approaches to HIV prevention. *Journal of the International AIDS Society* 14 (Suppl 2) S2.

Adams J and Neville S (2009) Men who have sex with men account for non-use of condoms. *Qualitative Health Research* 19 (12) 1669–77.

Adams V and Pigg S (eds) (2005) Sex *in Development: Science, Sexuality and Morality in Global Perspective*. London and Durham SC: Duke University Press.

AEGIS-IRIN (2009) Lesotho: Big Brands bring treatment to the factory floor. UN: IRIN (5 February).

Aggleton P (2009) Researching same-sex sexuality and HIV prevention. In V Reddy, T Sandfort and L Rispel *From Social Silence to Social Science*. Cape Town: HSRC Press.

Agyemang C, Bhopal R and Bruijnzeels M (2005) Negro, Black African, African Caribbean, African American or what? Labelling African origin populations in the health arena in the 21st century. *Journal of Epidemiology and Community Health* 59 (12) 1014–18.

AIDSTAR-Two (2010) *Men having sex with men in Eastern Europe: Implications of a Hidden HIV Epidemic*. Washington DC: USAID.

AIDS2031 (2010) *AIDS: Taking a Long Term View*. London: Financial Times Press.

Akintola O (2008) Unpaid HIV/AIDS care in Southern Africa: forms, content and implications. *Feminist Economics* 14 (4) 117–47.

Alcano MC (2009) Living and working in spite of antiretroviral therapies: strength in chronicity. *Anthropology and Medicine* 16 (2) 119–30.

Alkire S (2002) Dimensions of human development. *World Development* 30 (2) 181–205.

Alldis E (2009) *Primary Concern: Why Primary Health Care is Key to Tackling HIV and AIDS*. London: Action Aid.

Allen C, Mbonye M, Seeley J, Birungi J, Wolff B, Coutinho A, Jaffar, S (2011) ABC for people with HIV: responses to sexual behaviour recommendations among people receiving antiretroviral therapy in Jinja, Uganda. *Culture, Health and Sexuality* 13 (5) 529–43.

Allison E and Seeley J (2004) HIV and AIDS among fisherfolk: a threat to 'responsible fisheries'? *Fish and Fisheries* 5 (3) 215–34.

Alonzo A and Reynolds N (1995) Stigma, HIV and AIDS: an exploration and elaboration of a stigma trajectory. *Social Science and Medicine* 41 (3) 303–15.

Ambrosioni J, Calmy A, Hirschel B (2011) HIV treatment for prevention. *Journal of the International AIDS Society* 14 28.

Amoateng A, Richter L, Makiwane M. Rama S (2004). *Describing the Structure and Needs of Families in South Africa: Towards the Development of a National Policy Framework for Families*. A report commissioned by the Department of Social Development. Pretoria: Child Youth and Family Development, Human Sciences Research Council (HSRC).

Amon J (2008) Dangerous medicines: Unproven AIDS cures and counterfeit antiretroviral drugs. *Globalization and Health* 4 5.

Anderson M, Elam G, Gerver S, Solarin I, Fenton K, Easterbrook P (2008) HIV/AIDS related stigma and discrimination: accounts of HIV positive Caribbean people in the United Kingdom. *Social Science and Medicine* 67 (5) 790–98.

Anderson M, Elam G, Gerver S, Solarin I, Fenton K, Easterbrook P (2009) Liminal identities: Caribbean men who have sex with men in London, UK. *Culture, Health and Sexuality* 11 (3) 315–30.

Anderson T (2009) Innovative financing of health care. *BMJ* 339 4235.

Anema A, Vogenthaler N, Frongillo E, Kadiyala S, Weiser S (2009) Food insecurity and HIV/AIDS: current knowledge, gaps and research priorities. *Current HIV/AIDS Reports* 6 (4) 224–31.

Anema A, Weiser SP, Fernandes KA, Ding E, Brandson EK, Palmer A, Montaner JS, Hogg RS (2011) High prevalence of food insecurity among HIV-infected individuals receiving HAART in a resource rich setting. *AIDS Care* 23 (2) 221–30.

Angotti N (2010) Working outside of the box: How HIV counsellors in sub-Saharan Africa adapt western HIV testing norms. *Social Science and Medicine* 71 (5) 986–93.

Annandale E and Riska E (2009) New connections: towards a gender inclusive approach to women's and men's health. *Current Sociology* 57 (2) 123–33.

Ansell N, Robson E, Hajdu F, van Blerk L, Chipeta L (2009) The new variant famine hypothesis: moving beyond the household in exploring links between AIDS and food insecurity in Southern Africa. *Progress in Development Studies* 9 (3) 187–207.

Ansell N and van Blerk L (2004) Children's migration as a household/family strategy: coping with AIDS in southern Africa. *Journal of Southern African Studies* 30 (3) 673–90.

Antelman G, Smith Fawzi MC, Kaaya S, Mbwambo J, Msamanga G, Hunter DJ, Fawzi WW (2001) Predictors of HIV-1 serostatus disclosure: a prospective study among HIV-infected pregnant women in Dar es Salaam, Tanzania. *AIDS* 15 (14) 1865–74.

Antoniou T, Loutfy M, Glazier R, Strike C (2012) 'Waiting at the dinner table for scraps' a qualitative study of the help-seeking experiences of heterosexual men living with human immunodeficiency virus infection. *BMJ Open* 2 (4) e00697.

Appleton, J. (2000). 'At my age I should be sitting under the tree': The impact of AIDS on Tanzanian lakeshore communities. *Gender and Development* 8 (2) 19–27.

Ashford E (2007) The duties imposed by the human right to basic necessities. In T Pogge (ed.) *Freedom from Poverty as a Human Right*. New York: Oxford University Press.

Asia Catalyst (2012) *China's Blood Disaster: The Way Forward*. http://www. asiacatalyst.org.

Auerbach JD, Parkhurst JO, Caceres CF (2011) Addressing social drivers of HIV/AIDS for the long term response: conceptual and methodological considerations. *Global Public Health* 6 (Suppl 3) S293–309.

Babb DK, Pemba L, Seatlanye P, Charalambous S, Churchyard GJ, Grant AD (2007) Use of traditional medicines by HIV infected individuals in South Africa in the era of antiretroviral therapy. *Psychology, Health and Medicine* 12 (3) 314–20.

Backman G, Hunt P, Khosla R et al. (2008) Health systems and the right to health: an assessment of 194 countries. *Lancet* 372 (9655) 2047–85.

Baek N and Rutenberg C (2010) Implementing programs for the prevention of mother-to-child transmission in resource-constrained settings: Horizons Studies 1999–2007. *Public Health Report* 125 (2) 293–304.

Baggaley RF, White R, Boily M-C (2010) HIV transmission risk through anal intercourse: a systematic review, meta-analysis and implications for HIV prevention. *International Journal of Epidemiology* 39 (4) 1048–1063.

Baker B (2008) *Poverty, Racism, Globalization and Macroeconomic Fundamentalism: Structural Determinants of the Global AIDS Pandemic*. Boston: GAP, Northeastern University School of Law.

Baker BK (2010) The impact of the International Monetary Fund's macroeconomic policies on the AIDS pandemic. *International Journal of Health Services* 40 (2) 347–63.

Bangsberg D, Ware N, Simoni JM (2006) Adherence without access to antiretroviral therapy in sub-Saharan Africa? *AIDS* 20 (1) 140–41.

Baral S, Sifakis F, Cleghorn F, Beyrer C (2007) Elevated risk for HIV infection among men who have sex with men in low- and middle-income countries 2000–2006: a systematic review. *PLOS Medicine* 4 (12) e339.

Baral S, Beyrer C, Muessig K, Poteat T, Wirtz AL, Decker MR, Sherman SG, Kerrigan D. (2012) Burden of HIV among female sex workers in low and middle income countries *Lancet Infectious Diseases* 12 (7) 538–49.

Barker G and Ricardo C (2005) *Young Men and the Social Construction of Masculinity in Sub-Saharan Africa*. Washington DC: World Bank Social Development Papers.

Barker G and Veroni F (2008) *Men's Participation as Fathers in the Latin American and Caribbean Regions: A Critical Literature Review with Policy Considerations*. Brazil: Promundo and Save the Children.

Barnabas NN, Edin KE, Hurtig (2010) 'When I get better I will do the test': facilitators and barriers to HIV testing in Northwest Region of Cameroon with implications for TB and HIV/AIDS control programmes. *SAHARA Journal* 7 (4) 24–32.

Barnett T (2006) A long-wave event: HIV/AIDS, politics, governance and 'security': sundering the inter-generational bond? *International Affairs* 82 (2) 297–313.

Barnett T and Parkhurst J (2005) HIV/AIDS, sex, abstinence and behaviour change. *Lancet Infectious Diseases* 5 (9) 590–93.

Barnett T and Whiteside A (2002) Poverty and HIV: impact, coping and mitigation policy. in GA Cornia (ed.) *AIDS, Public Policy and Child Well-being*. Florence: UNICEF Innocenti Research Centre.

Barnett T and Whiteside A (2006) *AIDS in the 21st Century: Disease and Globalization*. London: Palgrave Macmillan.

Barnett T, Whiteside A, Desmond C (2001) The social and economic impact of HIV/AIDS in poor countries: A review of studies and lessons. *Progress in Development Studies* 1 (2) 151–70.

Barnighausen T, Bloom D, Humair S (2010) Universal antiretroviral treatment: the challenge of human resources. *Bulletin of the World Health Organisation* 88 (12) 951–2.

Barnighausen T, Hosegood V, Timaeus IM, Newell M-L (2007) The socioeconomic determinants of HIV incidence: evidence from a longitudinal, population-based study in rural South Africa. *AIDS* 21 (Suppl 7) S29–38.

Barr D, Amon JJ, Clayton M (2011) Articulating a rights based approach to HIV treatment and prevention interventions. *Current HIV Research* 9 (6) 396–404.

Bastian H (2000) A consumer trip into the world of DALY calculations: an Alice-in-Wonderland experience. *Reproductive Health Matters* 8 (15) 113–16.

Bastos FI, Caceres C, Galvao J, Veras MA, Castilho EA (2008) AIDS in Latin America: assessing the current status of the epidemic and the ongoing response. *International Journal of Epidemiology* 37 (4) 729–37.

Baumgartner L (2007) The incorporation of the HIV/AIDS identity into the self over time. *Qualitative Health Research* 17 (7) 919–31.

Bayer R (1996) AIDS prevention: sexual ethics and responsibility. *New England Journal of Medicine* 334 (23) 1540–42.

Bayer R and Edington C (2009) HIV testing, human rights and global AIDS policy: exceptionalism and its discontents. *Journal of Health Politics, Policy and Law* 34 (3) 301–23.

Baylies, C (2002) HIV/AIDS and older women in Zambia: concern for self, worry over daughters, towers of strength. *Third World Quarterly* 23 (2) 351–75.

Beard J, Feeley F, Rosen S (2009) Economic and quality of life outcomes of anti-retroviral therapy for HIV/AIDS in developing countries: a systematic literature review. *AIDS Care* 21 (11) 1343–56.

Beck (2004) *Antiretroviral Therapy in South Africa: An Investigation among Xhosa Speaking Men in Khayelitsha, Cape Town.* Cape Town: Centre for Social Science Research UCT.

Becker S (2007) Global perspectives on children's unpaid caregiving in the family. *Global Social Policy* 7 (1) 23–50.

Beckmann N and Bujra J (2010) 'The politics of the queue': the politicisation of people living with HIV/AIDS in Tanzania. *Development and Change* 41 (60) 1041–64.

Bekker LG, Egger M, Wood R (2007) Early antiretroviral therapy in resource-limited settings: what can we do about it? *Current Opinion in HIV and AIDS* 2 (4) 346–51.

Bekker L-G, Beyrer C, Quinn TC (2012) Behavioral and biomedical combination strategies for HIV prevention. *Cold Spring Harbour Perspectives in Medicine* 2 (8). http://perspectivesinmedicine.net/content/2/8/a007435.

Belden KA and Squires KE (2008) HIV infection in women: do sex and gender matter? *Current Infectious Diseases Reports* 10 (5) 423–431.

Bell E, Mthembu P, O'Sullivan S, Moody K (2007) Sexual and reproductive health services and HIV testing: perspectives and experiences of women and men living with HIV and AIDS. *Reproductive Health Matters* 15 (Suppl 29) 113–35.

Bell J (2004) *Children Care for their Dying Parents.* World Vision Cambodia. http://worldvision.org.kh/featuredet_35.html.

Benatar S and Doyal L (2009) Human rights abuses: toward balancing two perspectives. *International Journal of Health Services* 39 (1) 139–59.

Benatar S, Daar A, Singer P (2011) Global health ethics: the rationale for mutual caring. In S. Benatar and G Brock (eds) Global *Health and Global Health Ethics.* Cambridge: Cambridge University Press.

Benatar S, Gill S, Bakker I (2009) Making progress in global health: the need for new paradigms. *International Affairs* 2 347–371.

Benatar S, Gill S, Bakker I (2011) Global health and the global economic crisis. *American Journal of Public Health* 101 (4) 646–53.

Bene, C. and Merten S (2008) Women and fish-for-sex: transactional sex, HIV/ AIDS and gender in African fisheries. *World Development* 36 (5) 875–99.

Bennett R, Draper H, Frith L (2000) Ignorance is bliss? HIV and moral duties and legal duties to forewarn. *Journal of Medical Ethics* 26 (1) 9–15.

Berer M (1999) HIV/AIDS, pregnancy and maternal mortality and morbidity: implications for care. In M Berer and T Sundari Ravindran (eds) *Safe Motherhood Initiative: Critical Issues*. London: Blackwell Science for Reproductive Health Matters.

Bergenstrom AH and Abdul-Quader AS (2010) Injection drug use, HIV and the current response in selected low-income and middle-income countries. *AIDS* 24 (Suppl 3) S20–29.

Berger M (2004) *Workable Sisterhood: The Political Journey of Stigmatized Women*. Princeton NJ: Princeton University Press.

Berkman A, Garcia J, Munoz-Laboy M, Paiva V, Parker R (2005) A critical analysis of the Brazilian response to HIV/AIDS: lessons learned for controlling and mitigating the epidemics in developing countries. *American Journal of Public Health* 95 (7) 1162–72.

Bernatsky S, Souza R, de Jong K (2007) Mental health in HIV positive pregnant women: results from Angola. *AIDS Care* 19 (5) 674–6.

Bernays S and Rhodes T (2009) Experiencing uncertain HIV treatment delivery in a transitional setting: a qualitative study. *AIDS Care* 21 (3) 315–21.

Bernays S, Rhodes T, Barnett T (2007) Hope: a new way to look at the HIV epidemic. *AIDS* 21 (Suppl 5) S5–11.

Bernays S, Rhodes T, Terzic KJ (2010) 'You should be grateful to have medicines': continued dependence, altering stigma and the HIV treatment experience in Serbia. *AIDS Care* 22 (Suppl 1) 14–20.

Bernell, S. and Shinogle JA (2005) The relationship between HAART use and employment for HIV-positive individuals: an empirical analysis and policy outlook. *Health Policy* 71 (2) 255–64.

Beyeza-Kashesya J, Kaharuza F, Ekstrom AM, Mirembe F, Neema S, Kulane A (2010) My partner wants a child: a cross sectional study of the determinants of the desire for children among mutually disclosed sero-discordant couples receiving care in Uganda. *BMC Public Health* 10 247.

Beyeza-Kashesya J, Kaharuza F, Mirembe F, Neema S, Ekstrom AM, Kulane A (2009) The dilemma of safe sex and having children: challenges facing sero-discordant couples *African Health Sciences* 9 (1) 2–12.

Beyrer C, Baral S, Kerrigan D, El-Bassel N, Bekker L-G, Celentano DD (2011) Expanding the space: inclusion of most-at-risk populations in HIV prevention, treatment and care services. *Journal of Acquired Immune Deficiency Syndrome* 57 (Suppl 2) S96–9.

Bhagwanjee A, Petersen I, Akintola O, George G (2008) Bridging the gap between VCT and HIV treatment uptake: perspectives from a mining sector workplace in South Africa. *African Journal of AIDS Research* 7 (3) 271–9.

Bharat S (2011) A systematic review of HIV/AIDS-related stigma and discrimination in India: current understanding and future needs. *SAHARA Journal* 8 (3) 138–49.

Bhopal R (2008) *Ethnicity, Race and Health in Multicultural Societies: Foundations for Better Epidemiology, Public Health and Health Care.* Oxford: Oxford University Press.

Biehl J (2007) *The Will to Live: AIDS Therapies and the Politics of Survival.* Princeton NJ: Princeton University Press.

Black V, Brooke S, Chersich MF (2009) Effect of human immunodeficiency virus treatment on maternal mortality at a tertiary center in South Africa: a five-year audit. *Obstetrics and Gynecology* 114 (2 pt 1) 292–9.

Blair JM, Hanson DL, Jones JL, Dworkin MS (2004) Trends in pregnancy rates among women with human immunodeficiency virus. *Obstetrics and Gynecology* 103 (4) 663–8.

Blank MB, Metzger DS, Wingood GM, Di Clemente RJ (2008) The first national scientific meeting of the Social and Behavioural Sciences Research Network. *Journal of Acquired Immune Deficiency Syndrome* 47 (Suppl 1) S1–4.

Blas E, Gilson L, Kelly M, Labonte R et al. (2008) Addressing social determinants of health inequities : what can the state and civil society do? *Lancet* 372 (9650) 1684–9.

Bloom D, Reddy Bloom L, Steven D, Weston M (2006) *Business and HIV/ AIDS: A Healthier Partnership? A Global Review of the Business Response to HIV/AIDS 2005–2006.* Geneva: World Economic Forum Global Health Initiative.

Blystad A and Moland K (2009) Technologies of hope? Motherhood, HIV and infant feeding in Eastern Africa. *Anthropology and Medicine* 16 (2) 105–18.

Boily MC, Baggaley RF, Wang L, Masse B, White RG, Hayes RJ, Alary M (2009) Heterosexual risk of HIV-1 infection per sexual act: systematic review and meta-analysis of observational studies. *Lancet Infectious Diseases* 9 (2) 118–29.

Bond V and Nyblade L (2006) The importance of addressing the unfolding TB-HIV stigma in high HIV prevalence settings. *Journal of Community and Applied Social Psychology* 16 (6) 452–61.

Bond V (2010) 'It is not an easy decision on HIV especially in Zambia': opting for silence, limited disclosure and implicit understanding to retain a wider identity. *AIDS Care* 22 (Suppl 1) 6–13.

Bor J et al. (2012) Dramatic increases in adult life expectancy and economic benefits after ART roll out in rural South Africa. 19th International Conference on AIDS. Abstract TULBE05. Washington DC.

Boutayeb A (2009) The impact of HIV/AIDS on human development in African countries *BMC Public Health* 9 (Suppl 1) S3.

Bowleg L (2004) Love, sex and masculinity in socio-cultural context: HIV concerns and condom use among African-American men in heterosexual relationships. *Men and Masculinities* 7 (2) 166–86.

Bowleg L (2008) When Black + lesbian + women = Black lesbian woman: the methodological challenges of qualitative and quantitative intersectionality research. *Sex Roles* 59 (5–6) 312–25.

Boyce P, Huang Soo Lee M, Jenkins C, Mohamed S, Overs C, Paiva V, Reid E, Tan M, Aggleton P (2007) Putting sexuality (back) into HIV/AIDS: issues, theory, and practice. *Global Public Health* 2 (1) 1–34.

Boyer S, Marcellin F, Ongolo-Zogo P, Abega S et al. (2009) Financial barriers to HIV treatment in Yaounde, Cameroon: first results of a national cross sectional survey. *Bulletin of the World Health Organization* 87 (4) 279–87.

Braitstein P, Brinkhof M, Dabis F et al. (2006) Mortality of HIV-1-infected patients in the first year of antiretroviral therapy: comparison between low-income and high-income countries. *Lancet* 367 (9513) 817–24.

Brandt R (2009a) Mental health of people living with HIV/AIDS in Africa: a systematic review. *African Journal of AIDS Research* 8 (2)123–33.

Brandt R (2009b) Putting mental health on the agenda for HIV+ women: a review of evidence from sub-Saharan Africa. *Women and Health* 49 (2–3) 215–28.

Braveman PA, Cubbin C, Egerter S, Chideya S, Marchi K, Metzler M, Posner S (2005) Socioeconomic status in health research: one size does not fit all. *Journal of the American Medical Association* 294 (22) 2879–88.

Bray R and Brandt R (2007) Child care and poverty in South Africa: ethnographic challenge to conventional interpretations. *Journal of Children and the Family* 13 (1) 1–19.

Bredstrom A (2006) Intersectionality: a challenge for feminist HIV/AIDS research? *European Journal of Women's Studies* 13 (3) 229–43.

Breuer E, Myer L, Struthers H, Joska J (2011) HIV/AIDS and mental health research in sub-Saharan Africa: a systematic review. *African Journal of AIDS Research* 10 (2) 101–22.

Brickley DB, Le Dung Hanh D, Nguyen LT, Mandel JS, Giang LT, Sohn AH (2009) Community, family and partner-related stigma experienced by pregnant and postpartum women with HIV in Ho Chi Minh City, Vietnam. *AIDS and Behavior* 13 (6) 1197–204.

Brock D, Wikler D (2009) Ethical Challenges in long term funding for HIV/AIDS. *Health Affairs (Millwood)* 28 (6) 1966–1976.

Brock G (2009) *Global Justice: A Cosmopolitan Account*. Oxford: Oxford University Press.

Brock G (2011) International taxation. In S Benatar and G Brock (eds) *Global Health and Global Health Ethics*. Cambridge: Cambridge University Press.

Brown GW and Labonte R (2011) Globalization and its methodological discontents: contextualising globalization through the study of HIV/AIDS. *Globalization and Health* 7 (29).

Bunkenborg M (2003) *Crafting Diabetic Selves: An Ethnographic Account of a Chronic Illness in Beijing.* Masters thesis. University of Copenhagen.

Bunnell R, Ekwaru P, Solberg N, Wamai W et al. (2006) Changes in sexual behaviour and risk of HIV-transmission after antiretroviral therapy and prevention interventions in rural Uganda. *AIDS* 20 (1) 85–92.

Burchardt M (2010) 'Life in Brackets': biographical uncertainties of HIV positive women in South Africa. *Forum of Qualitative Social Research* 11 (1) Art3.

Burns F and Fenton KA (2006) Access to care amongst migrant Africans in London: what are the issues? *Psychology, Health and Medicine* 11 (1) 117–25.

Burris S, Cameron E (2008) The case against criminalisation of HIV transmission. *Journal of the American Medical Association* 300 (5) 578–81.

Bury M (1982) Chronic illness as a biographical disruption. *Sociology of Health and Illness* 4 (2) 165–82.

Butler D and Smith D (2007) Seropositivity can potentially increase HIV transmission. *AIDS* 21 (9) 1218–20.

Butt L (2011) Can you keep a secret? Pretences of confidentiality in HIV/AIDS counselling and treatment in Eastern Indonesia. *Medical Anthropology* 30 (3) 319–38.

Caceres C (2002) HIV among gay and other men who have sex with men in Latin America and the Caribbean: a hidden epidemic? *AIDS* 16 (Suppl 3) S23–33.

Caceres C, Konda K, Pecheny M, Chatterjee A, Lyeria R (2006) Estimating the number of men who have sex with men in low and middle income countries. *Sexually Transmitted Infections* 82 (Suppl 3) iii 3–9.

Cairns G (2012) *Treatment as Prevention.* London: NAM http://www.aidsmap.com.

Cameron E and Sherratt K (2005) *Witness to AIDS.* Cape Town: Tafelberg Press.

Campbell C, Foulis CA, Maimane S, Sibiya Z (2005) 'I have an evil child at my house': stigma and HIV/AIDS management in a South African community. *American Journal of Public Health* 95 (5) 808–15.

Campbell C, Nair Y, Maimane S, Nicholson J (2007) 'Dying Twice': a multi-level model of the roots of AIDS stigma in South African communities. *Journal of Health Psychology* 27 (12) 403–16.

Campbell C, Scott K, Madanhire C, Nyamukapa C, Gregson S (2011a) A 'good hospital': Nurse and patient perceptions of good clinical care for HIV-positive people on antiretroviral treatment in rural Zimbabwe – a mixed-methods qualitative study. *International Journal of Nursing Studies* 48 (2) 175–83.

Campbell C, Skovdal M, Madanhire C, Mugurungi O, Gregson S, Nyamukapa C (2011b) We, the AIDS people: How antiretroviral therapy enables Zimbabweans living with AIDS to cope with stigma. *American Journal of Public Health* 101 (6) 1004–10.

Caney S (2005) *Justice Beyond Borders: A Global Political Theory.* Oxford: Oxford University Press.

Carballo-Dieguez A, Ventuneac A, Bauermeister J, Dowsett GW, Dolezal C et al. (2009) Is 'bareback' a useful construct in primary HIV prevention? Definitions, identity and research. *Culture, Health and Sexuality* 11 (1) 51–65.

Case A and Menendez A (2009) *Requiescat in pace? The Consequences of the High Cost of Funerals in South Africa.* Cambridge MA: National Bureau of Economics Working Paper no. 14998.

Cassidy R and Leach M (2009) *AIDS, Citizenship and Global Funding: A Gambian Case Study* IDS Working Paper no. 325 Brighton: Institute of Development Studies.

Castro P and Farmer P (2005) Understanding and addressing AIDS-related stigma: from anthropological theory to clinical practice in Haiti. *American Journal of Public Health* 95 (1) 53–9.

Cataldo F (2008) New forms of citizenship and socio-political inclusion: accessing anti-retroviral therapy in a Rio de Janeiro favela. *Sociology of Health and Illness* 30 (6) 900–12.

Centers for Disease Control and Prevention (2006) Cases of HIV infection and AIDS in the United States by race/ethnicity 2000–2004. *HIV/AIDS Surveillance Report* 12 (1) 14–16.

Chakrapani V, Newman PA, Shunmugam M, Kurian AK, Dubrow R (2008) Secondary HIV prevention among kothi-identified MSM in Chennai, India. *Culture, Health and Sexuality* 10 (4) 313–27.

Chakrapani V, Newman P, Shunmugam M, Kurian AK, Dubrow R (2009) Barriers to free anti-retroviral treatment access for female sex workers in Chennai, India *AIDS Patient Care* 11 (9) 73–80.

Chazan M (2008) Seven deadly assumptions: unravelling the implications of HIV/AIDS among grandmothers in South Africa and beyond. *Ageing and Society* 28 (7) 935–58.

Chazan M and Whiteside A (2007) The making of vulnerabilities: understanding the differentiated effects of HIV and AIDS among street traders in Warwick Junction, Durban, South Africa. *African Journal of AIDS Research* 6 (2) 165–73.

Chen S, Gibson M, Katz MH, Klausner JD, Dilley JW, Schwarcz SK, Kellog TA, McFarland W (2002) Continuing increases in sexual risk behaviour and sexually transmitted diseases among men who have sex with men: San Francisco, Calif. 1999–2001 USA. *American Journal of Public Health* 92 (9) 1387–8.

Chi BK, Hanh NT, Rasch V, Gammeltoft T (2010) Induced abortion among HIV-positive women in Northern Vietnam: exploring reproductive dilemmas. *Culture Health and Sexuality* 12 (Suppl 1) S41–54.

Chigwedere P, Seage GR, Gruskin S, Lee T-H and Essex M (2008) Estimating the lost benefits of antiretroviral drug use in South Africa. *Journal of Acquired Immune Deficiency Syndrome* 49 (4) 410–15.

Chileshe M and Bond VA (2010) Barriers and outcomes: TB patients co-infected with HIV accessing antiretroviral therapy in rural Zambia. *AIDS Care* (Suppl 1) 51–9.

Chimwaza AF and Watkins SC (2004) Giving care to people with symptoms of AIDS in rural sub-Saharan Africa. *AIDS Care* 16 (7) 795–807.

Chin J (2007) *The AIDS Pandemic: The Collision of Epidemiology with Political Correctness.* Oxford: Radcliffe.

Choi KH, Lui H, Guo Y, Mandel J (2006) Lack of HIV testing and awareness of HIV infection among men who have sex with men in Beijing, China. *AIDS Education and Prevention* 18 (1) 33–43.

Chopra M, Kendall C, Hill Z, Schaay N, Nkonki L, Doherty TM (2006) 'Nothing new': responses to the introduction of antiretroviral drugs in South Africa. *AIDS* 20 (15) 1975–7.

Ciambrone D (2001) Illness and other assaults on the self: the relative impact of HIV/AIDS on women's lives. *Sociology of Health and Illness* 23 (4) 517–40.

Ciambrone D (2002) Informal networks among women with HIV/AIDS: present support and future prospects. *Qualitative Health Research* 12 (7) 876–96.

Clark SJ, Collinson MA, Kahn K. Drullinger K, Tollman SM (2007) Returning home to die: circular labour migration and mortality in South Africa. *Scandinavian Journal of Public Health* 69 (Suppl) 35–44.

Coates TJ, Richter L, Caceres C (2008) Behavioural strategies to reduce HIV transmission: how to make them work better. *Lancet* 372 (9639) 669–84.

Cloete A, Simbayi L, Kalichman S, Strebel A, Henda N (2009) Stigma and discrimination: experiences of HIV-positive men who have sex with men in Cape Town, South Africa. *AIDS Care* 20 (9) 1105–10.

Coetzee D, Hildebrand K, Boulle A, Maartens G, Louis F, Labatala V, Reuter H, Ntwana N, Goemaere F. (2004) Outcomes after two years of providing antiretroviral treatment in Khayelitsha, South Africa. *AIDS* 18 (6) 887–95.

Cohen J (2009) *Human Rights and HIV/AIDS: Now more than ever. Ten reasons why human rights should occupy the center of the global AIDS struggle.* Open Society Foundation

Cohen J (2010) Late for the epidemic: HIV/AIDS in Eastern Europe. *Science* 329 (5988) 160–64.

Cohen MS, Chen YQ, McCauley M et al. for the HPTN 052 Study Team (2011) Prevention of HIV infection with early antiretroviral therapy. *New England Journal of Medicine* 365 (6) 493–505.

Collins C, Coates T, Szekeres G (2008a) Accountability in the global response to HIV: measuring progress driving change. *AIDS* 22 (Suppl 2) S105–11.

Collins C, Coates TJ, Curran J (2008b) Moving beyond the alphabet soup of HIV prevention. *AIDS* 22 (Suppl 2) S5–8.

Collins F (2004) What we do and don't know about 'race', 'ethnicity', genetics and health at the dawn of the genome era. *Nature Genetics* Supplement 36 (11) S13–15.

Collins P (2000) 'It's all in the family': intersections of gender, race and nation. In U Narayan and S Harding (eds) *Decentering the Center: Philosophy for a Multicultural, Postcolonial and Feminist World*. Bloomington: Indiana University Press.

Collins PY, Holman AR, Freeman MC, Patel V (2006) What is the relevance of mental health to HIV/AIDS care and treatment programs in developing countries? A systematic review. *AIDS* 20 (12) 1571–82.

Colvin CJ and Robins S (2009) Positive men in hard neo-liberal times: engendering health citizenship in South Africa. In J Boesten and N Poku (eds) *Gender and HIV/AIDS: Critical Perspective from the Developing World*. Farnham: Ashgate.

Colvin CJ, Robins S and Leavens J (2010) Grounding 'responsibilisation talk': masculinities, citizenship and HIV in Cape Town, South Africa. *Journal of Development Studies* 46 (7) 1179–95.

Connell R and Messerschmidt J (2005) Hegemonic masculinity: rethinking the concept. *Gender and Society* 19 (6) 829–59.

Connelly P and Rosen S (2006) Treatment for HIV/AIDS at South Africa's largest employers: myth and reality. *South African Medical Journal* 96 (2) 128–33.

Conyers L, Boomer KB, McMahon BT (2005). Workplace discrimination and HIV/AIDS: the national EECC ADA research project. *Work* 25 (1) 37–48.

Cooper D, Harris J, Myer L, Orner P, Bracken H (2007) 'Life is still going on': reproductive intentions among HIV positive women and men in South Africa. *Social Science and Medicine* 65 (2) 274–83.

Cooper D, Moodley J, Zweigenthal V, Bekker LG, Shah I, Myer L (2009) Fertility intentions and reproductive health care needs of people living with HIV in Cape Town, South Africa: implications for integrating reproductive health and HIV care services. *AIDS Behaviour* 13 (Suppl 1) 38–46.

Coovadia H (2009) Current issues in prevention of mother to child transmission of HIV-1. *Current Opinion in HIV/AIDS* 4 (4) 319–24.

Cornell M, Myer L, Kaplan R, Bekker LG, Wood R (2009) The impact of gender and income on survival and retention in a South African antiretroviral therapy programme. *Tropical Medicine and International Health* 14 (7) 722–31.

Cotton S, Puchalski CM, Sherman SN et al. (2006) Spirituality and religion in patients with HIV/AIDS. *Journal of General and Internal Medicine* 21 (Suppl 6) S5–13.

Cottingham J, Germain A, Hunt P (2012) Use of human rights to meet the unmet need for family planning. *Lancet* 380 (9837) 172–80.

Courtenay-Quirk C, Wolitski RJ, Parsons JT, Gomez CA (Seropositive Urban Men's Study Team) (2006) Is HIV/AIDS stigma dividing the gay community? Perceptions of HIV-positive men who have sex with men. *AIDS Education and Prevention* 18 (1) 56–67.

Courtney W (2000) Constructions of masculinity and their influence on men's health. *Social Science and Medicine* 50 (10) 1385–401.

Coutsoudis A, Coovadia HM, Wilfert CM (2008) HIV, infant feeding and more perils for poor people: new WHO guidelines encourage review of formula milk policies. *Bulletin of World Health Organization* 86 (3) 210–14.

Crenshaw WK (1994) Mapping the margins: intersectionality, identity politics and violence against women of colour. In MA Fineman and R Mykitiuk (eds) *The Public Nature of Private Violence*. New York: Routledge.

Crepaz N and Marks G (2002) Towards an understanding of sexual risk behaviour in people living with HIV: a review of social, psychological and medical findings. *AIDS* 16 (2) 135–49.

Crepaz N, Hart TA, Marks G (2004) Highly active antiretroviral therapy and sexual risk behavior: a meta-analytic review. *Journal of the American Medical Association* 292 (2) 224–36.

Csete J and Elliot R (2011) Criminalization of HIV transmission and exposure: in search of rights based public health alternatives to criminal law. *Future Virology* 6 (8) 941–50.

Daftary A (2012) HIV and tuberculosis : the construction and management of double stigma. *Social Science and Medicine* 74 (10) 1512–1519.

Dahab M, Charalambous S, Hamilton R, Fielding K, Kielmann K, Churchyard G, Grant A (2008) 'That is why I stopped the ART': patients' and providers' perspectives on barriers to and enablers of HIV treatment adherence in a South African workplace programme *BMC Public Health* 8 63.

Damar A, and du Plessis G (2010) Coping versus grieving in a 'death accepting society: AIDS-bereaved women living with HIV in Indonesia. *Asian and African Studies* 45 (4) 421–431.

Daniels N (2008) *Just Health: Meeting Health Needs Fairly*. Cambridge: Cambridge University Press.

Daniels N and Sabin J (1997) Limits to health care: fair procedures, democratic deliberation, and the legitimacy problem for insurers. *Philosophy and Public Affairs* 26 (4) 303–50.

Datye V, Kielmann K, Sheikh K, Deshmukh D, Deshpande S, Porter J, Rangan S (2006) Private practitioners' communications with patients around HIV testing in Pune, India. *Health Policy and Planning* 21 (5) 343–52.

Davies JB, Sandstrom S, Shorrocks A, Wolff EN (2008) *The World Distribution of Household Wealth*. Working Papers DP2008/03. World Institute for Development Economic Research (UNU-WIDER).

Davis M (2007) The 'loss of community' and other problems for sexual citizenship in recent HIV prevention. *Sociology of Health and Illness* 30 (2) 182–96.

Davis M and Flowers P (2011) Love and HIV sero-discordance in gay men's accounts of life with their regular partners. *Culture, Health and Sexuality* 13 (7) 737–49.

Dawson A and Verweij M (2007) *Ethics, Prevention and Public Health*. Oxford: OUP.

de Bruyn M (2005) *HIV/AIDS and Reproductive Health. Sensitive and Neglected Issues: A Review of the Literature and Recommendations for Action.* Chapel Hill NC: IPAS.

de Bruyn M and Paxton S (2005) HIV testing of pregnant women: what is needed to protect positive women's needs and rights? *Sexual Health* 2 (3) 143–52.

de Cock KM, Bunnell R, Mermin J (2006) Unfinished business: expanding HIV testing in developing countries. *New England Journal of Medicine* 354 (5) 440–42.

de Paoli MM, Manongi R, Klepp KI (2002) Counsellors' perspectives on antenatal HIV testing and infant feeding dilemmas facing women with HIV in northern Tanzania. *Reproductive Health Matters* 10 (20) 144–56.

de Waal A (2006) *AIDS and Power.* London: Zed Books.

de Waal A and Whiteside A (2003) New variant famine: AIDS and food crisis in Southern Africa. *Lancet* 362 (9391) 1234–7.

de Wit JB, Aggleton P, Myers T, Crewe M (2011) The rapidly changing paradigm of HIV prevention: time to strengthen social and behavioural approaches. *Health Education Research* 26 (3) 381–92.

Deacon H (2006) Towards a sustainable theory of health-related stigma: lessons from the HIV/AIDS literature. *Journal of Community and Applied Social Psychology* 16 (6) 418–25.

Deacon H, Stephney I, Prosalendis S et al. (2006) *Understanding HIV/AIDS Stigma: A Theoretical and Methodological Analysis.* Cape Town: HSRC Press.

Dean H (2010) *Understanding Human Need.* Bristol: Policy Press.

Delvaux T and Nostlinger C (2007) Reproductive choice for women and men living with HIV: contraception, abortion and fertility. *Reproductive Health Matters* 15 (Suppl 29) 46–66.

Demmer C (2007) AIDS and palliative care in South Africa. *American Journal of Hospice and Palliative Care* 24 (7) 7–12.

Demmer C (2010) Experiences of women who have lost young children to AIDS in KwaZulu-Natal, South Africa: a qualitative study. *Journal of the International AIDS Society* 13 50.

Denis P and Ntsimane R (2006) Absent fathers: why do men not feature in stories of families affected by HIV/AIDS in Kwazulu Natal? In L Richter and R Morrell (eds) *Baba: Men and Fatherhood in South Africa* Johannesburg: HSRC Press.

Denison JA, O'Reilly KP, Schmid GP, Kennedy CE, Sweat MD (2008) HIV voluntary counseling and testing and behavioral risk reduction in developing countries : a meta-analysis 1990–2005. *AIDS and Behavior* 12 (3) 363–73.

Deol A and Heath-Toby A (2009) *HIV risk for Lesbians, Bisexuals and Other Women Who Have Sex with Women.* New York: Women's Institute at Gay Men's Health Crisis.

Desclaux A and Alfieri C (2009) Counseling and choosing between infant-feeding options: overall limits and local interpretations by health care providers and women living with HIV in resource poor countries (Burkina Faso, Cambodia and Cameroon). *Social Science and Medicine* 69 (6) 821–9.

DiClementi, J, Ross M, Mallo C, Johnson S (2005) Predictors of successful return to work from HIV related disability. *Journal of HIV/AIDS and Social Services* 3 (3) 89–96.

Dieleman M, Biemba G, Mphuka S, Sichinga-Sichali K, Sissolak D, van der Kwaak A, van der Witt AJ (2007) 'We are also dying like any other people: we are also people': perceptions of the impact of HIV/AIDS on health workers in two districts in Zambia. *Health Policy and Planning* 22 (3) 139–48.

Dilger H (2008) 'We are all going to die': kinship, belonging and the morality of HIV/AIDS-related illnesses and deaths in rural Tanzania. *Anthropological Quarterly* 81 (1) 207–32.

Dilger H, Burchardt M, van Dijk R (2010) Introduction: the redemptive moment: HIV treatments and the production of new religious spaces. *African Journal of AIDS Research* 9 (4) 373–383.

Dodds, J, Johnson, A. Parry J, Mercey, D (2007). A tale of three cities: persisting high HIV prevalence, risk behaviour and undiagnosed infection in community samples of men who have sex with men. *Sexually Transmitted Infections* 83 (5) 392–6.

Dodds JP, Mercey DE, Parry JV, Johnson AM (2004) Increasing risk behaviour and high levels of undiagnosed HIV infection in a community sample of homosexual men. *Sexually Transmitted Infections* 80 (3) 236–40.

Doherty T, Chopra M, Nkonki L, Jackson D, Greiner T (2006) Effect of the HIV epidemic on infant feeding in South Africa: 'When they see me coming with the tins they laugh at me.' *Bulletin of the World Health Organization* 84 (2) 90–96.

Douglas N (2009) *I Just Get On With It ... A Study Of The Employment Experiences Of Gay And Bisexual Men And Black African Men And Women Living With HIV in the UK*. London: National AIDS Trust.

Dowsett G (2003) Some considerations on sexuality and gender in the context of AIDS. *Reproductive Health Matters* 11 (22) 21–9.

Doyal L (1995) *What Makes Women Sick? Gender and the Political Economy of Health*. London: Macmillan.

Doyal Len (1995) Needs, rights and equity: moral quality in health care rationing. *Quality in Health Care* 4 273–283.

Doyal L (1997a) Human need and the right of patients to privacy. *Journal of Contemporary Health Law and Policy* 14 1–21.

Doyal L (1997b) Rationing within the NHS should be explicit: the case for BMJ 314:1114.

Doyal L (1998) Public participation and the moral quality of health care rationing. *Quality in Health Care* 7 (2) 98–102.

Doyal L (2001) Sex, gender and health: the need for a new approach. *BMJ* 323 (7320) 1061–3.

Doyal L (2009a) Challenges in researching life with HIV/AIDS: an intersectional analysis of black African migrants in London. *Culture, Health and Sexuality* 11 (2) 173–88.

Doyal L (2009b) What do we know about men living with and/or dying from AIDS? *Journal of Men's Health* 6 (3) 155–7.

Doyal L and Gough I (1991) *A Theory of Human Need*. London: Macmillan.

Doyal L and Harris R (1983) The practical foundations of human understanding. *New Left Review* 139 (May–June) 59–78.

Doyal L and Payne S (2011) Gender and global health: inequality and differences. In S Benatar and G Brock (eds) *Global Health and Global Health Ethics*. Cambridge: Cambridge University Press.

Doyal L, Paparini S, Anderson J (2008) Elvis died and I was born: Black African men negotiating same sex desire in London. *Sexualities* 11 (1) 171–192.

Doyal L, Anderson J, Paparini S (2009) You are not yourself: exploring masculinities among heterosexual African men living with HIV in London. *Social Science and Medicine* 68 (10) 1901–7.

Dray-Spira, R, Gueguen A, Lert F for VESPSA Study Group (2008) Disease severity, self-reported experience of workplace discrimination and employment loss during the course of chronic HIV disease: differences according to gender and education. *Occupational and Environmental Medicine* 65 (2) 112–19.

du Plessis, G (2003). *HIV and Fertility in South African: Some Theoretical and Methodological Considerations. Fertility: The Current South African Issues*. Cape Town: Health Science Research Council. http://www.hsrcpress.ac.za [accessed 20 September 2012].

Dubois-Arber F and Moreau-Gruet F (2007) Men having sex with men and HIV/ AIDS prevention in Switzerland: 1987–2000. *Euro Surveillance* 7 (2) pii=347.

Dworkin R (1984) Rights as trumps. In J Waldron (ed) *Theories of Rights*. Oxford: Oxford University Press.

Dworkin R (1993) *Life's Dominion*. London: HarperCollins.

Dworkin R (1977) *Taking Rights Seriously*. London: Duckworth.

Dworkin S (2005) Who is epidemiologically fathomable in the HIV/AIDS epidemic? Gender, sexuality and intersectionality in public health. *Culture, Health and Sexuality* 7 (6) 615–23.

Dyer ST, Abrahams N, Mokoena NE, van der Spuy ZM, (2004) 'You are a man because you have children': experiences, reproductive health knowledge and treatment-seeking behaviour among men suffering from couple infertility in South Africa. *Human Reproduction* 19 (4) 960–67.

Dylan B (1992) A Hard Rain's A Gonna Fall. New York: Columbia Records.

Eholie S, Nolan M, Gaumon A, Mambo J, Kouamé-Yebouet Y, Aka-Kakou R et al. (2003) *Antiretroviral Treatment Can Be Cost-Saving for Industry and Life-Saving for Workers: A Case Study from Côte d'Ivoire's Private Sector. Economics of AIDS and Access to HIV/AIDS Care in Developing Countries, Issues and Challenges*. Paris: Agence Nationale de Recherches sur le Sida.

England R (2008) The writing is on the wall for UNAIDS. *BMJ* 336 1072.

Elam G, Macdonald N, Hickson FC, Imrie J for Insight Collaboration Research Team (2008) Risky sexual behaviour in context: qualitative results from an investigation into risk factors for sero-conversion among gay men who test for HIV. *Sexually Transmitted Infections* 84 (6) 473–7.

Elford J and Hart G (2005) HAART, viral load and sexual risk behaviour *AIDS* 19 (2) 205–7.

Elford J, Ibrahim F, Bukutu C, Anderson J (2007) Sexual behaviour of people living with HIV in London: implications for HIV transmission. *AIDS* 21p S63–70.

Elford J, Ibrahim F, Bukutu C, Anderson J (2008a) HIV-related discrimination reported by people living with HIV in London, UK. *AIDS Behaviour* 12 255–264.

Elford J, Ibrahim F, Bukutu C, Anderson J (2008b) Over fifty and living with HIV in London. *Sexually Transmitted Infections* 84 (6) 468–72.

Elson D (ed.) (2003) *Progress of the World's Women 2002*. New York: UNIFEM.

Elul B, Delvaux T, Munyana E et al. (2009) Pregnancy desires and contraceptive knowledge and use among prevention of mother- to-child transmission clients in Rwanda. *AIDS* 23 (Suppl 1) S19–26.

Essack Z and Strode A (2012) 'I feel like half a women all the time': the impact of coerced and forced sterilisations on HIV-positive women in South Arica *Agenda: Empowering Women for Gender Equity* 26 (2) 24–34.

European Centre for Disease Prevention and Control (2010) *Migrant Health: Epidemiology of HIV and AIDS in Migrant Communities and Ethnic Minorities in EU/EEA Countries*. Stockholm: ECDC.

Evans R and Becker S (2009) *Children Caring for Parents with HIV/AIDS: Global Issues and Policy Responses*. Bristol: Policy Press.

Evans R and Thomas F (2009) Emotional interactions and an ethics of care: caring relations in families affected by HIV and AIDS. *Emotion, Space and Society* 2 (2) 111–19.

Exley C (2004) Review article: the sociology of dying, death and bereavement. *Sociology of Health and Illness* 26 (1) 110–22.

Ezekiel MJ, Talle A, Juma JM, Klepp K-I (2009) 'When in the body it makes you look fat and HIV negative': the constitution of antiretroviral therapy in local discourse among youth in Kahe, Tanzania. *Social Science and Medicine* 68 (5) 957–64.

Fakoya I, Reynolds R, Caswell G, Shirpind I (2008) Barriers to HIV testing for migrant black Africans in Western Europe. *HIV Medicine* 9 (Suppl 2) S23–5.

Farmer P (2001) *Infections and Inequalities: The Modern Plagues*. Berkeley: University of California Press.

Farmer P (2004) An anthropology of structural violence. *Current Anthropology* 45 (3) 305–25.

Farmer P (2008) Challenging orthodoxies: the road ahead for health and human rights. *Health and Human Rights* 10 (1) 5–19.

Farmer P (2010) *Partner to the Poor: a Paul Farmer Reader*. Berkeley: University of California Press.

Farmer P, Leanadre K, Mukerjhee J, Claude M, Nevil P, Smith-Fawzi M, Koenig S et al. (2001) Community based approaches to HIV treatment in resource poor settings. *Lancet* 358 (9279) 404–9.

Fassin D (2007) *When Bodies Remember: Experiences and Politics of AIDS in South Africa*. Berkeley: University of California Press.

Fee E and Parry M (2008) Jonathan Mann, HIV/AIDS and human rights. *Journal of Public Health Policy* 29 (1) 54–71.

Feldman R and Maposhere C (2003) Safe sex and reproductive choice: findings from 'Positive women: voices and choices' in Zimbabwe. *Reproductive Health Matters* 11 (2) 126–73.

Fidler D (2008) Architecture and anarchy: global health's quest for governance *Global Governance* 1 (1) 1–17.

Fidler D (2008–09) After the revolution: global politics in a time of economic crisis and threatening future trends. *Global Health Governance* 2 (9).

Fiore S, Heard I, Thorne C, Savasi V, Coll O, Malyuta R, Niemiec T, Martinelli P, Tibaldi C, Newell ML (2008) Reproductive experience of HIV-infected women living in Europe. *Human Reproduction* 23 (9) 2140–44.

Fisher J, Smith L, Lenz E (2010) Secondary prevention of HIV in the United States: past, current and future perspectives. *Journal of Acquired Immune Deficiency Syndrome* 55 (Suppl 2) S106–15.

Fisher M and Cooper V (2012) HIV and ageing: premature ageing or premature conclusions? *Current Opinion in Infectious Diseases* 25 1–3.

Fitzgerald M, Collumbien M, Hosegood V (2010) No one can ask me 'Why do you take that stuff?': men's experiences of antiretroviral treatment in South Africa. *AIDS Care* 22 (3) 355–60.

Fleury S (2011) Brazil's health care reform: social movements and civil society. *Lancet* 377 (9739) 1724–5.

Flowers P, Smith J, Sheeran P, Beail N (1997) Health and romance: understanding unprotected sex in relationships between gay men. *British Journal of Health Psychology* 2 (1) 73–86.

Foley E (2005) HIV/AIDS and African immigrant women in Philadelphia: structural and cultural barriers to care *AIDS Care* 17 (8) 1030–43.

Ford CL, Whetten KD, Hall SA, Kaufman JS, Thrasher AD (2007) Black sexuality, social construction and research targeting the 'Down Low' ('the DL'). *Annals of Epidemiology* 17 (3) 209–16.

Forde I and Raine R (2008) Placing the individual within a social determinants approach to health inequality. *Lancet* 372 (9650) 1694–6.

Forman L (2011) Global AIDS funding and the re-emergence of AIDS 'exceptionalism'. *Social Medicine* 6 (1) 45–51.

Forsyth B, Vandormael A, Kershaw T, Grobbelaar J (2008) The political context of AIDS-related stigma and knowledge in a South African township community. *SAHARA Journal* 5 (2) 74–82.

Fox A and Mason Mcier B (2009) Health as freedom: Addressing social determinants of global health inequities through the human right to development. *Bioethics* 23 2 112–122.

Fox MP and Rosen S (2010) Patient retention in antiretroviral therapy programs up to three years on treatment in sub-Saharan Africa 2007–2009: systematic review. *Tropical Medicine and International Health* (Suppl 1) 1–15.

Frank E (2009) The relation of HIV testing and treatment to identity formation in Zambia. *African Journal of AIDS Research* 8 (4) 515–24.

Franke MF, Murray MB, Muñoz M, Hernández-Díaz S, Sebastián JL, Atwood S, Caldas A, Bayona J, Shin S (2010) Food insufficiency is a risk factor for suboptimal antiretroviral therapy adherence among HIV-infected adults in urban Peru. *AIDS and Behavior* 15 (7) 1483–9.

Fried C (1978) *Right and Wrong*. Cambridge MA: Harvard University Press.

Friedman SR, Kippax SC, Phaswana-Mafuya N, Rossi D, Newman CE (2006) Emerging future issues in HIV/AIDS social research. *AIDS* 20 (7) 959–65.

Fultz E and Frances J (2011) Employer-sponsored programs for prevention and treatment of HIV/AIDS: recent experience in sub-Saharan Africa. *International Social Security Review* 64 (3) 1–19.

Galvao J (2005) Brazil and access to HIV/AIDS drugs: a question of human rights and public health. *American Journal of Public Health* 95 (7) 1110–16.

Gangoli G (1999) Unmet needs: sex workers and health care. *Indian Journal of Medical Ethics* 7 (3).

Garrett L (2007) The Challenge of Global Health. *Foreign Affairs* (Jan/Feb).

Gasper D (2007) Conceptualising human needs and well-being. In I Gough and A McGregor (eds) *Well-being in Developing Countries* Cambridge: Cambridge University Press.

Gebhardt M (2005) Recent trends in new diagnoses of HIV infections in Switzerland: probable increase in MSM despite an overall decrease. *Euro Surveillance* 10 (12) E051208 2.

Gerver SM, Chadborn TR, Ibrahim F, Vatsa B, Delpech VC, Easterbrook PJ (2010) High rate of loss of clinical follow up among African HIV infected patients attending a London clinic: a retrospective analysis of a clinical cohort. *Journal of the International AIDS Society* 13 (29).

Gibbs A and Smith J (2010) *Annotated Bibliography on Care in the Context of HIV and AIDS*. Durban: HEARD, University of KwaZulu-Natal.

Giddens A (1984) *The Constitution of Society: An Outline of Structuration*. Berkeley and Los Angeles: University of California Press.

Gil S (2007) Body image, wellbeing and sexual satisfaction: a comparison between heterosexual and gay men. *Sexual and Relationship Therapy* 22 (2) 237–44.

Gilabert P (2006) Basic positive duties of justice and Narveson's libertarian challenge. *Southern Journal of Philosophy* 44 193–216.

Gilbert L and Walker L (2009) 'They (ARVs) are my life without them I am nothing': experiences of patients attending an HIV/AIDS clinic in Johannesburg, South Africa. *Health and Place* 15 (4) 1123–9.

Gilbert L and Walker L (2010) 'My biggest fear was that people would reject me once they knew my status'. Stigma as experienced by patients in an HIV/ AIDS clinic in Johannesburg, South Africa. *Health and Social Care in the Community* 18 (2) 139–46.

Giles ML, Hellard ME, Lewin SR, O'Brien ML (2009) The 'work' of women when considering and using interventions to reduce mother to child transmission (MTCT) of HIV. *AIDS Care* 21 (10) 1230–37.

Gill CJ, Hamer DH, Simon JL, Thea DM, Sabin LL (2005) No room for complacency about adherence to anti-retroviral therapy in sub-Saharan Africa. *AIDS* 19 (12) 1243–9.

Gill S and Bakker I (2011) The global crisis and global health. In S Benatar and G Brock (eds) *Global Health and Global Health Ethics*. Cambridge: Cambridge University Press.

Gillespie S, Greener R, Whiteside A, Whitworth J (2007a) Investigating the empirical evidence for understanding vulnerability and the associations between poverty, HIV infection and AIDS impact. *AIDS* 21 (Suppl 7) S1–4.

Gillespie S, Kadiyala S, Greener R (2007b) Is poverty or wealth driving HIV transmission? *AIDS* 21 (Supp 7) S5–16.

Gillett H and Parr J (2011) Disclosure among HIV positive women: the role of HIV/AIDS support groups in Kenya. *African Journal of AIDS Research* 9 (4) 337–44.

Global Commission on HIV and the Law (2012) *Risks, Rights and Health*. New York: UNDP HIV/AIDS Working Group.

Goffman E (1963) *Stigma: Notes on the Management of Spoiled Identity*. Englewood Cliffs NJ: Prentice-Hall.

Gogna M, Pecheny M, Ibarlucia I, Manzelli H, Lopez SB (2009) The reproductive needs and rights of people living with HIV in Argentina: health services users' and providers' perspectives. *Social Science and Medicine* 69 (6) 813–20.

Golub S, Operario D, Gorbach PM (2010) Pre-exposure prophylaxis: state of the science: analogies for research and implementation. *Current HIV/AIDS Reports* 7 (4) 201–9.

Gorna R (1996) *Vamps, Virgins and Victims: How Can Women Fight AIDS?* London: Cassell.

Gostin L and Mok E (2009) Grand challenges in global health governance. *British Medical Bulletin* 90 7–18.

Gough I (2003) Lists and thresholds: comparing the Doyal-Gough theory of human need with Nussbaum's capabilities approach. ESRC WeD Working Paper 01.

Granich R, Crowley S, Vitoria M, Smyth C, Kahn JG, Bennett R, Lo YR, Souteyrand Y, Williams B (2010) Highly active antiretroviral treatment as prevention of HIV transmission: review of scientific evidence and update. *Current Opinion in HIV AIDS* 5 (4) 298–304.

Grant GE, Logie D, Masura M, Gorman D, Murray SA (2008) Factors facilitating and challenging access and adherence to antiretroviral therapy in a township in the Zambian Copperbelt: a qualitative study *AIDS Care* 20 (10) 1155–60.

Gravlee CC (2009) How race becomes biology: embodiment of social inequality. *American Journal of Physical Anthropology* 139 (1) 7–57.

Gravlee CC and Sweet E (2008) Race, ethnicity and racism in medical anthropology 1977–2002. *Medical Anthropology Quarterly* 22 (1) 27–51.

Gray G and Berger P (2007) Pain in women with HIV/AIDS. *Pain* 132 (Suppl 1) S13–21.

Gready P (2008) Rights-based approaches to development: what is the value-added? *Development in Practice* 18 (6) 735–47.

Gruskin S and Daniels N (2008) Process is the point. Justice and human rights: priority setting and fair deliberative processes. *American Journal of Public Health* 98 (9) 1573–7.

Gruskin S and Tarantola D (2008) Universal access to HIV prevention, treatment and care: assessing the inclusion of human rights in international and national strategic plans. *AIDS* 22 (Suppl 2) S123–32.

Gruskin S, Ferguson L, O'Malley J (2007a) Ensuring sexual and reproductive rights for people living with HIV: an overview of key human rights, policy and health systems issues. *Reproductive Health Matters* 15 (Suppl 29) 4–26.

Gruskin S, Mills E, Tarantola D (2007b) History, principles and practice of health and human rights. *Lancet* 370 (9585) 449–55.

Gruskin S, Firestone R, MacCarthy S, Ferguson L (2008) HIV and pregnancy intentions: do services adequately respond to women's needs? *American Journal of Public Health* 98 (10) 1746–50.

Gupta GR (2002) How men's power over women fuels the HIV epidemic. *BMJ* 324 (7331) 3–4.

Gupta GR, Parkhurst JO, Ogden JA, Aggleton P, Mahal A (2008) Structural approaches to HIV prevention. *Lancet* 372 (9640) 766–75.

Gupta J, Raj A, Decker MR, Reed E, Silverman J (2009) HIV vulnerabilities of sex-trafficked Indian women and girls. *International Journal of Gynaecology and Obstetrics* 107 (1) 30–34.

Gurevich M, Mathieson C, Bower J, Dhanyanandhan (2007) Disciplining bodies, desires and subjectivities: sexuality and HIV positive women. *Feminism and Psychology* 17 (1) 9–30.

Gysels M, Pell C, Straus L, Pool R (2011) End of life care in sub-Saharan Africa: a systematic review of the qualitative literature. *BMC Palliative Care* 10 6.

Haddad B, Olivier J, De Gruchy S (2008) *The Potential and Perils of Partnership: Christian Religious Entities and Collaborative Stakeholders Responding to HIV and AIDS in Kenya, Malawi and the DRC*. Study commissioned by Tearfund and UNAIDS. Interim Report. African Religious Health Assets Program.

Hamilton C, Okoko D, Tolhurst R, Kilonzo N, Theobald S, Taegtmeyer M (2008) Potential for abuse in the VCT counselling room: service providers' perceptions in Kenya. *Health Policy and Planning* 23 (6) 390–96.

Hancock A-M (2007) When multiplication doesn't equal quick addition: examining intersectionality as a research paradigm. *Perspectives on Politics* 5 (1) 63–79.

Hankins CA and Zalduondo BO (2010) Combination prevention: a deeper understanding of HIV prevention. *AIDS* 24 (Suppl 4) S70–80.

Hankivsky O (2012) Women's health, men's health and gender and health: implications of intersectionality. *Social Science and Medicine* 74 (11) 1712–20.

Haour-Knipe M (2009) Families, children, migration and AIDS. *AIDS Care* 21 (Suppl 1) 43–8.

Harawa NT, Williams JK, Ramamurthi HC, Bingham TA (2006) Perceptions towards condom use, sexual activity and HIV disclosure among African American men who have sex with men: implications for heterosexual transmission. *Journal of Urban Health* 83 (4) 682–94.

Hardon AP, Akurut D, Comoro C, Ekezie C, Irunde H et al (2007) Hunger, waiting time and transport costs: time to confront challenges to ART adherence in Africa *AIDS Care* 19 (5) 658–65.

Hardon A, Desclaux A, Egrot M, Simon E, Micollier E, Kyakuwa M (2008) Alternative medicines for AIDS in resource- poor settings: insights from exploratory anthropological studies in Asia and Africa *Journal of Ethnobiology and Ethnomedicine* 4 16.

Hardy C and Richter M (2006) Disability grants or antiretrovirals? A quandary for people with HIV/AIDS in South Africa. *African Journal of AIDS Research* 5 (1) 85–96.

Harries AD, Nyangulu DS, Hargreaves NJ, Kaluwa O, Salaniponi FM (2001) Preventing antiretroviral anarchy in sub-Saharan Africa. *Lancet* 358 (9279) 410–14.

Harries J, Cooper D, Myer L, Bracken H, Zweigenthal V, Orner P (2007) Policy maker and health care provider perspectives on reproductive decision making amongst HIV infected individuals in South Africa. *BMC Public Health* 7 282.

Hazra R, Siberry GK, Mofenson LM (2010) Growing up with HIV: children, adolescents, and young adults with perinatally acquired HIV infection. *Annual Review of Medicine* 61 169–85.

Haytmanek E, Cuff P, Ostapkovitch K (2010) *Preparing for the future of HIV/AIDS in Africa: A Shared Responsibility*. Washington DC: Institute of Medicine.

Heard I, Sitta R, Lert F, VESPA Study Group (2007) Reproductive choice in men and women living with HIV: evidence from a large representative sample of outpatients attending French hospitals (ANRS–EN12-VESPA Study). *AIDS* 21 (Suppl 1) S77–82.

Hecht R, Bollinger L, Stover J, McGreevey W, Muhib F, Emas Madavo C, de Ferranti D (2009) Critical choices in financing the response to the global HIV/AIDS pandemic. *Health Affairs* (Millwood) 28 (6) 1591–605.

Hedsrom P and Ylikoski P (2010) Causal mechanisms in the social sciences. *Annual Review of Sociology* 36 49–67.

Hein W and Kickbusch I (2012) Global health governance and the intersection of health and foreign policy. In T Schrecker (ed.) *The Ashgate Research Companion to Globalization of Health*. Farnham: Ashgate.

Hein W and Kohlmorgen L (2008) Global health governance: conflicts on global social rights. *Global Social Policy* 8 (1) 80–108.

Held D (1995) *Democracy and the Global Order: From the Modern State to Cosmopolitan Governance*. Cambridge: Polity Press.

Henry J Kaiser Family Foundation (2012) *The HIV/AIDS Epidemic in the United States*. Fact Sheet July 2012. Menlo Park CA: KFF.

Herbst JH, Jacobs ED, Finlayson TJ, McKleroy VS, Neumann MS, Crepaz N (2008) Estimating HIV prevalence and risk behaviours of transgender persons in the United States: a systematic review. *AIDS and Behavior* 12 (1) 1–17.

Heunis C, Wouters E, Norton WE, Engelbricht MC, Kigozi NG, Sharma A, Ragin C (2011) Patient and delivery level factors related to acceptance of HIV counseling and testing services among tuberculosis patients in South Africa: a qualitative study with community health workers and program managers. *Implementation Science* 6 27.

Higgins JA, Hoffman S, Dworkin SL (2010) Rethinking gender, heterosexual men and women's vulnerability to HIV/AIDS: time to shift the paradigm. *American Journal of Public Health* 100 (3) 435–45.

Hirsch JS (2007) Gender, sexuality and antiretroviral therapy: using social science to enhance outcomes and inform secondary prevention strategies. *AIDS* 21 (Suppl 5) S21–9.

Hodge DR and Roby JL (2010) Sub-Saharan African women living with HIV/AIDS: an exploration of general and spiritual coping strategies. *Social Work* 55 (1) 27–37.

Holt M (2011) Gay men and ambivalence about 'gay community': from gay community attachment to personal communities. *Culture, Health and Sexuality* 13 (8) 857–71.

Holzemer WL, Hudson A, Kirksey KM, Hamilton MJ (2001) The revised sign and symptom check-list for HIV (SSC-HIV rev). *Journal of the Association of Nurses in AIDS Care* 12 (5) 60–70.

Hopkins K, Maria Barbosa R, Riva Knauth D, Potter JE (2005) The impact of health care providers on female sterilization among HIV-positive women in Brazil. *Social Science and Medicine* 61 (3) 541–54.

Horrox R (1994) *The Black Death*. Manchester: Manchester University Press.

Horstmann E, Brown J, Islam F, Buck J, Agins BD (2010) Retaining HIV infected patients in care: Where are we? Where do we go from here? *Clinical Infectious Diseases* 50 (5) 752–61.

Horton R (2009) The global financial crisis: an acute threat to health. *Lancet* 373 (9661) 355–6.

Hosegood V, McGrath N, Herbst K, Timaeus IM (2004) The impact of adult mortality on household dissolution and migration in rural South Africa. *AIDS* 18 (11) 1585–90

Hosegood V, Floyd S, Marston M, Hill C, McGrath N, Isingo R, Crampin A, Zaba B (2007a) The effects of high HIV prevalence on orphanhood and living arrangements of children in Malawi, Tanzania, and South Africa. *Population Studies* 61 (3) 327–36.

Hosegood V, Preston-Whyte E, Busza J, Moitse S, Timaeus I.(2007b) Revealing the full extent of households' experiences of HIV and AIDS in rural South Africa. *Social Science and Medicine* 65 (6) 1249–59.

Human Rights Watch (2004) *Hated to Death: Homophobia, Violence and Jamaica's HIV Epidemic*. New York: HRW.

Human Rights Watch (2007) *Hidden in the Mealie Meal: Gender Based Abuses and Women's HIV Treatment in Zambia*. New York: HRW.

Human Rights Watch (2011) *'We'll Show You You're a Woman': Violence and Discrimination against Black Lesbians and Transgender Men in South Africa*. Johannesburg: HRW.

Hunger Watch (2008) *Local Voices: A Community Perspective on HIV and Hunger in Zambia*. London: ACF International Network.

Hunt P (2007) *Neglected Diseases: A Human Rights Framework*. Geneva: WHO.

Hunter L (2007) *Understanding How HIV/AIDS and Agricultural Food Systems Are Linked*. Washington DC: Population Reference Bureau.

Hunter LM, Twine W, Patterson L (2007) 'Locusts are now our beef': adult mortality and household dietary use of local environmental resources in rural South Africa. *Scandinavian Journal of Public Health* 35 (Suppl 69) 165–74.

Hunter D and Dawson A (2011) Is there a need for global health ethics? For and against. In S Benatar and G Brock (eds) *Global Health and Global Health Ethics*. Cambridge: Cambridge University Press.

Hurst S, Mezger N, Mauron A (2011) Allocating resources in humanitarian medicine. In S Benatar and G Brock (eds) *Global Health and Global Health Ethics* Cambridge: Cambridge University Press.

Imrie J, Elford J, Kippax S, Hart G (2007) Biomedical HIV prevention – and social science. *Lancet* 370 (9581) 10–11.

Ingram D and Hutchison SA (2000) Double binds and the reproductive and mothering experiences of HIV positive women. *Qualitative Health Research* 10 (1) 117–32.

Inhorn M and Whittle K (2001) Feminism meets the 'new 'epidemiologies': towards an appraisal of anti-feminist biases in epidemiological research on women's health. *Social Science and Medicine* 53 (5) 553–67.

International Community of Women Living with HIV/AIDS (2004) *HIV Positive Women, Poverty and Gender Inequality*. London: ICW Vision Paper.

International Gay and Lesbian Human Rights Coalition (2007) *Off the Map: How HIV/AIDS Programming is Failing Same-Sex Practicing People in Africa*. New York: IGLHRC.

International Labour Organisation (2012) *ILO Concept Note on the post-2015 Development Agenda*. Geneva ILO.

International Treatment Preparedness Coalition (2007) *Missing the Target: A Report on HIV/AIDS Treatment Access from the Front Lines*. http://www.soros.

org/reports/missing-target-5-improving-aids-drug-access-and-advancing-health-care-all [accessed 20 September 2012].

International Treatment Preparedness Coalition (2009) *Missing the Target: Failing Women, Failing Children: HIV, Vertical Transmission and Women's Health*. ITPC Treatment Access Project. http://aidsdatahub.org/en/reference-librarycols2/item/21997-missing-the-target-7-failing-women-failing-children-hiv-vertical-transmission-and-women%E2%80%99s-health-international-treatment-preparedness-coalition-2009 [accessed 20 September 2012].

Ironson G, Stuezle R, Fletcher M (2006) An increase in religiousness/spirituality occurs after HIV diagnosis and predicts slower disease progression over 4 years in people with HIV. *Journal of General Internal Medicine* 21 (Suppl 5) S62–8.

Isingo R, Zaba B, Marston M et al. (2007) Survival after HIV infection in the pre-antiretroviral therapy era in a rural Tanzanian cohort. *AIDS* 21 (Suppl 6) S5–13.

Jeske D (2008) Special obligations. In E Zalta (ed.) *The Stanford Encyclopedia of Philosophy*. http://plato.stanford.edu/archives/fall2008/entries/special-obligations.

Jewkes R, Abrahams N, Mvo Z (1998) Why do nurses abuse patients? Reflections from South African obstetric services. *Social Science and Medicine* 47 (11) 1781–95.

Johri M, Chung R, Dawson A, Schrecker T (2012) Global health and national borders: the ethics of foreign aid in a time of financial crisis. *Global Health* 8 (19).

Johnston D (2008) Bias, not error: assessments of the economic impact of HIV/AIDS using evidence from micro-studies in sub-Saharan Africa. *Feminist Economics* 14 (4) 87–115.

Office of the United Nations High Commissioner for Human Rights and Joint United Nations Programme on HIV/AIDS (2006) *International Guidelines on HIV/AIDS and Human Rights*. Geneva: UNAIDS.

Jones C (1999) *Global Justice: Defending Cosmopolitanism*. Oxford: Oxford University Press.

Jones PS (2012) Mind the gap: access to ARV medication, rights and the politics of scale in South Africa. *Social Science and Medicine* 74 (1) 28–35.

Joseph S, Kielmann K, Kuhale A, Sheikh K, Shinde S, Porter J, Rangan S (2010) Examining sex differentials in the uptake and process of HIV testing in three high prevalence districts of India. *AIDS Care* 22 (3) 286–95.

JRF, Terrence Higgins Trust and Age UK (2010) *50 Plus: A National Study of People over 50 Living with HIV*. London: JRF, THT and Age UK.

Juma M, Okeyo T, Kidenda G (2004) *'Our Hearts Are Willing, But ... ': Challenges of Elderly Caregivers in Rural Kenya*. Nairobi: Population Council (Horizons Research Update).

Jurgens R, Csete J, Amon JJ, Baral S, Beyrer C (2010) People who use drugs, HIV and human rights. *Lancet* 376 (9730) 475–85.

Kaida A, Andia I, Maier M, Strathdee SA, Bangsberg DR et al. (2006) The potential impact of ARV therapy on fertility in Sub Saharan Africa *Current HIV/AIDS Report* 3 (4) 187–94.

Kaida A, Laher F, Strathdee S, Janssen P, Money D, Hogg R, Gray G (2011) Childbearing intentions of HIV-positive women of reproductive age in Soweto, South Africa: the influence of expanding access to HAART in an HIV hyperendemic setting. *American Journal of Public Health* 101 (2) 350–58.

Kaiser Family Foundation (2012) *Fact Sheet: The HIV/AIDS Epidemic in the United States*. Menlo Park CA: KFF.

Kandiyoti D (1998) Gender, power and contestation: 'Rethinking bargaining with patriarchy'. In: C Jackson and R Pearson (eds) *Feminist Visions of Development: Gender Analysis and Policy*. London: Routledge.

Kanniappan S, Jeyapaul M, Kalyanwala S (2008) Desire for motherhood: exploring HIV positive women's desires, intentions and decision making in attaining motherhood. *AIDS Care* 20 (6) 625–30.

Kates J et al. (2011) *Financing the Response to AIDS in Low and Middle Income Countries: Income Assistance from Donor Governments in 2010*. Menlo Park CA: Kaiser Family Foundation and UNAIDS.

Katz A (2009) Prospects for a genuine revival of primary health care through the visible hand of social justice rather than the invisible hand of the market Part 1. *International Journal of Health Services* 39 (3) 567–85.

Katz A (2010) Prospects for a genuine revival of primary health care through the visible hand of social justice rather than the invisible hand of the market Part 2. *International Journal of Health Services* 40 (1) 119–37.

Keikelame, M, Ringheim K, Woldehanna S (2010) Perceptions of HIV/AIDS leaders about faith based organisations' influence on HIV/AIDS stigma in South Africa. *African Journal of AIDS Research* 9 (1) 63–70.

Kelly C, Lohan M, Alderdice F, Spence D (2011) Negotiation of risk in sexual relationships and reproductive decision making amongst HIV sero-different couples. *Culture Health and Sexuality* 13 (7) 815–27.

Kelly M and Field D (1996) Medical Sociology, chronic illness and the body. *Sociology of Health and Illness* 18 (2) 241–57.

Kendall T (2009) Reproductive rights violations reported by Mexican women with HIV. *Health and Human Rights* 11 (2) 77–87.

Kerrigan D, Bastos F, Malta M, Carneiro-da-Cunha C, Pilotto J, Strathdee S (2006) The search for social validation and the sexual behaviour of people living with HIV in Rio de Janeiro, Brazil: understanding the role of treatment optimism in context. *Social Science and Medicine* 62 (10) 2386–96.

Kiapi E (2010) Why waste ARVs on sex workers? *Inter Press Service (IPS)* 3 December.

Kickbusch I (2011) Advancing the global health agenda. *UN Chronicle* online. http://www.un.org/wcm/content/site/chronicle/home/archive/issues2011/7billionpeople1unitednations/advancingtheglobalhealthagenda [accessed 28 October 2012].

Kickbusch I, Hein W, Silberschmidt G (2010) Addressing global health governance through a new mechanism: the proposal for a committee C for the World Health Assembly. *Journal of Law, Medicine and Ethics* 38 (3) 550–563.

Kickbusch I and Gleicher D (2012) *Governance for Health in the 21st Century*. Geneva : WHO

Kim J, Lutz B, Dhaliwal M, O'Malley J (2011) The 'AIDS and MDGs' approach: what is it, why does it matter and how do we take it forward? *Third World Quarterly* 32 (1) 141–163

King R, Lifshay J, Nakayiwa S, Katuntu D, Lindkvist P, Bunnell R (2008) The virus stops with me: HIV infected Ugandans' motivations in preventing HIV transmission. *Social Science and Medicine* 68 (4) 749–57.

Kippax S (2008) Understanding and integrating the structural and biomedical determinants of HIV infection: a way forward for prevention. *Current Opinion in HIV and AIDS* 3 (4) 489–94.

Kippax S and Holt M (2009) *The State of Social and Political Science Research Related to HIV: A Report for the International AIDS Society*. Geneva: IAS.

Kippax S, Reis E, de Wit J (2011) Two sides to the HIV prevention coin: efficacy and effectiveness. *AIDS Education and Prevention* 23 (5) 393–6.

Kirshenbaum SB, Hirky AE, Correale J, Goldstein RB, Johnson M, Rotheramborus MJ and Ehrhardt AA (2004) 'Throwing the dice' reproductive decision making among HIV positive women in four US cities. *Perspectives on Sexual and Reproductive Health* 36 (3) 106–13.

Kizito D, Woodburn PW, Kesande B, Amoke C, Nabulime J, Muwanga M, Grosskurth H, Elliot AM (2008) Uptake of HIV and syphilis testing of pregnant women and their male partners in a programme for prevention of mother to child transmission in Uganda. *Tropical Medicine and International Health* 13 (5) 680–82.

Kleinert S and Horton R (2011) Brazil: towards sustainability and equity in health. *Lancet* 377 (9779) 1721–2.

Knodel J and Van Landingham M (2003) Return migration in the context of parental assistance in the AIDS epidemic: the Thai experience. *Social Science and Medicine* 57 (2) 327–42.

Koh H (2003) *On American Exceptionalism*. Faculty Scholarship Series. Paper 1778. http://digitalcommons.law.yale.edu/fss_papers/1778.

Koivusalo M (2011) Trade and health: the ethics of global rights, regulation and redistribution. In S Benatar and G Brock (eds) *Global Health and Global Health Ethics* Cambridge: Cambridge University Press.

Koricho A (2008) *The Fear of Mother's Milk in the Era of HIV: A Qualitative Study among HIV Positive Mothers and Health Professionals*. Addis Ababa: Centre for International Health, Bergen: University of Bergen.

Krieger N (1999) Embodying inequality: A review of concepts, measures, and methods for studying health consequences of discrimination. *International Journal of Health Services* 29 (2) 295–352.

Krieger N (2001) Theories for social epidemiology in the 21st century: an eco-social perspective. *International Journal of Epidemiology* 30 (4) 668–77.

Krieger N (2003a) Does racism harm health? Did child abuse exist before 1962? On explicit questions, critical science and current controversies: an ecosocial perspective *American Journal of Public Health* 93 (2) 194–9.

Krieger N (2003b) Gender, sexes and health: what are the connections and why does it matter? *International Journal of Epidemiology* 32 (4) 652–7.

Krieger N (2008) Proximal, distal and the politics of causation: what's level got to do with it? *American Journal of Public Health* 98 (2) 221–30.

Krieger N, Williams D, Moss N (1997) Measuring social class in US public health research: concepts, methodologies and guidelines. *Annual Review of Public Health* 18 341–78.

Krishna V, Bhatti R, Chandra P, Juvva S (2005) Unheard voices: experiences of families living with HIV/AIDS in India. *Contemporary Family Therapy* 27 (2) 483–506.

Kumarasamy N, Safren SA, Raminani SR, Pickard R, James R et al. (2005) Barriers and facilitators to antiretroviral medication adherence among patients with HIV in Chennai India: a qualitative study. *AIDS Patient Care and STDs* 19 (8) 526–37.

Kuoh M and Best K (2001) HIV positive women have different needs. *Network* 20 (4).

Kymlicka W (1996) *Multicultural Citizenship: A Liberal Theory of Minority Rights*. Oxford: Clarendon Press.

Kymlicka W (2001) *Politics in the Vernacular: Nationalism, Multiculturalism and Citizenship*. Oxford: Oxford University Press.

Kymlicka W (2002) *Contemporary Political Philosophy*. 2nd ed. Oxford: Oxford University Press.

Labonte R (2012) Commentary: global action on social determinants of health. *Journal of Public Health Policy* 33 (2) 139–47.

Labonte R and Schrecker T (2011) The state of global health: a radically unequal world: patterns and prospects. In S Benatar and G Brock (eds) *Global Health and Global Health Ethics*. Cambridge: Cambridge University Press.

Laher F, Todd CS, Stibich MA, Phofa R, Behane X, Mohapi L, Gray G (2009) A qualitative assessment of decisions affecting contraceptive utilisation and fertility intentions among HIV positive women in Soweto, South Africa. *AIDS and Behavior* June 13 (Suppl 1) S47–54.

Laher F, Todd CS, Stibich MA Phofa R, Behane X, Mohapi L, Martinson N Gray G (2010) Role of menstruation in contraceptive choice among HIV infected women in Soweto, South Africa. *Contraception* 81 (6) 547–51.

Lambert S, Keegan A, Petrak J (2005) Sex and relationships for HIV positive women since HAART: a quantitative study. *Sexually Transmitted Infections* 8 (1) 333–7.

Lancet (2011) HIV treatment as prevention: it works. *Lancet* 377 (9779) 1719 (no authors listed).

Lane M (2004) *HIV/AIDS and the Black Death*. Report of a discussion meeting held on 24 May at Centre for History and Economics, King's College, Cambridge.

Larson BA, Fox MP, Rosen S, Bii M, Sigei C, Shaffer D, Sawe F, McCoy K, Wasunna M, Simon J. (2009) Do the socioeconomic impacts of antiretroviral therapy vary by gender? A longitudinal study of Kenyan agricultural worker employment outcomes. *BMC Public Health* 9 240.

Lavery JV, Boyle J, Dickens BM, Maclean H, Singer PA (2001) Origins of the desire for euthanasia and assisted suicide in people with HIV-1 or AIDS: a qualitative study. *Lancet* 358 (9279) 362–7.

Lawton J (2009) *Sociology of Health and Illness*. Virtual special issue on 'Illness, Biography and Narrative', editorial. http://www.blackwellpublishing.com/shil_enhanced/virtual3_full.asp.

Lazarus R, Struthers H, Violari A (2009) Hopes, fears, knowledge and misunderstandings: responses of HIV-positive mothers to early knowledge of the status of their baby. *AIDS Care* 21 (3) 329–34.

Leach-Lemens C (2010) Preventing unintended pregnancies in women living with HIV in resource-poor settings. *HATIP (HIV/AIDS Treatment in Practice)* 155.

Leclerc-Madlala S (2006) 'We will eat when I get the grant': negotiating AIDS, poverty and antiretroviral treatment in South Africa. *African Journal of AIDS Research* 5 (3) 249–56.

Lee M, Wu Z, Rotheram-Borus MJ, Detels R, Guan J, Li L (2005) HIV-related stigma among market workers in China. *Health Psychology* 24 (4) 435–38.

Lemke S (2003) Empowered women and the need to empower men; gender relations and food security in black South African households. *Studies of Tribes and Tribals* 1 (1) 59–67.

Lert F and Kazatchkine M (2007) Antiretroviral treatment and care for injecting drug users: an evidence based overview. *International Journal of Drug Policy* 18 (4) 255–61.

Leshabari SC, Blystad A, Moland KM (2007) Difficult choices: infant feeding experiences of HIV positive mothers in Northern Tanzania. *SAHARA Journal* 4 (1) 544–55.

Levy J and Storeng K (2007) Living positively: narrative strategies of women living with HIV in Cape Town, South Africa. *Anthropology and Medicine* 14 (1) 55–68.

Li, L, Sheng W, Zunyou W, Sun S, Cui H, Jia M (2006) Understanding family support for people living with HIV/AIDS in Yunnan, China. *AIDS and Behavior* 10 (5) 509–17.

Liamputtong P, Haritavorn N, Kiatying-Angsulee N (2009) HIV and AIDS, stigma and AIDS support groups: perspectives from women living with HIV and AIDS in central Thailand. *Social Science and Medicine* 69 (6) 862–8.

Liu J (2007) The use of herbal medicines in early drug development for the treatment of HIV and AIDS infections. *Expert Opinion in Investigating Drugs* 16 (9) 1355–64.

Lockhart C (2008) The life and death of a street boy in East Africa: everyday violence in the time of AIDS. *Medical Anthropology Quarterly* 22 (1) 94–115.

Loevinsohn M and Gillespie S (2003) *HIV/AIDS, Rural Livelihoods and Food Security: Understanding and Responding.* Washington DC: Food Policy Research Institute.

Logie CH, James L, Tharao W, Loutfy MR (2011) HIV, gender, race, sexual orientation and sex work: a qualitative study of intersectional stigma experienced by HIV positive women in Ontario, Canada. *PLOS Medicine* 8 (11).

Logie CH, James L, Tharao W, Loutfy MR (2012) 'We don't exist': a qualitative study of marginalization experienced by HIV-positive lesbian, bisexual queer and transgender women in Toronto, Canada. *Journal of the International AIDS Society* 15 (2) 17392.

London L (2002) Human rights and public health: dichotomies or synergies in developing countries? Examining the case of HIV in South Africa. *Journal of Law, Medicine and Ethics* 30 (4) 677–91.

London L and Schneider H (2012) Globalisation and health inequalities: can a human rights paradigm create space for civil society action? *Social Science and Medicine* 74 (1) 6–13.

London L, Orner P, Myer L (2008) 'Even if you're positive you still have rights because you are a person': human rights and the reproductive choice of HIV-positive persons. *Developing World Bioethics* 8 (1) 11–22.

Long C (2009a) *Contradicting Maternity: HIV-Positive Motherhood in South Africa.* Johannesburg: Wits University Press.

Long C (2009b) HIV positive women on secrets, condoms and gendered conversations. *Sexualities* 12 (6) 701–20.

Long S (2003) *More Than a Name: State-Sponsored Homophobia and its Consequences in Southern Africa.* New York: Human Rights Watch and International Gay and Lesbian Human Rights Commission.

Lopez Gonzales L (2012) Will the world pay up to end HIV? Global AIDS funding. *NAM Aidsmap* issue 212.

Lorenc T, Marrero-Guillamon I, Aggleton P, Cooper C, Llewellyn A, Lehmann A, Lindsay C (2011) HIV testing among men who have sex with men (MSM): systematic review of qualitative evidence. *Health Education Research* 26 (5) 834–46.

Loutfy MR, Hart TA, Mohammed SS, Su D, Ralph ED et al. (2009) Fertility desires and intentions of HIV-positive women of reproductive age in Ontario, Canada: a cross-sectional study. *PLOS ONE* 4 (12) e7925.

Luginaah I, Elkins D, Maticka-Tyndale E, Landry T, Mathul M (2005) Challenges of a pandemic: HIV-AIDS related problems affecting Kenyan widows. *Social Science and Medicine* 60 (6) 1219–28.

Luzi K, Guaraldi G, Murri R, de Paola M et al. (2009) Body image is a major determinant of sexual dysfunction in stable HIV-infected women. *Antiviral Therapy* 14 (1) 85–92.

Lyttleton C (2004) Fleeing the fire: transformation and gendered belonging in Thai HIV/AIDS support groups. *Medical Anthropology* 23 (1) 1–10.

MacCarthy S, Laher F, Nduna M, Farlane L, Kaida A (2009) Responding to her question: a review of the influence of pregnancy on HIV disease progression in the context of expanded access to HAART in sub-Saharan Africa. *AIDS and Behavior* (Suppl 1) 66–71.

MacDevette M (2011) *Disease Burden, Proportionality and the AIDS Funding Debate: Towards Clarity on Whether the World is Spending 'Too Much' on HIV/AIDS.* Working Paper 297 CSSR. Cape Town: UCT.

MacPhail C, Terris-Prestholt F, Kumaranayake L, Ngoako P, Watts C, Rees H (2009) Managing men: women's dilemmas about covert and overt use of barrier methods for HIV prevention. *Culture, Health and Sexuality* 11 (5) 485–97.

Madhavan S and Schatz EJ (2007) Coping with change: household structure and composition in rural South Africa, 1992–2003. *Scandinavian Journal of Public Health* 69 85–93.

Mahajan AP, Colvin M, Rudatsikira JB, Etti D (2007) An overview of HIV/AIDS workplace policies and programmes in southern Africa. *AIDS* 21 (Suppl 3) S31–9.

Mahajan AP, Sayles JN, Patel VA, Remien RH, Sawires S, Ortiz DJ, Szekeres G, Coates TJ (2008) Stigma in the HIV/AIDS epidemic: a review of the literature and recommendations for the way forward. *AIDS* 22 (Suppl 2) S67–79.

Malebranche D (2008) Bisexually active black men in the United States and HIV: acknowledging more than the 'Down Low'. *Archives of Sexual Behaviour* 37 (5) 810–16.

Maman S, Abler L, Parker L, Lane T, Chirowodza A et al. (2009a) A comparison of HIV stigma and discrimination in five international sites: the influence of care and treatment resources in high prevalence settings. *Social Science and Medicine* 68 (12) 2271–8.

Maman S, Cathcart R, Burkhardt G, Omba S, Behets F (2009b) The role of religion in HIV-positive women's disclosure experiences and coping strategies in Kinshasa, Democratic Republic of Congo. *Social Science and Medicine* 68 (5) 965–70.

Mantell JE, Smit JA, Stein ZA (2009) The right to choose parenthood among HIV-infected women and men. *Journal of Public Health Policy* 30 (4) 367–78.

Marks S (2002) An epidemic waiting to happen? The spread of HIV/AIDS in South Africa in social and historical perspective. *African Studies* 61 (1) 13–26.

Masanjala W (2007) The poverty–AIDS nexus in Africa: a livelihood approach. *Social Science and Medicine* 64 (5) 1032–41.

Mason Meier B (2012) Global health takes a normative turn: the expanding purview of international health law and global health politics to meet the public health challenges of the 21st century. In *The Global Community: Yearbook of International Law and Jurisprudence*. Dobbs Ferry NY: Oceana Publications.

Mathambo V and Gibbs A (2008) Qualitative accounts of family and household changes in response to the effects of HIV and AIDS: a review with pointers to action. Joint Learning Initiative on Children and HIV/AIDS (JLICA) Learning Group 1 – Strengthening Families.

Mathers BM, Degenhardt L, Phillips B, Wiessing L et al. (for 2007 Reference Group to the UN on HIV and injecting drug use) (2008) Global epidemiology of injecting drug use and HIV among people who inject drugs: a systematic review. *Lancet* 372 (9719) 1733–45.

Mathers BM, Degenhardt L, Ali H, Wiessing L, Hickman M et al. (2010) HIV prevention, treatment and care services for people who inject drugs: a systematic review of global, regional and national coverage. *Lancet* 375 (9719) 1014–28.

Mattes D (2011) 'We are just supposed to be quiet': the production of adherence to antiretroviral treatment in urban Tanzania. *Medical Anthropology* 30 (2) 158–82.

Mattes D (2012) 'I am also a human being!' Antiretroviral treatment in local moral worlds. *Anthropology and Medicine* 19 (1) 75–84.

Maughan-Brown B (2010) Stigma rises despite antiretroviral roll-out: a longitudinal analysis in South Africa. *Social Science and Medicine* 70 (3) 368–74.

Mayfield Arnold E, Rice E, Flannery D, Rotheram-Borus MJ (2008) HIV disclosure among adults living with HIV. *AIDS Care* 20 (1) 80–92.

McDonald K (2011) 'The old-fashioned way': conception and sex in sero-discordant relationships after ART. *Culture, Health and Sexuality* 13 (10) 1119–33.

McGreal C (2002) Thabo Mbeki's catastrophe. *Prospect* 20 (March) 42–47.

McInnes C and Rushton S (2010) HIV, AIDS and security: where are we now? *International Affairs* 86 (1) 225–45.

McIntyre J (2010) Use of antiretrovirals during pregnancy and breastfeeding in low-income and middle-income countries. *Current Opinion on HIV and AIDS* 5 (1) 48–53.

McIntyre L and Rondeau K (2011) Food security and global heath. In S Benatar and G Brock (eds) *Global Health and Global Health Ethics*. Cambridge: Cambridge University Press.

McNamara R (2003) *Female Genital Health and the Risk of HIV Transmission.* New York: UNDP.

Médecins Sans Frontières (2007) *Confronting the Health Care Worker Crisis to Expand Access to HIV/AIDS Treatment*. Johannesburg: MSF.

Médecins Sans Frontières (2009) *Punishing Success? Early Signs of a Retreat from Commitment to HIV/AIDS Care and Treatment*. Geneva: MSF.

Médecins Sans Frontières (2010) *No Time to Quit: HIV Treatment Gap Widening in Africa*. Geneva: MSF.

Medley A, Garcia-Moreno C, McGill S, Maman S (2004) Rates, barriers and outcomes of HIV serostatus disclosure among women in developing countries: implications for prevention of mother-to-child transmission. *Bulletin of the World Health Organisation* 82 (4) 299–307.

Mcdley AM, Kennedy CE, Lunyolo S, Sweat MD (2009) Disclosure outcomes, coping strategies and life changes among women living with HIV in Uganda. *Qualitative Health Research* 19 (12) 1744–54.

Merten S, Kenter E, McKenzie O, Mushekc M, Ntalasha H, Martin-Hiber A (2010) Patient reported barriers and drivers of adherence to antiretrovirals in sub-Saharan Africa: a meta-ethnography. *Tropical Medicine and International Health* 15 (Suppl 1) 16–33.

Mfecane S (2011) Negotiating therapeutic citizenship and notions of masculinity in a South African village. *African Journal of AIDS Research* 10 (2) 129–38.

Miller D (1988) The ethical significance of nationality. *Ethics* 98 647–63.

Miller D (1995) *On Nationality*. Oxford: Clarendon Press.

Miller D (1999) Justice and inequality. In A Hurrell and M Woods (eds) *Inequality, Globalization and World Politics*. Oxford: Oxford University Press.

Miller D (2000) *Citizenship and National Identity*. Cambridge: Polity Press.

Mills EJ, Montori V, Perri D, Phillips E, Koren G (2005) Natural health product-HIV drug interaction: a systematic review. *International Journal of STDs and AIDS* 16 (3) 181–6.

Mills E, Barnighausen T, Negin J (2012) HIV and aging: preparing for the challenges ahead. *New England Journal of Medicine* 366 1270–73.

Mills EJ, Nachega JB, Buchan I, Orbinski J et al. (2006) Adherence to antiretroviral therapy in sub-Saharan Africa and North America: a meta-analysis. *Journal of the American Medical Association* 296 (6) 679–90.

Milloy M-J, Montaner J, Wood E (2012) Barriers to HIV treatment among people who use injection drugs: implications for 'treatment as prevention'. *Current Opinion in HIV and AIDS* 7 (4) 332–8.

Mimiaga M, Safren S, Dvoryak S, Reisner S, Needle R, Woody G (2010) 'We fear the police and the police fear us': structural and individual barriers and facilitators to HIV medication adherence among injection drug users in Kiev, Ukraine. *AIDS Care* 22 (11) 1305–13.

Mishra V, Assche SB, Greener R, Vaessen M, Hong R, Ghys PD, Boerma JT, Van Assche A, Khan S, Rutstein S (2007) HIV does not disproportionately affect the poorer in sub-Saharan Africa. *AIDS* (Suppl 7) S17–28.

MMWR (2008) Persons tested for HIV – United States, 2006. *Morbidity and Mortality Weekly Report* 8 August 57 (31) 845–9. Centers for Disease Control and Prevention (CDC).

Mnyani CN and McIntyre JA (2009) Preventing mother to child transmission of HIV. *British Journal of Obstetrics and Gynaecology* 116 (Suppl 1) 71–6.

Moatti JP, Spire B, Kazatchkine M (2004) Drug resistance and adherence to HIV/AIDS antiretroviral treatment: against a double standard between the north and the south. *AIDS* 18 (Suppl 3) S55–61.

Moatti JP and Souteyrand Y (2000) Editorial: HIV/AIDS social and behavioural research: past advances and thoughts about the future. *Social Science and Medicine* 50 (11) 1519–32.

Moland KM, de Paoli M, Sellen D, van Esterik P, Leshabari SC, Blystad A (2010) Breastfeeding and HIV: experiences from a decade of postnatal HIV transmission in sub-Saharan Africa. *International Breastfeeding Journal* 5 10.

Montaner J et al. (eds) (2011) *Proceedings of First International HIV Treatment as Prevention (TasP) Workshop*. Vancouver.

Montaner JS, Hogg R, Wood E, Kerr T, Tyndall M, Levy A, Harrigan P (2006) The case for expanding access to highly active antiretroviral therapy to curb the growth of the HIV epidemic. *Lancet* 368 (9534) 531–6.

Montgomery CM, Hosegood V, Busza J, Timaeus IM, (2006) Men's involvement in the South African family: engendering change in the AIDS era. *Social Science and Medicine* 62 (10) 2411–19.

Montgomery CM and Poole R (2011) Critically engaging: integrating the social and the biomedical in international microbicides research. *Journal of the International AIDS Society* 14 (Suppl 2) S4.

Moore AR and Amey F (2008) Sexual responses to living with HIV/AIDS in Lome, Togo. *Culture, Health and Sexuality* 10 (3) 287–96.

Moore AR and Henry D (2005) Experiences of older informal caregivers to people with HIV/AIDS in Lome, Togo. *Ageing International* 30 (2) 147–66.

Moore AR and Oppong J (2007) Sexual risk behaviour among people living with HIV/AIDS in Togo. *Social Science and Medicine* 64 (5) 1057–66.

Morrell R (2001) *Changing Men in Southern Africa*. London: Zed Books.

Morell R and Jewkes R (2011) Carework and caring: a path to gender equitable practices among men in South Africa? *International Journal of Equity and Health*. 10:17

Morgan,D, Mahe C, Mayanja B. Okongo JM, Lubega R. Whitworth JA (2002) HIV-1 infection in rural Africa: is there a difference in median time to AIDS and survival compared with that in industrialized countries? *AIDS* 16 (4) 597–603.

Msishi W, Kapiga S, Earls F, Subramanian S (2008) Socioeconomic status and HIV seroprevalence in Tanzania: a counterintuitive relationship. *International Journal of Epidemiology* 37 (6) 1297–303.

Munoz-Laboy M, Garcia J, Moon-Howard J, Wilson PA, Parker R (2011) Religious responses to HIV and AIDS: understanding the role of religious cultures and institutions in confronting the epidemic. *Global Public Health* 6 (Suppl 2) S127–31.

Murphy D, Roberts KJ, Herbeck DM (2012) HIV-positive mothers with late adolescent/early adult children: 'empty nest' concerns. *Health Care for Women International* 33 (4) 387–402.

Murphy L, Harvey P, Silvestre E (2005) How do we know what we know about the impact of AIDS on food and livelihood insecurity? A review of empirical research from rural sub-Saharan Africa. *Human Organization* 64 (3) 265–75.

Murray LK, Semrau K, McCurley E, Thea DM, Scott N et al. (2009) Barriers to acceptance and adherence of antiretroviral therapy in urban Zambian women: a qualitative study. *AIDS Care* 21 (1) 78–86.

Murungi K and Mabele N (2002). Anti-lesbian rape, HIV and the human rights of South African lesbians. International Conference on AIDS, 7–12 July (14) abstract no. ThOrG1419. New York: IGLHRC c/o Human Rights Watch.

Mutangadura G (2005) Gender, HIV/AIDS and rural livelihoods in Southern Africa: addressing the challenges. *JENdA: A Journal of Culture and African Women Studies* 7.

Muula A, Ngulube TJ, Siziya S, Makupe CM, Umar E, Prozesky HW, Wiysonge CS, Mataya RH (2007) Gender distribution of adult patients on highly active antiretroviral therapy (HAART) in Southern Africa: a systematic review. *BMC Public Health* 7 63.

Myer L, Rebe K, Morroni C (2007) Missed opportunities to address reproductive health care needs among HIV positive women in antiretroviral therapy programmes. *Tropical Medicine and International Health* 12 (12) 1484–9.

Mykhalovskiy E and Rosengarten M (2009a) HIV/AIDS in its third decade: renewed critique in social and cultural analysis – an introduction. *Social Theory and Health* 7 (3) 187–95.

Mykhalovskiy E and Rosengarten M (2009b) Commentaries on the nature of social and cultural research: interviews on HIV/AIDS with Judy Auerbach, Susan Kippax, Steven Epstein, Didier Fassin, Barry Adam and Dennis Altman. *Social Theory and Health* 7 (3) 284–304.

Nachega JB, Mills EJ, Schechter M (2010) Antiretroviral therapy adherence and retention in care in middle-income and low-income countries: current status of knowledge and research priorities. *Current Opinion in HIV and AIDS* 5 (1) 70–77.

Namakhoma I, Bongololo G, Bello G, Nyirenda L, Phoya A, Phiri S, Theobald S, Obermeyer CM (2010) Negotiating multiple barriers: health workers' access to counselling, testing and treatment in Malawi. *AIDS Care* 22 Supp 1 68-76

Narveson J (2000) Libertarianism. In H Lafollette (ed.) *The Blackwell Guide to Ethical Theory*. Oxford: Blackwell.

Narveson J (2003) We don't owe them a thing! A tough-minded but soft-hearted view of aid to the faraway needy. *The Monist* 86 (3) 419–33.

Narveson J (2004) Welfare and wealth, poverty and justice in today's world. *Journal of Ethics* 8 (4) 305–48.

Natrass N (2005) Trading off income and health? AIDS and the disability grant in South Africa. *Journal of Social Policy* 35 (1) 3–19.

Natrass N (2006a) *AIDS, Gender and Access to Antiretroviral Treatment in South Africa*. CSSR Working Paper no. 178 Cape Town: UCT.

Natrass N (2006b) What determines cross-country access to antiretroviral treatment? *Development Policy Review* 24 (3) 321–37.

Nattabi B, Li J, Thompson SC, Orach CG, Earnest J (2009) A systematic review of factors influencing fertility desires and intentions among people living with HIV/AIDS: implications for policy and service delivery. *AIDS and Behavior* 13 (5) 949–68.

Navarro V (2009) What do we mean by social determinants of health? *Global Health Promotion* 16 5–16.

Navarro V (2011) The importance of politics in policy. *Australian and New Zealand Journal of Public Health* 35 (4) 313.

Ndlovu V (2009) Considering childbearing in the age of highly active antiretroviral therapy (HAART): views of HIV positive couples. *SAHARA Journal* 6 (2) 58–68.

Nduna M and Farlane L (2009) Women living with HIV in South Africa and their concerns about fertility. *AIDS and Behavior* 13 (Suppl 1) S62–5.

Negin J and Cumming GR (2010) HIV infection in older adults in sub-Saharan Africa: extrapolating prevalence from existing data. *Bulletin of World Health Organization* 88 (11) 847–55.

Newman P (2009) Social and behavioural challenges of HIV vaccines: implications for social work and social science. *Journal of HIV/AIDS and Social Services* 8 (4) 313–30.

Ng N and Ruger PJ (2011) Global health governance at a crossroads. *Global Health Governance* 3 2.

Nguyen T, Oosterhoof P, Yen P, Wright P, Hardon A (2008) Barriers to access prevention of mother to child transmission for HIV-positive women in a well resourced setting in Vietnam. *AIDS Research and Therapy* 5 (7).

Nguyen V-K (2008) Antiretroviral globalism, biopolitics and therapeutic citizenship. In A Ong and S Collier (eds) *Global Assemblages: Technology, Politics and Ethics as Anthropological Problems*. Oxford: Blackwell.

Nguyen V-K, Ako CY, Niamba P, Sylla A, Tiendrebeogo I (2007) Adherence as therapeutic citizenship: impact of the history of access to antiretroviral drugs on adherence to treatment. *AIDS* 21 (Suppl 5) S31–5.

Nguyen, V-K, Bajos N, Dubois-Arber F, O'Malley J, Pirkle CM (2011) Remedicalising an epidemic: from HIV treatment as prevention to HIV treatment is prevention. *AIDS* 25 (3) 291–3.

Nickle J (2007) *Making Sense of Human Rights*. London: Blackwell.

Nieburg P and Carty L (2011) *HIV Prevention among Injection Drug Users in Kenya and Tanzania: New Opportunities for Progress*. Washington DC: Center for Strategic and International Studies.

Niehaus I (2007) Death before dying: understanding AIDS stigma in the South African Lowveld. *Journal of South African Studies* 33 (4) 845–60.

Nixon S and Renwick R (2003) Experiences of contemplating returning to work for people living with HIV/AIDS. *Qualitative Health Research* 13 (9) 1272–90.

Nkurunziza E and Rakodi C (2005) *Urban Families under Pressure: Conceptual and Methodological Issues in the Study of Poverty, HIV/AIDS And Livelihood Strategies*. Working Paper no. 1 University of Birmingham International Development Department.

Norman LR, Carr R, Jimenez J (2006) Sexual stigma and sympathy: attitudes towards persons living with HIV in Jamaica. *Culture Health and Sexuality* 8 (5) 423–33.

Nostlinger CM, Gordillo V, Borms R, Murphy C, Bogner J, Csepe P, Colebunder R (2008) Differences in perceptions on sexual and reproductive health between service providers and people living with HIV: a qualitative elicitation study. *Psychology Health and Medicine* 13 (5) 516–28.

Novogrodsky N (2009) The duty of treatment: human rights and the HIV/AIDS pandemic. *Yale Human Rights and Development Law Journal* 12 1–61.

Nozick R (1974) *Anarchy, State and Utopia.* Oxford: Blackwell.

Nussbaum M (2000) *Women and Human Development.* New York: Cambridge University Press.

Nussbaum M (2011) *Creating Capabilities.* Cambridge MA: Harvard University Press.

Nussbaum M (2012) *New Religious Intolerance: Overcoming the Politics of Fear in an Anxious Age.* Cambridge MA: Harvard University Press.

Nzioka C (2000) The social meanings of death from HIV/AIDS: an African interpretative view. *Culture, Health and Sexuality* 2 (1) 1–14.

Obermeyer CM (2005) Reframing research on sexual behaviour and HIV. *Studies in Family Planning* 36 (1) 1–12.

Obermeyer CM (2006) HIV in the Middle East. *BMJ* 333 (7573) 851–4.

Obermeyer CM and Osborn M (2007) The utilisation of testing and counseling for HIV: a review of the social and behavioral evidence. *American Journal of Public Health* 97 (10) 1762–72.

Ogden J, Esim S, Grown C (2006) Expanding the care continuum for HIV/AIDS: bringing carers into focus. *Health Policy and Planning* 21 (5) 333–42.

O'Leary A and Wolitski RJ (2009) Moral agency and the sexual transmission of HIV. *Psychological Bulletin* 135 (3) 478–94.

Oliva J (2009) HIV positive women are less likely to find work than men affected by the virus. *Health Economics Letters* 19 491–500.

O'Neill O (1996) *Towards Justice and Virtue.* Cambridge: Cambridge University Press.

O'Neill O (2000) *Bounds of Justice.* Cambridge: Cambridge University Press.

O'Neill O (2005) The dark side of human rights. *International Affairs* 81 (2) 427–39.

Oosterhoff P, Anh NT, Yen PN, Wright P, Hardon A (2008a) HIV-positive mothers in Vietnam: using their status to build support groups and access essential services. *Reproductive Health Matters* 16 (32) 162–70.

Oosterhoff P, Anh NT, Hanh NT, Yen PN, Wright P (2008b) Holding the line: family responses to pregnancy and the desire for a child in the context of HIV in Vietnam. *Culture, Health and Sexuality* 10 (4) 403–16.

Operario D, Soma T, Underhill K (2008) Sex work and HIV status among transgender women: systematic review and meta-analysis. *Journal of Acquired Immune Deficiency Syndromes* 48 (1) 97–103.

Oppenheimer G and Bayer R (2009) The rise and fall of AIDS exceptionalism. *Virtual Monitor* 11 (12) 988–92.

Orbach D (2007) *Committed to Caring: Older Women and HIV/AIDS in Cambodia, Thailand and Vietnam*. London: Help Age International.

Orner P, de Bruyn M, Cooper D (2011a) 'It hurts but I don't have a choice, I'm not working and I am sick': decisions and experiences regarding abortion of women living with HIV in Cape Town, South Africa. *Culture, Health and Sexuality* 13 (7) 781–95.

Orner PJ, de Bruyn M, Barbosa RM, Boonstra H, Gatsi-Mallet J, Cooper DD (2011b) Access to safe abortion: building choices for women living with HIV and AIDS. *Journal of International AIDS Society* 14 (54).

Østergaard LR and Bula A (2010) 'They call our children "nevirapine babies"': a qualitative study about exclusive breastfeeding among HIV positive mothers in Malawi. *African Journal of Reproductive Health* 14 (3) 213–22.

Over M (2008) *Prevention Failure: The Ballooning Entitlement Burden of US global AIDS Spending and What To Do About It*. Working Paper 144. Washington DC: Center for Global Development.

Overs C and Hawkins K (2011) Can rights stop the wrongs? Exploring the connections between the framing of sex workers' rights and sexual and reproductive health. *International Health and Human Rights* 11 (Suppl 3) S6.

Owen G (2008) An 'elephant in the room'? Stigma and hepatitis C transmission among HIV positive 'serosorting' gay men. *Culture, Health and Sexuality* 10 (6) 601–10.

Owen G and Catalan J (2012) 'We never expected this to happen.' Narratives of ageing with HIV among gay men in London. *Culture, Health and Sexuality* 14 (1) 59–72.

Oxfam (2013) *The cost of inequality: how wealth and income extremes hurt us all*. Media Briefing 18 Jan 2013

Padian NS, Buve A, Balkus J, Serwadda D, Cates W Jr (2008) Biomedical intervention to prevent HIV infection: evidence, challenges and the way forward. *Lancet* 372 (9638) 585–99.

Padilha A (2011) Brazil calls for pact on social factors to improve health. *Bulletin of World Health Organization* 89 (10) 714–15.

Padilla M, Castellanos D, Guilamo-Ramos V, Reyes AM, Sánchez Marte LE, Soriano MA.(2008) Stigma, social inequality and HIV disclosure among Dominican male sex workers. *Social Science and Medicine* 67 (3) 380–88.

Paiva V, Filipe EV, Santos N, Lima TN, Segurado A (2003) The right to love: the desire for parenthood among men living with HIV. *Reproductive Health Matters* 11 (22) 91–100.

Paiva V, Segurado AC, Filipe EV (2011) Self-disclosure of HIV diagnosis to sexual partners by heterosexual and bisexual men: a challenge for HIV/AIDS care and prevention. *Cad. Saude Publica* 27 (9) 1699–710.

Palitza K (2006) AIDS puts African funeral traditions under pressure. *Inter Press Service* 24 February.

Pallikadavath S, Garda L, Apte H, Freedman J, Stones RW (2005) HIV/AIDS in rural India: context and health care needs. *Journal of Biosocial Science* 37 (5) 641–55.

Pang T, Daulaire N, Keusch G et al. (2010) The new age of global health governance holds promise. *Nature Medicine* 16 1181.

Paparini S, Doyal L, Anderson J (2008) 'I count myself as being in a different world': African gay and bisexual men living with HIV in London. An exploratory study. *AIDS Care* 20 (5) 601–5.

Paraskevis D, Nikolopoulos G, Tsiara C, Paraskeva D et al. (2012) HIV-1 outbreak among injecting drug users in Greece 2011: a preliminary report. *Euro Surveillance* 16 (36).

Parker R and Aggleton P (2003) HIV and AIDS-related stigma and discrimination: a conceptual framework and implications for action. *Social Science and Medicine* 57 (1) 13–24.

Parker R and Gagnon JH (eds) (1995) *Conceiving Sexuality: Approaches to Sex Research in a Modern World*. New York: Routledge.

Parkhurst JO (2010) Understanding the correlations between wealth, poverty and human immunodeficiency virus infection in African countries. *Bulletin of the World Health Organization* 88 (7) 519–26.

Patten A (1999) The autonomy argument for liberal nationalism. *Nations and Nationalism* 5 (1) 1–17.

Payne S (2006) *The Health of Women and Men*. Cambridge: Polity Press.

Peacock D, Stemple L, Sawires S, Coates TJ (2009) Men, HIV/AIDS and human rights. *Journal of Acquired Immune Deficiency Syndrome* 51 (Suppl 3) S119–25.

Peberdy S and Dinat N (2007) *Migrants and Domestic Work in South Africa: Worlds of Work Health and Mobility in Johannesburg*. Johannesburg: South African Migrants Project.

Peltzer K and Phaswana-Mafuya N (2008) The symptom experience of people living with HIV and AIDS in the Eastern Cape, South Africa. *BMC Health Services Research* 8 271.

Peltzer K, Chao LN, Dana P (2009) Family Planning among HIV positive and negative prevention of mother-to-child transmission (PMTCT) clients in a resource poor setting in South Africa. *AIDS and Behavior* 13 (5) 973–9.

Peltzer K, Preez NF, Ramlagan S, Fomundam H (2008) Use of traditional, complementary and alternative medicine for HIV patients in KwaZulu-Natal, South Africa. *BMC Public Health* 8 255.

Persson A and Richards W (2008) Vulnerability, gender and 'proxy negativity': women in relationships with HIV-positive men in Australia. *Social Science and Medicine* 67 (5) 799–807.

Persson A (2005) Facing HIV: body shape change and the (in) visibility of illness. *Medical Anthropology* 24 (3) 237–64.

Persson A (2011) HIV-negativity in serodiscordant relationships: the absence enactment and liminality of serostatus identity. *Medical Anthropology* 30 (6) 569–90.

Persson A (2012) The undoing and doing of sexual identity among heterosexual men with HIV in Australia. *Men and Masculinities* 15 (3) 311–28.

Persson A and Newman C (2012) When HIV positive children grow up: a critical analysis of the transition literature in developed countries. *Qualitative Health Research* 22 (5) 656–667.

Persson A, Elland J, Newman C, Holt M, de Wit J (2011) Human rights and universal access for men who have sex with men and people who inject drugs: a qualitative analysis of the 2010 UNGASS narrative country progress reports. *Social Science and Medicine* 73 (3) 467–74.

Peters P, Walker P, Kambewa D (2008) Striving for normality in a time of AIDS in Malawi. *Journal of Modern African Studies* 46 (4) 659–87.

Peters P, Kambewa D, Walker PA (2010) Contestations over tradition and culture in a time of AIDS. *Medical Anthropology* 29 (3) 278–302.

Peterson J and Jones K (2009) HIV prevention for black men who have sex with men in the United States. *American Journal of Public Health* 99 (6) 976–80.

Petrak JA, Doyle AM, Smith A, Skinner C, Hodge B (2001) Factors associated with self-disclosure of HIV serostatus to significant others. *British Journal of Health Psychology* 6 (Pt 1) 69–79.

Pierret J (2000) Everyday life with AIDS/HIV; surveys in the social sciences. *Social Science and Medicine* 50 (11) 1589–98.

Pierret J (2001) Interviews and biographical time: the case of long term HIV non-progressors. *Sociology of Health and Illness* 23 (2) 159–79.

Pillay N (2008) 'Sexual orientation and gender identity'. New York: United Nations Meeting On Human Rights, 18 December.

Pinkham S and Malinowska-Sempruch K (2008) Women, harm reduction and HIV. *Reproductive Health Matters* 16 (31)168–81.

Pisani E (2008) *The Wisdom of Whores: Bureaucrats, Brothels and the Business of AIDS*. London and New York: Granta and WW Norton.

Piot P, Kazatchkine M, Dybul M, Lob-Levyt J (2009) AIDS: lessons learnt and myths dispelled. *Lancet* 374 (9685) 260–63.

Podmore M, Mburu G, Nieuwenhuys B (2012) *Don't Stop Now: How Underfunding the Global Fund to Fight AIDS, TB and Malaria Impacts on the HIV Response*. London: International HIV/AIDS Alliance.

Pogge T (1992) Cosmopolitanism and sovereignty. *Ethics* 103 (1) 48–75.

Pogge T (2005) Real world justice. In G Brock and D Moellendorf (eds) *Current Debates in Global Justice*. Dordrecht: Springer.

Pogge T (2008) *World Poverty and Human Rights*. Cambridge: Polity Press.

Pogge T (ed.) (2007) *Freedom from Poverty as a Human Right*. Oxford: Oxford University Press.

Pogge T (2011) The Health Impact Fund: how to make new medicines accessible to all. In S Benatar and G Brock (eds) *Global Health and Global Health Ethics*. Cambridge: Cambridge University Press.

Pool R, Hart G, Green G, Harrison S, Nyanzi S, Whitworth J (2000) Men's attitudes to condoms and female controlled means of protection against HIV and STDs in South Western Uganda. *Culture, Health and Sexuality* 2 (2) 197–211.

Posel D, Kahn K, Walker L (2007) Living with death in a time of AIDS: a rural South African case study. *Scandinavian Journal of Public Health* 69 (Suppl 1) 138–46.

Posse M, Meheus F, van Asten H, van der Ven A, Baltussen R (2008) Barriers to access to antiretroviral treatment in developing countries. *Tropical Medicine and International Health* 13 (7) 904–13.

Powers M and Faden R (2006) *Social Justice: The Moral Foundations of Public Health and Health Policy*. New York: Oxford University Press.

Pradha B and Sunda R (2006) *Gender Impact of HIV and AIDS in India*. New Delhi: UNDP.

Prince M, Patel V, Saxena S, Maj M, Maselko M, Phillips M, Rahman A (2007) No health without mental health. *Lancet* 370 (9590) 859–77.

Prior L, Wood F, Lewis G, Pill R (2003) Stigma alone does not explain non-disclosure of psychological symptoms in general practice. *Evidence Based Mental Health* 6 (4) 128.

Radley A and Billig M. (1996) Accounts of health and illness: dilemmas and representations. *Sociology of Health and Illness* 18 (2) 220–40.

Raj A and Bowleg L (2011) Heterosexual risk for HIV among black men in the United States: a call to action against a neglected crisis in black communities. *American Journal of Men's Health* 6 (3) 178–81.

Rao D, Angell B, Lam C, Corrigan P (2008) Stigma in the workplace: employer attitudes about people with HIV in Beijing, Hong Kong, and Chicago. *Social Science and Medicine* 67 (10) 1541–9.

Raphael D (ed.) (1967) *Political Theory and the Rights of Man*. London: Macmillan.

Ravishankar N, Gubbins P, Cooley R, Leach-Lemon K, Michaud CM, Jamison DT, Murray CJ (2009) Financing of global health : tracking development assistance for health from 1990 to 2007. *Lancet* 373 (9681) 2113–24.

Rawls J (1972) *A Theory of Justice*. Oxford: Oxford University Press.

Rawls J (1987) The idea of an overlapping consensus. *Oxford Journal of Legal Studies* 7 (1) 1–25.

Rawls J (1997) The idea of public reason. In J Bohman and W Rehg (eds) *Deliberative Democracy*. Cambridge MA: MIT Press.

Raymond HF and McFarland W (2009) Racial mixing and HIV risk among men who have sex with men. *AIDS and Behavior* 13 (4) 630–37.

Rees D, Murray J, Nelson G, Sonnenberg P (2010) Oscillating migration and the epidemics of silicosis, tuberculosis and HIV infection in South African gold miners. *American Journal of Industrial Medicine* 53 (4) 398–404.

Reid A, Scano F, Getahun H, Williams B et al (2006) Toward universal access to HIV prevention, treatment, care and support: the role of tuberculosis /HIV collaboration. *Lancet Infectious Diseases* 6 (8) 483–95.

Relf M, Bishop T, Lachat M, Schiavone D et al. (2009) A qualitative analysis of partner selection, HIV sero-status disclosure and sexual behaviours among HIV positive urban men. *AIDS Education and Prevention* 21 (3) 280–97.

Remoto D (2009) Rina, overseas Filipino Worker, HIV positive. *UNDP Philippines News* 4 August.

Reynolds N (2004) Adherence to antiretroviral therapies: state of the science. *Current HIV Research* 2 (3) 207–14.

Reynolds W, van der Geest S, Hardon A (2006) *Social Lives of Medicines*. Cambridge: Cambridge University Press.

Reynolds Whyte S (2009) Health, identities and subjectivities: the ethnographic challenge. *Medical Anthropology Quarterly* 23 (1) 6–15.

Rhodes T and Cusick L (2000) Love and intimacy in relationship risk management: HIV positive people and their sexual partners. *Sociology of Health and Illness* 22 (1) 1–26.

Rhodes T, Bernays S, Terzic KJ (2009) Medical promise and the recalibration of expectation: hope and HIV treatment in a transitional setting. *Social Science and Medicine* 68 (6) 1050–59.

Richey L (2005) Lover, mother or worker: women's multiple roles and the HIV/AIDS and reproductive health agenda in Tanzania. *African Journal of AIDS Research* 4 (2) 83–90.

Richey L (2006) *Gendering the Therapeutic Citizen: ARVs and Reproductive Health*. CSSR Working Paper no. 175. Cape Town: UCT Press.

Richter L and Morrell R (2006) *Baba: Men and Fatherhood in South Africa*. Cape Town: HSRC Press.

Ridge D, Ziebland S, Anderson J, Williams I, Elford J (2007) Positive prevention: contemporary issues facing HIV positive people negotiating sex in the UK *.Social Science and Medicine* 65 (4) 755–70.

Ridge D, Williams I, Anderson J, Elford J (2008) Like a prayer: the role of spirituality and religion for people living with HIV in the UK. *Sociology of Health and Illness* 30 413–428.

Rispel L and Metcalfe C (2009) Breaking the silence: South African HIV policies and the needs of men who have sex with men. *Reproductive Health Matters* 17 (33) 133–42.

Rispel L, Metcalfe C, Cloete A, Moorman J, Reddy V (2011) 'You become afraid to tell them that you are gay': health service utilisation by men who have sex with men in South African cities. *Journal of Public Health Policy* 32 (Suppl 1) 37–151.

Robson E (2004) Hidden child workers: young carers in Zimbabwe. *Antipode* 36 (2) 227–48.

Robson E, Ansell N, Huber U, Gould W, Young L (2006) Young caregivers in the context of the HIV/AIDS pandemic in sub-Saharan Africa. *Population, Space and Place* 12 (2) 93–111.

Rohleder P, Gibson K (2005) *'We Are Not Fresh' HIV Positive Women Talk of their Experiences of Living with their Spoiled Identity*. Cape Town: Centre for Social Sciences Research, UCT.

Rosen S, Fox MD, Gill CJ (2007) Patient retention in antiretroviral therapy programs in sub-Saharan Africa: a systematic review. *PLOS Medicine* 4 (10) e298.

Ross-Degnan D, Pierre-Jacques M, Zhang F et al. (2010) Measuring adherence to antiretroviral treatment in resource-poor settings: the clinical validity of key indicators. *BMC Health Services* Research 10 42.

Ruanjahn G, Roberts D, Monterosso L (2010) An exploration of factors influencing adherence to highly active antiretroviral therapy (HAART) among people living with HIV/AIDS in northern Thailand. *AIDS Care* 22 (12) 1555–61.

Rudin J and Sanders D (2011) Debt, structural adjustment and health. In S Benatar and G Brock (eds) *Global Health and Global Health Ethics*. Cambridge: Cambridge University Press.

Ruger JP (2010) *Health and Social Justice*. Oxford: Oxford University Press.

Rugulema G (2000) Coping or struggling? A journey into the impact of HIV/AIDS in Southern Africa. *Review of African Political Economy* 86 537–45.

Russell S, Seeley J, Ezati E, Wamai N, Were W, Bunnell R (2007) Coming back from the dead: living with HIV as a chronic condition. *Health Policy and Planning* 22 (5) 344–7.

Russell S and Seeley J (2010) The transition to living with HIV as a chronic condition in rural Uganda: working to create order and control when on antiretroviral therapy. *Social Science and Medicine* 703 (3) 375–82.

Russell S, Seeley J, Whiteside A (2010) Expanding antiretroviral therapy provision in resource-constrained settings; social processes and their policy challenges *AIDS Care* 22 (Suppl 1) 1–5.

Rutledge SE, Abell N, Padmore J, McCann TJ (2009) AIDS stigma in health services in the Eastern Caribbean. *Sociology of Health and Illness* 31 (1) 17–34.

Saavedra J, Izazola-Licea JA, Beyrer C (2008) Sex between men in the context of HIV: The AIDS 2008 Jonathan Mann Memorial Lecture in health and human rights. *Journal of the International AIDS Society* 11 9.

Sabin LL, Desilva MB, Hamer DH, Keyi X et al. (2008) Barriers to adherence to antiretroviral medications among patients living with HIV in southern China: a qualitative study. *AIDS Care* 20 (10) 1242–50.

Saggurti N, Schensul SV, Verma RK (2009) Migration, mobility and sexual risk behaviour in Mumbai, India: mobile men with non-residential wife show increased risk. *AIDS and Behavior* 13 (5) 921–7.

Samia A, Mezger N, Mauron A (2011) Allocating resources in humanitarian medicine. In S Benatar and G Brock (eds) *Global Health and Global Health Ethics*. Cambridge: Cambridge University Press.

Samuels F and Rutenberg N (2008) HIV, Food and Drugs: livelihoods, nutrition and anti-retroviral therapy (ART) in Kenya and Zambia. London: ODI Briefing Paper. http://www.odi.org.uk.

Samuelsen H, Norgaard O, Ostergaard LR (2012) Social and cultural aspects of HIV and AIDS in West Africa: a narrative review of qualitative research. *SAHARA Journal* 9 (2) 64–73.

Sandfort T and Dodge B (2005) Researching same-sex sexuality and HIV prevention. In V Reddy, T Sandfort, L Rispel (eds) *From Social Silence to Social Science*. Cape Town: HSRC Press.

Sanjobo N, Frich JC, Fretheim A (2008) Barriers and facilitators to patients' adherence to antiretroviral treatment in Zambia: a qualitative study. *SAHARA Journal* 5 (3) 136–43.

Sarna A, Chersich M, Okal J, Luchters S et al. (2009) Changes in sexual risk taking with antiretroviral treatment: influence of context and gender norms in Mombasa, Kenya. *Culture Health and Sexuality* 11(8) 783–97.

Sauer M (2006) American physicians remain slow to embrace the reproductive needs of human immuno-deficiency virus-infected patients. *Fertility and Sterility* 85 (2) 295–7.

Sawers L, Stillwaggon E, Hertz T (2008) Cofactor infections and HIV epidemics in developing countries: implications for treatment. *AIDS Care* 20 (4) 488–94.

Scambler G (2009) Health-related stigma. *Sociology of Health and Illness* 31 (3) 441–55.

Scambler G and Paoli F (2008) Health work, female sex workers and HIV/AIDS: global and local dimensions of stigma and deviance as barriers to effective interventions. *Social Science and Medicine* 66 (8) 1848–62.

Schatz E (2007) 'Taking care of my own blood': older women's relationships to their households in rural South Africa. *Scandinavian Journal of Public Health* (Suppl 69) 147–54.

Schatz E and Ogunmefun C (2007) Caring and contributing: the role of older women in rural South African multi-generational households in the HIV/AIDS era. *World Development* 35 (8) 1390–403.

Schensul S, Mekki-Berrada A, Nastasi B, Singh R, Burleson J, Bojko M (2006) Men's extramarital sex, marital relationships and sexual risk in urban poor communities in India. *Journal of Urban Health* 83 (4) 614–24.

Scheper Hughes N and Bourgeois P (2004) Introduction: making sense of violence. In N Scheper Hughes and P Bourgeois (eds) *War and Peace: An Anthology*. Oxford: Blackwell.

Shiffman J (2008) Has donor prioritization of HIV/AIDS displaced aid for other health issues? *Health Policy and Planning* 23 (2) 95–100.

Schiltz MA and Sandfort TG (2000) HIV-positive people, risk and sexual behaviour. *Social Science and Medicine* 50 (11) 1571–88.

Schmid GP, Williams BG, Garcia-Calleja JM, Miller C, Segar E, Southworth M, Tonyan D, Wacloff J, Scott J (2009) The unexplained story of HIV and ageing. *Bulletin of the World Health Organization* 87 (3) 162–162A.

Schneider H, Blaauw D, Gilson L, Nzapfurundi N, Goudge J (2006) Health systems and access to antiretroviral drugs for HIV in Southern Africa: service delivery and human resources challenges. *Reproductive Health Matters* 14 (27) 12–23.

Schneider H, Hlophe H, van Rensburg D (2008) Community health workers and the response to HIV/AIDS in South Africa: tensions and prospects *Health Policy and Planning* 23 (3) 179–87.

Schrecker T (2008) Denaturalizing scarcity: a strategy of enquiry for public health. *Bulletin of World Health Organization* 86 (8) 600–605.

Schrecker T, Chapman A, Labonte R, de Vogli R (2010) Advancing health equity in the global marketplace: how human rights can help. *Social Science and Medicine* 71 (8) 1520–26.

Schrecker T, Labonte R, de Vogli R (2008) Globalisation and health: the need for a global vision. *Lancet* 372 (9650) 1670–76.

Schumaker LL and Bond VA (2008) Antiretroviral therapy in Zambia: colours, 'spoiling', 'talk' and the meaning of antiretrovirals. *Social Science and Medicine* 67 (12) 2126–34.

Scott J, Minichiello V, Marino R, Harvey GP, Jamieson M, Browne J (2005) Understanding the new context of the male sex work industry. *Journal of Interpersonal Violence* 20 (3) 320–42.

Seale C (2000) Changing patterns of death and dying. *Social Science and Medicine* 51 (6) 917–30.

Seedat F (2011) The reminder of corruption in HIV and AIDS prevention and treatment: clarifying the facts. Consultancy Africa Intelligence. http://www.consultancyafrica.com/index.php?option=com_contentandview=articleandid.

Seeley J (2002) *Thinking with the Livelihoods Framework in the Context of the HIV/AIDS Epidemic*. Research Paper. Livelihoods Connect. University of Sussex: Institute of Development Studies.

Seeley J and Pringle C (2001) *Sustainable Livelihoods Approaches and the HIV/AIDS Epidemic: A Preliminary Resource Paper*. Norwich: UEA School of Development Studies.

Seeley J and Russell S (2010) Social rebirth and social transformation? Rebuilding social lives after ART in rural Uganda. *AIDS Care* 22 (Suppl 1) 44–50.

Seeley J, Grellier R, Barnett T (2004) Gender and HIV/AIDS impact mitigation in sub- Saharan Africa: recognizing the constraints. *SAHARA Journal* 1 (2) 87–98.

Seeley J, Russell S, Khana K, Ezati E, King R, Bunnell R (2009) Sex after ART: sexual partnerships established by HIV infected persons taking anti-retroviral therapy in Eastern Uganda. *Culture, Health and Sexuality* 11 (7) 703–16.

Segurado AC and Paiva V (2007) Rights of HIV positive people to sexual and reproductive health: parenthood. *Reproductive Health Matters* 15 (29 Suppl 1) 27–45.

Sen A (1992) *Inequality Reexamined*. Oxford: Clarendon Press.

Sen A (2009) *The Idea of Justice*. London, Penguin.

Setswe G (2009) Best practice workplace HIV/AIDS programmes in South Africa: a review of case studies and lessons learned. *African Journal of Primary Health Care and Family Medicine* 1 1.

Shamos S, Hartwig KA, Zindela N (2009) Men's and women's experiences with HIV and stigma in Swaziland. *Qualitative Health Research* 19 (12) 1678–89.

Shannon K, Bright V, Duddy J, Tyndall M (2005) Access and utilization of HIV treatment among women sex workers in downtown eastside Vancouver. *Journal of Urban Health* 82 (3) 488–97.

Shannon M and Lee K (2008) HIV-infected mothers' perceptions of uncertainty, stress, depression and social support during HIV viral testing of their infants. *Archives of Women's Mental Health* 11 (4) 259–67.

Sharma A, Feldman JG, Golub ET, Schmidt J, Silver S, Robison E, Minkoff H (2007) Live birth patterns among human immunodeficiency virus-infected women before and after the availability of highly antiretroviral therapy. *American Journal of Obstetrics and Gynecology* 196 (6) 541 e1–6.

Sharma M, Oppenheimer E, Saidel T, Loo V, Garg R (2009) A situation update on HIV epidemics among people who take drugs and national responses in South East Asia Region. *AIDS* 23 (11) 1405–13.

Shaxson N, Christense J, Mathiason N (2012) *Inequality: you don't know the half of it.* Tax Justice Network. http://www.taxjustice.net [accessed 20 September 2012].

Shebaya S (2009) Global and local sovereignties. *Public Reason* 1 (1) 125–40.

Shelton J, Cassell M, Adetunji J (2005) Is poverty or wealth at the root of HIV? *Lancet* 366 (9491) 1057–8.

Sherr L (2010) Fathers and HIV: considerations for families. *Journal of the International AIDS Society* 13 (Suppl 2) S4.

Sherr L and Barry N (2004) Fatherhood and HIV positive heterosexual men. *HIV Medicine* 5 (4) 258–63.

Shilts R (1987) *And the Band Played On: Politics, People, and the AIDS Epidemic.* London: Souvenir Press.

Shin S, Munoz M, Caldas A, Ying Wu, Zeladita J et al. (2011) Mental health burden among impoverished HIV-positive patients in Peru. *Journal of the International Association of Physicians in AIDS Care* 10 (1) 18–25.

Shue H (1996) *Basic Rights, Subsistence and US Foreign Policy.* Princeton NJ: Princeton University Press.

Siegel K, Scrimshaw EW, Lekas HM (2006) Diminished sexual activity, interest and feelings of attractiveness among HIV infected women in two eras of the AIDS epidemic. *Archives of Sexual Behaviour* (35) 437–49.

Siegel K, Scrimshaw E, Lekas H, Parsons J (2008) Sexual behaviours of non-gay indentified non-disclosing men who have sex with men and women. *Archives of Sexual Behaviour* (37) 720–35.

Sienaert A (2008) *The Labour Supply Effects of the South African State Old Age Pension: Theory, Evidence and Implications.* Working Paper no. 20. Cape Town: SALDRU University of Cape Town.

Silverman JG, Decker MR, Gupta J, Dharmadhikari A, Seage GR, Raj A (2008) Syphilis and hepatitis B Co-infection among HIV-infected, sex-trafficked women and girls in Nepal. *Emerging Infectious Diseases* 14 (6) 932–4.

Silverman JG, Decker MR, Gupta J, Maheshwari A, Willis BM, Raj A (2007). HIV prevalence and predictors of infection in sex-trafficked Nepalese girls and women. *Journal of the American Medical Association* 298 (5) 536–42.

Simbayi LL, Kalichman S, Strebel A, Cloete A, Henda N, Mqeketo A (2007) Internalised stigma, discrimination and depression among men and women living with HIV/AIDS in Cape Town, South Africa. *Social Science and Medicine* 64 (9) 1823–31.

Simbayi L, Strebel A, Cloete A, Henda N, Mqeketo A, Kalichman S (2006) Disclosure of HIV status to sex partners and sexual risk behaviours among HIV positive men and women in Cape Town, South Africa. *Sexually Transmitted Infections* 83 (1) 29–34.

Simoni JM and Pantalone DN (2004) Secrets and safety in the age of AIDS: does HIV disclosure lead to safer sex? *Topics in HIV Medicine* 12 (4) 109–18.

Singer PA and Bowman KW (2002) Quality end-of-life care: a global perspective *BMC Palliative Care* 1 (i) 4.

Singhanetra-Renard A, Chongsatitmun C, Aggleton P (2001). Care and support for people living with HIV/AIDS in northern Thailand: Findings from an in-depth qualitative study. *Culture, Health and Sexuality* 3 (2) 167–82.

Sinha G, Peters DH, Bollinger RC (2008) Strategies for gender-equitable HIV services in rural India. *Health Policy and Planning* 24 (3) 197–208.

Skeen S, Lund C, Kleintjes S, Flisher A (2010) Meeting the millennium development goals in sub-Saharan Africa: what about mental health? *International Review of Psychiatry* 22 (6) 624–31.

Skovdal M and Ogutu VO (2009) 'I washed and fed my mother before going to school': understanding the psychosocial well-being of children providing chronic care for adults affected by HIV/AIDS in Western Kenya. *Globalization and Health* 5 8.

Skovdal M, Campbell C, Madanhire C, Mupambireyi Z, Nyamukapa C, Gregson S (2011) Masculinity as a barrier to men's use of HIV services in Zimbabwe. *Globalization and Health* 15 7.

Skovdal M, Ogutu VO, Aoro C, Campbell C (2009) Young carers as social actors: coping strategies of children caring for ailing or aging guardians in Western Kenya. *Social Science and Medicine* 69 (4) 587–95.

Smit P, Brady M, Carter M, Fernandes R, Lamore L et al. (2012) HIV-related stigma within communities of gay men: a literature review. *AIDS Care* 24 (4) 405–12.

Smith A, Tapsoba P, Peshu N, Sanders EJ, Jaffe HN (2009) Men who have sex with men and HIV/AIDS in sub-Saharan Africa. *Lancet* 374 (9687) 416–22.

Smith DJ and Mbakwem BC (2010) Antiretroviral therapy and reproductive life projects: mitigating the stigma of AIDS in Nigeria. *Social Science and Medicine* 71 (2) 345–52.

Smith J and Whiteside A (2010) The history of AIDS exceptionalism. *Journal of the International AIDS Society* 13 47.

Smith J, Ahmed K, Whiteside A (2011) Why HIV/AIDS should be treated as exceptional: arguments from sub-Saharan Africa and Eastern Europe. *African Journal of AIDS Research* 10 (Suppl) 345–56.

Society for Women's Health Research (2009) *Sex Differences in HIV/AIDS*. http://www.womenshealthresearch.org/site/PageServer?pagename=hs_healthfacts [accessed 20 September 2012].

Sontag D and Thompson G (2010) On street tracing Haiti's pain, survival goes on. *New York Times* 24 January.

Sontag S (1991) *Illness as Metaphor and AIDS and Its Metaphors*. London: Penguin.

Souteyrand Y, Collard V, Moatti J, Grubb I, Guerma T (2008) Free care at the point of service delivery: a key component for reaching universal access to HIV/AIDS treatment in developing countries. *AIDS* 22 (Suppl 1) S161–8.

Sprague C (2008) Women's health, HIV/AIDS and the workplace in South Africa. *African Journal of AIDS Research* 7 (3) 341–52.

Sri Krishnan A, Hendricksen S, Vallabha S, Johnson N et al. (2007) Sexual behaviours of individuals with HIV living in south India: a qualitative study. *AIDS Education and Prevention* 19 (4) 334–45.

Ssengonzi R (2007) The plight of older persons as caregivers to people infected/affected by HIV/AIDS: evidence from Uganda. *Journal of Cross-Cultural Gerontology* 22 (4) 339–53.

Stadler J (2003) Rumor, gossip and blame: implications for HIV/AIDS prevention in the South African Lowveld. *AIDS Education and Prevention* 15 (4) 357–68.

Stadler J and Delaney S (2006) The 'healthy brothel': the context of clinical services for sex workers in Hillbrow, South Africa. *Culture, Health and Sexuality* 8 (5) 451–64.

Steinbrook R (2007) HIV in India: a complex epidemic. *New England Journal of Medicine*. 356 (11) 1089–93.

Stemple L (2008) Health and human rights in today's fight against HIV/AIDS. *AIDS* 22 (Suppl 2) S113–21.

Stevens PE and Galvao L (2007) 'He won't use condoms': HIV-infected women's struggles in primary relationships with serodiscordant partners. *American Journal of Public Health* 97 (6) 1015–22.

Steward WT, Herek GM, Ramakrishna J, Bharat S, Chandy S, Wrubel J, Ekstrand ML (2008) HIV related stigma: adapting a theoretical framework for use in India. *Social Science and Medicine* 67 (8) 1225–35.

Stewart H (2012) Wealth doesn't just trickle down –it just floods offshore, new research reveals. *The Guardian* 23 July.

Tamir Y (1995) *Liberal Nationalism*. Princeton NJ: Princeton University Press.

Tapp C, Millry MJ, Kerr T Zhang R, Guillemi S, Hogg RS, Montaner J, Wood E (2011) Female gender predicts lower access and adherence to antiretroviral therapy in a setting of free health care. *BMC Infectious Diseases* 11 86.

Taylor L and Dickinson C (2006) *The Link between Corruption and HIV/AIDS: Global Corruption Report*. Berlin: Transparency International.

Tasioulas J (2007) The moral reality of human rights. In: T Pogge (ed) *Freedom from Poverty as a Human Right*. Oxford: Oxford University Press.

Tersbol B (2006) 'I just ended up here, no job and no health …': men's outlook on life in the context of economic hardship and HIV/AIDS in Namibia. *SAHARA Journal* 3 (1) 403–16.

Thomas F (2006) Stigma, fatigue and social breakdown: exploring the impact of HIV/AIDS on patient and carer wellbeing in the Caprivi Region, Namibia. *Social Science and Medicine* 63 (12) 3174–87.

Thomas F (2008) Indigenous narratives of HIV/AIDS: morality and blame in a time of change. *Medical Anthropology* 27 (3) 227–56.

Thomas F, Aggleton P, Anderson J (2009) 'Experts', 'partners' and 'fools': exploring agency in HIV treatment seeking among African migrants in London. *Social Science and Medicine* 70 (5) 736–43.

Tijou Traoré A, Querre M, Brou H, Leroy V, Desclaux A, Desgrees-du Lou A (2009) Couples, PMTCT programs and infant feeding decision-making in Ivory Coast. *Social Science and Medicine* 69 (6) 830–37.

Tucker JO, Henderson GE, Wang TF, Huang YY, Parish W, Pan SM, Chen XS, Cohen, MS (2005) Surplus men, sex work, and the spread of HIV in China. *AIDS* 19 (6) 539–47.

Tuller DM, Bangsberg DR, Senfungu J, Ware NC, Emenyonu N, Weiser SD (2010) Transportation costs impede sustained adherence and access to HAART in a clinic population in southwestern Uganda: a qualitative study. *AIDS and Behavior* 14 (4) 778–84.

Turan JM, Miller S, Bukusi EA, Sande J, Cohen CR (2008) HIV/AIDS and maternity care in Kenya: how fears of stigma and discrimination affect uptake and provision of labor and delivery services. *AIDS Care* 20 (8) 938–45.

UK Health Protection Agency (2011) *HIV in the UK 2011 Report*. London: HPA.

UN (2005) *Progress of the World's Women 2005: Women, Work and Poverty*. New York: UNIFEM.

UN (2011) *Discriminatory laws and practices and acts of violence against individuals based on their sexual orientation and gender identity*. New York: UN

UN (2012) The Millennium Development Goals Report 2012. New York: UN

UNAIDS (2007) *Handbook on HIV and Human Rights for National Human Rights Institutions*. Geneva: UNAIDS: Office of High Commissioner for Human Rights and Joint United Nations programme on HIV/AIDS.

UNAIDS (2009) *HIV Transmission in Intimate Personal Relationships in Asia*. Geneva: UNAIDS.

UNAIDS (2011) *Terminology Guidelines*. Geneva: UNAIDS

UNAIDS (2012a) *A Progress Report on the Global Plan towards the Elimination of New HIV Infections among Children by 2015 and Keeping their Mothers Alive*. Geneva: UNAIDS.

UNAIDS (2012b) *AIDS Dependency: Sourcing African Solutions*. Geneva: UNAIDS.

UNAIDS (2012c) *World AIDS Day Report*. Geneva: UNAIDS.

UN Department of Economic and Social Affairs (2011) *Trends in International Migration*. New York: UN

Undie CC, Ziraba AK, Madise N, Kebaso J, Kimani-Murage E (2009) 'If you start thinking positively you won't miss sex': narratives of sexual (in)activity among people living with HIV in Nairobi's informal settlements. *Culture, Health and Sexuality* 11 (8) 767–82.

UNDP (2008) *HIV Vulnerabilities of Migrant Women from Asia to the Arab States*. Colombo: UNDP

Urbanus AT, van de Laar TJ, Stolte IG, Schinkel J et al. (2009) Hepatitis C virus infections among HIV-infected men who have sex with men: an expanding epidemic. *AIDS* 23 (12) F1–7.

Urdang S (2006) The care economy: gender and the silent AIDS Crisis. *Journal of Southern African Studies* 32 (1) 165–77.

Uys L, Chirwa M, Dlamini P et al. (2005) 'Eating plastic', 'winning the lotto', 'joining the WWW': descriptions of HIV/AIDS in Africa. *Journal of the Association of Nurses in AIDS Care* 16 (3) 11–21.

Valencia-Garcia D, Starks H, Strick L, Simoni J (2008) After the fall from grace: negotiation of new identities among HIV-positive women in Peru. *Culture, Health and Sexuality* 10 (7) 739–52.

Van Blerk L and Ansell N (2007) Alternative care giving in the context of HIV/AIDS in Southern Africa: complex strategies for care. *Journal of International Development* 19 (7) 865–84.

Van der Spuy Z (2009) HIV and reproductive health: a South African experience *Reproductive Biomedicine Online* 18 (Suppl 2) S3–10.

Van de Laar M, Likatavicius G, Stengaard A, Donoghoe M (2008) HIV/AIDS surveillance in Europe: update 2007. *Eurosurveillance*, 13 50.

Van Griensven F, van Wijngaarden J, Baral S, Grulich A (2009) The global epidemic of HIV infection among men who have sex with men. *Current Opinion in HIV and AIDS* 4 (4) 300–307.

Van Hollen C (2007) Negotiating HIV, pregnancy and childbearing in South India: pragmatics and constraints in women's decision making. *Medical Anthropology* 26 (7) 7–52.

Van Hollen C (2011) Breast or bottle? HIV-positive women's responses to global health policy on infant feeding in India. *Medical Anthropology Quarterly* 25 (4) 499–518.

Van Kesteren N, Hospers HJ, van Empelen P, van Breukelen G, Kok G. (2005) Sexuality and sexual risk behaviour in HIV positive men who have sex with men. *Qualitative Health Research* 15 (2) 145–68.

Van Rompaey S, Kimfuta J, Kimbondo P, Monn C, Buve A (2011) Operational assessment of access to ART in rural Africa: the example of Kisantu in Democratic Republic of the Congo. *AIDS Care* 23 (6) 686–93.

Vanable P, Carey M, Brown J, Littlewood R, Bostwick R, Blair D (2011) What HIV positive MSM want from sexual risk reduction strategies: findings from a qualitative study *AIDS and Behavior* 16 (3) 354–63.

Vance C (1991) Anthropology rediscovers sexuality: a theoretical comment. *Social Science and Medicine* 33 (8) 875–84.

Veenstra N, Whiteside A, Lalloo D, Gibbs A (2010) Unplanned antiretroviral treatment interruptions in Southern Africa: how should we be managing these? *Globalization and Health* 6 4.

Visser M, Neufield S, de Villiers A, Makin J, Forsyth B (2008) To tell or not to tell: South African women's disclosure of HIV status during pregnancy. *AIDS Care* 20 (9) 1138–45.

Waldron J (1988) The philosophy of rights. In G Parkinson et al. (eds) *Encyclopedia of Philosophy*. London: Routledge.

Waldron J (1993) *Liberal Rights: Collected Papers 1981–1991*. Cambridge: Cambridge University Press.

Waldron J (1995) Minority cultures and the cosmopolitan alternative. In W Kymlicka *The Rights of Minority Cultures*. Oxford: Oxford University Press.

Wamoyi J, Mbonye M, Seeley J, Birung J, Jaffar S (2011) Changes in sexual desires and behaviours of people living with HIV after initiation of ART: implications for HIV prevention and health promotion. *BMC Public Health* 11 633.

Ware N, Idoko J et al. (2010) Explaining adherence success in sub-Saharan Africa: an ethnographic study. *PLOS Medicine* 6 1.

Watt M, Maman S, Earp J, Eng E, Setel P, Golin C, Jacobson M (2009) 'It's all the time in my mind': facilitators of adherence to antiretroviral therapy in a Tanzanian setting. *Social Science and Medicine* 68 (10) 1793–800.

Watt M, Maman S, Jacobson M, Laiser J, John M (2009) Missed opportunities for religious organisations to support people living with HIV/AIDS : findings from Tanzania *AIDS Patient Care and STDs* 23 (5) 389–94.

Weeks J (2009) *Sexuality (Key Ideas)*. London: Routledge.

Westaway E, Seeley J and Allison E (2007) Feckless and reckless or forbearing and resourceful? Looking behind the stereotypes of HIV and AIDS in 'fishing communities'. *African Affairs* 106 (425) 663–79.

White J and Robinson E (2000) *HIV/AIDS and Rural Livelihoods in Sub-Saharan Africa*. London: University of Greenwich Natural Resources Institute.

Whiteside A (2008) *HIV/AIDS: A Very Short Introduction*. Oxford: Oxford University Press.

Whiteside A and Smith J (2009) Exceptional Epidemic: AIDS still deserves a global response. *Globalisation and Health* 5 (15).

Wikipedia. http://en.wikipedia.org/wiki/Homosexuality_laws_of_the_world.

Wilcher R and Cates W (2009) Reproductive choices for women with HIV. *Bulletin of the World Health Organization* 87 (11) 833–9.

WHO, UNICEF and UNAIDS (2011) *Progress Report: Global HIV/AIDS Response. Epidemic Update and Health Sector Progress towards Universal Access*. Geneva: UNAIDS.

Williams A and Tumwekwase G (2001) Multiple impacts of the HIV/AIDS epidemic on the aged in rural Uganda. *Journal of Cross-Cultural Gerontology* 16 (3) 221–36.

Wilsher D (2011) *Immigration Detention: Law, History, Politics.* Cambridge: Cambridge University Press.

Wilson S (2007) 'When you have children, you're obliged to live': motherhood, chronic illness and biographical disruption. *Sociology of Health and Illness* 29 (4) 610–26.

Wizeman T and Pardue M (eds) (2001) *Exploring the Biological Contributions to Human Health: Does Sex Matter?* Washington DC: Institute of Medicine.

Wojcicki J (2005) Socioeconomic status as a risk factor for HIV infection in women in East, Central and Southern Africa: a systematic review. *Journal of Biosocial Science* 37 (1) 1–36.

Wolfe D, Carrieri M, Shepard D (2010) Treatment and care for injecting drug users with HIV infection: a review of barriers and ways forward. *Lancet* 376 (9738) 355–66.

Wolff J (2012) *The Human Right to Health.* New York and London: Amnesty International and WW Norton.

Wolff J and De-Shalit A (2007) *Disadvantage.* New York: Oxford University Press.

Wolitski R and Fenton K (2011) Sexual Health, HIV and Sexually Transmitted Infections among gay, bisexual and other men who have sex with men in the United States. *AIDS and Behavior* 15 (1) S9–17.

Wood E, Montaner J, Bangsberg D, Tyndall M, Strathdee S, O'Shaughnessy M, Hogg R (2003) Expanding access to antiretroviral therapy among marginalised populations in the developed world. *AIDS* 17 2419–27.

World Bank (2011) *HIV/AIDS and Mining Toolkit.* http://go.worldbank.org/MF87JJ43Z0.

World Bank (2012) World Development Report on Gender Equality and Development. Washington DC: World Bank

World Economic Forum (2013) *Global Risks 2013 : 8th Edition.* Geneva: World Economic Forum

World Health Organization (2003) *Gender Dimensions of HIV Status Disclosure to Sexual Partners: Rates, Barriers and Outcomes: A Review Paper.* Geneva: WHO.

World Health Organization (2008a) *Medical Eligibility for Contraceptive Use* 4th ed. Geneva: WHO.

World Health Organization (2008b) *Closing the Gap in a Generation: Health Equity Through Action on the Social Determinants of Health. Final Report of the Commission on Social Determinants of Health.* Geneva: WHO.

World Health Organization (2009) *WHO Guide to Identifying the Economic Consequences of Disease and Injury.* Geneva: WHO.

World Health Organization (2010a) *Antiretroviral Drugs for Treating Pregnant Women and Preventing HIV Infection in Infants: 2010 Revision.* Geneva: WHO.

World Health Organization (2010b) *Prevention of Mother to Child Transmission of HIV to Reach UNGASS and Millennium Development Goals 2010–15.* Geneva: WHO.

World Health Organization (2010c) *Guidelines on HIV and Infant Feeding 2010: Principles and Recommendations for Infant Feeding in the Context of HIV and a Summary of Evidence*. Geneva: WHO.

World Health Organization (2011) *HIV/TB Facts 2011*. Geneva: WHO.

World Health Organisation (2012a) *Antiretroviral treatment as prevention (TASP) of HIV and TB*. Geneva: WHO

World Health Organization (2012b) *Hormonal Contraception and HIV: Technical Statement*. Geneva: WHO.

Yamin A (2011) *What next for a global development agenda that takes human rights seriously?* Geneva: UNICEF Research Watch

Young L and Ansell N (2003). Fluid households, complex families: the impacts of children's migration as a response to HIV/AIDS in Southern Africa. *The Professional Geographer* 55 (4) 464–76.

Young RM and Meyer IH (2005) The trouble with 'MSM' and 'WSW': erasure of the sexual-minority person in public health discourse. *American Journal of Public Health* 95 1144–9.

Yu D, Souteyrand Y, Banda M, Kaufman J, Perriens J (2008) Investing in HIV and AIDS programs: does it help strengthen health systems in developing countries? *Globalisation and Health* 4 8.

Zhang L, Li X, Kaljee L, Fang X, Lin X, Zhao G, Zhao J, Hong Y. (2009) 'I felt I have grown up as an adult': caregiving experience of children affected by HIV/AIDS in China. *Child Care, Health and Development* 5 (4) 542–50.

Zhou Y (2007) 'If you get AIDS you have to endure it alone': understanding the social construction of HIV/AIDS in China. *Social Science and Medicine* 65 (2) 284–95.

Zhou Y (2008) Help seeking in a context of AIDS stigma: understanding the health care needs of people with HIV/AIDS in China. *Health and Social Care in the Community* 17 (2) 202–8.

Zhou Y (2010) The phenomenology of time: lived experiences of people with HIV/AIDS in China. *Health* 14 310–25.

Zimbabwe Lawyers for Human Rights (2010) *Corruption Burns: Universal Access to Treatment*. Harare: ZLHR.

Zou J, Yamanaka Y, John M, Watt M, Ostermann J, Thielman N (2009) Religion and HIV in Tanzania: influence of religious beliefs on HIV stigma, disclosure and treatment attitudes. *BMC Public Health* 9 75.

Zwahlen and Egger (2006) *Progression and Mortality of HIV-Positive Individuals Living in Resource-Limited Settings*. Report on UNAIDS Obligation HQ/05/422204. University of Berne.

Index